IMAGES
of America

THE SCHOHARIE VALLEY

AF807510

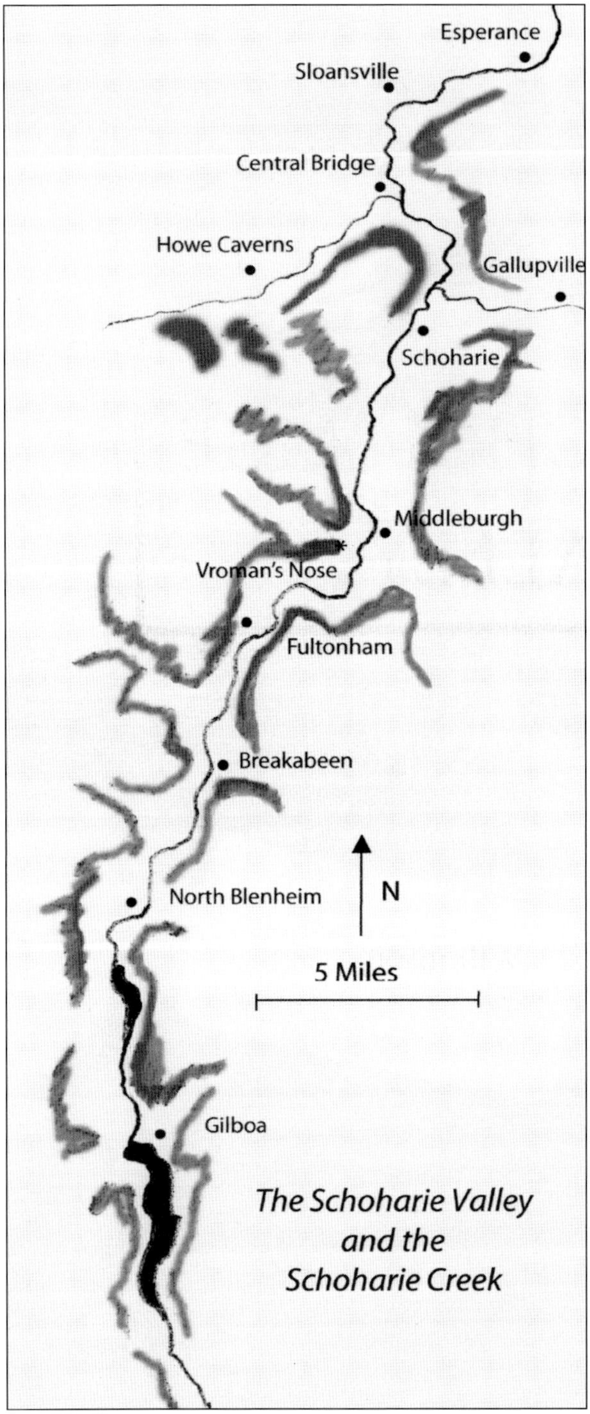

MAP OF SCHOHARIE VALLEY. This map shows the Schoharie Valley and the Schoharie Creek with the hamlets and villages of Gilboa, North Blenheim, Breakabeen, Fultonham, Middleburgh, Schoharie, Gallupville, Central Bridge, Howe's Cave, Sloansville, and Esperance. The location of the iconic mountain Vroman's Nose is also shown. (Courtesy of author's collection.)

ON THE COVER: In this c. 1890 photograph, four people in Victorian clothing look out onto the Schoharie Valley and the Schoharie Creek from the peak of Vroman's Nose. The mountain was named after Adam Vroman, an early settler of the region. The Native Americans called the mountain Onistagrawa, meaning "Corn Mountain." (Courtesy of Dolores Shaul.)

IMAGES
of America

THE SCHOHARIE VALLEY

John P.D. Wilkinson

ARCADIA
PUBLISHING

Copyright © 2012 by John P.D. Wilkinson
ISBN 978-0-7385-9140-7

Published by Arcadia Publishing
Charleston, South Carolina

Printed in the United States of America

Library of Congress Control Number: 2011938596

For all general information, please contact Arcadia Publishing:
Telephone 843-853-2070
Fax 843-853-0044
E-mail sales@arcadiapublishing.com
For customer service and orders:
Toll-Free 1-888-313-2665

Visit us on the Internet at www.arcadiapublishing.com

This book is dedicated to all those in the Schoharie Valley whose homes, businesses, farms, and crops were damaged or lost in Hurricane Irene and the flood of August 28, 2011, and to the thousands of volunteers who came to help in the valley's recovery.

Contents

ACKNOWLEDGMENTS

It was Jean Harra, president of the Schoharie Colonial Heritage Association and curator of the association's Schoharie Valley Railroad Museum, who first suggested that I develop this book. I am indebted to several collectors and historians for their generous sharing of vintage photographs: Robert Holt for his help on Central Bridge and Howe Caverns, Ken Jones for his collection on Esperance and Sloansville, and Kenneth Clark and Samantha Clark for their photographs of Gilboa. Lester Hendrix kindly lent his editorial experience toward improving the text, for which I am grateful.

I am indebted to farming families for allowing me to use their personal photographs: Dolores Shaul and the extended Shaul family, Cindy Barber and the Barber family, Kristen Wyckoff, and Naomi Zimmer Wikane. Many people generously gave of their time, knowledge, and collections, including Edwin Truax, Willis Truax Jr., Betsy Colyer Guernsey, Skip Edmonds, Richard Ball, Rick Colyer, Sally Scranton Law, Anne and Lester Hendrix, Arlene Price, Robert Loden, Lois Gruner, Susan Kintz McGiver, Todd Rolfe, Rose Mace, and Greg Starheim. Historians were also generous with their knowledge: Town of Conesville historian Beatrice Mattice, Town of Fulton historian Gerald Hamm, and Fulton Historical Society president Elizabeth Coons.

I was privileged to have been allowed to view and use photographs from numerous museums: the Old Stone Fort Museum (OSFM) and director Carle Kopecky and curator Dan Beams, the Middleburgh Library History Room (MLHR) and Steven LaMont and Marian Lyons Bouck, the New York Power Authority Blenheim Gilboa Visitors Center and Stephen Ramsey and Adrienne Gallup, the Gilboa Museum, the Esperance Historical Museum, the Schoharie Chapter National Society of the Daughters of the American Revolution, and the collection of Howe Caverns, Inc.

I acknowledge the foresight of collectors of historical information, those who are no longer with us: Chester Zimmer, Edward Scribner, Helene Farrell, Russell Bergh, Robert Mahar, Willis Truax Sr., Edward Hagan, and Samuel A. Scranton (1875–1947), the photographer who recorded many scenes of the village of Schoharie in the 1900s on glass plates.

Finally, I wish to thank Wanda and Rick Colyer for allowing me and my wife, Ruth Anne, to stay in their home when our own home in the village of Schoharie was damaged by the 2011 flood and had to be rebuilt.

Introduction

The fertile fields of the Schoharie Valley were formed during the time of the Ice Age when the glaciers that covered much of upstate New York began to recede. A large lake formed covering the entire valley. Streams flowed from the valley walls, bringing silt and sediments with them. The silt filled the valley forming the flat fields in the valley bottom. The Schoharie Creek became the main channel for water to flow from its watershed in the northern Catskill Mountains. The creek flows north and empties into the Mohawk River. In the 10,000 years from the glacial period, the creek has changed course many times, and traces of the meander can still be seen in the valley fields. The name *Schoharie* is said to come from an Indian word meaning "driftwood," after a large driftwood heap that was located in the Schoharie Creek near Middleburgh.

The first permanent European settlers were the Palatine Germans, who came to America in 1710 and began settling the area. The area around Middleburgh was settled 300 years ago in 1712. Several settlements around the present village of Schoharie were established a year later. The newcomers were from the German Palatinate and also from Holland. They spoke German or Dutch. Reformed churches were established in the 1720s in both Middleburgh and Schoharie. The churches shared a minister until around 1790. The Lutheran church in Schoharie was established not long afterwards before 1734.

The Schoharie Valley became known as the "Breadbasket of the Revolution" because of the rich soils that produced grain for Gen. George Washington's forces during the American Revolution. The landmark now known as the Old Stone Fort Museum in Schoharie was originally built in 1772 as a Reformed church. During the American Revolution, in October 1780, the British and their Iroquois Indian allies attacked the Schoharie Valley. They wanted to prevent the settlers from sending grain to Washington's troops. At that time, the church was stockaded and turned into a fort. Many houses, barns, and crops were destroyed in the attack. Several houses that were attacked at the time still stand today. Much of the population sided with the patriots, and the men joined the local militias. Many, however, remained loyal to the British crown. After the American Revolution, the loyalists left the area and settled elsewhere. By 1795, Schoharie County had been officially formed with the village of Schoharie as the county seat. The county was eventually divided into 16 towns, and the major villages were incorporated by the mid-1800s.

A significant factor in the prosperity of the Schoharie Valley was the building of the railroad from Middleburgh, through Schoharie, and then to Schoharie Junction where the trains met the Albany & Susquehanna Railroad (which later became the Delaware & Hudson Railroad). Curiously, though operated as a unit, the railroads in the valley were incorporated by two entities: the Middleburgh & Schoharie Railroad ran from Middleburgh to Schoharie while the Schoharie Valley Railroad continued from Schoharie north to Schoharie Junction. The railroads were built in 1867, soon after the construction of the Albany & Susquehanna Railroad in 1865. The railroads carried valley produce to the outside world and in turn brought goods and visitors to the valley. The small railroads gradually became unprofitable due to competition from trucks and had ceased operation by the 1940s. The rails were scrapped for the war effort.

Farming has been the major industry in the Schoharie Valley. The fertile valley flats, as the bottom fields are called, lent themselves to intensive crop production. During the late 1800s and early 1900s, hops were extensively grown. The hop vine grew on tall poles. In the fall, hops were picked by men, women, and children from the area and beyond. The flowers of the hop vine were harvested and sent to breweries elsewhere as an ingredient for making beer. Unfortunately, a disease invaded the hop plants in the early 1900s, putting the hop industry in jeopardy. On the Pindar farm in Middleburgh, the last hops were grown in the early 1950s.

Though hops were no longer grown, many other crops superseded it. Buckwheat, oats, and wheat were popular crops. Mills in Central Bridge and Esperance were built to grind the grains into flour. The dairy industry also prospered. Later, corn became the dominant crop, and later still, vegetables, such as carrots, potatoes, peas, squash, spinach, and pumpkins, were grown and sold at local farm stands or shipped elsewhere. Farming not only produced prosperity for the farming families, but engendered small enterprises in the hamlets and villages, such as general stores, blacksmith shops, and carriage makers. Inns were built to shelter visitors. As the automobile became popular, the general stores sold gasoline and oil, and service stations later sprang up.

New York City had long been in need of a source of water for its inhabitants. By 1916, surveys had been done in the Schoharie Valley to make a dam that would contribute to this need. The Gilboa Dam was built by 1926 and created the Schoharie Reservoir from which water eventually reached the city aqueducts. The result was that the small village of Gilboa was destroyed and its inhabitants scattered. Later, in the 1970s, the Blenheim-Gilboa pumped storage project was developed to produce peak electric power. This dammed the Schoharie Creek downstream from the Gilboa Dam.

This book follows the path of the Schoharie Creek within the borders of Schoharie County. Because farming is so important to the area, the narrative begins with vintage photographs of agricultural activities in the valley. The subsequent chapters trace the settlements in the Schoharie Valley from south to north along the path of the creek: Gilboa, North Blenheim, Breakabeen, Fultonham, Middleburgh, Schoharie, Gallupville, Central Bridge, Howe's Cave, Sloansville, and Esperance. The communities are linked not only by the Schoharie Creek, but also, for the most part, by New York State Route 30, also known as the Timothy Murphy Trail after a local hero of the American Revolution. Murphy, a sharpshooter with Daniel Morgan's Rifle Corps, is reputed to have mortally wounded the British general Simon Fraser during the Battle of Saratoga in 1777.

The flood of August 28, 2011, is fresh in the minds of the residents of the Schoharie Valley. It is hoped that this book of vintage photographs will help heal the damage inflicted on the valley by Hurricane Irene. Some of the structures shown in the book were destroyed or badly damaged by the flood. The last photograph in the book shows the flood in full progress in the town of Fulton in a view taken from Vroman's Nose. It is a reminder that the elements are never tamed, and that the valley's inhabitants are hardy and will rebuild for the future.

This book recognizes the 300th anniversary of the settling of Middleburgh in 1712. Schoharie will celebrate its 300th anniversary a year later. Those 300 years have seen great changes, but the spirit of the inhabitants is still the same: we treasure our history, and we love our valley.

One

Farming in the Schoharie Valley

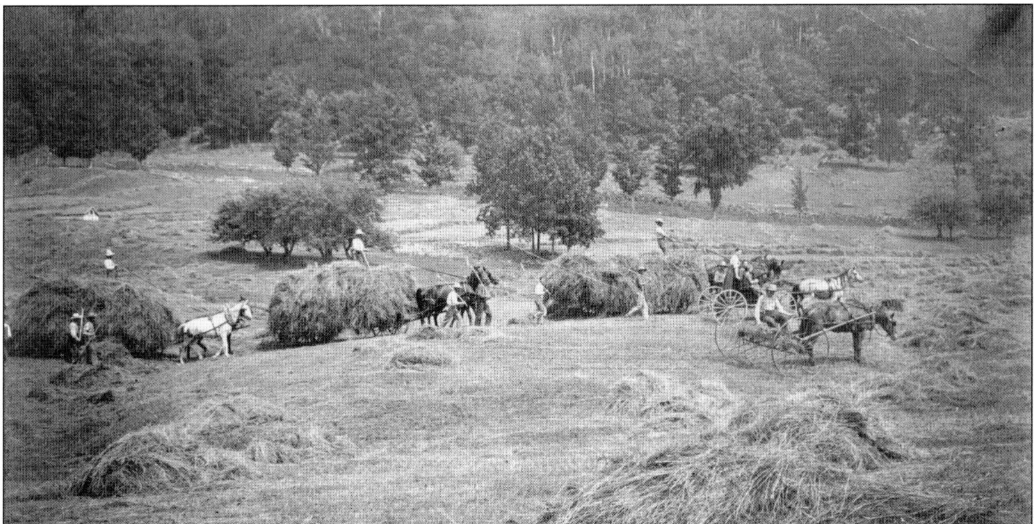

Haying on the Wyckoff Farm, Gilboa. Teams of horses pull loaded hay wagons while men with pitchforks walk beside them in this 1895 view of the Wyckoff farm. The men on top of the hay wagons are holding the reins. At right, a man is using a horse-drawn hay rake. (Courtesy of Kristen Wyckoff.)

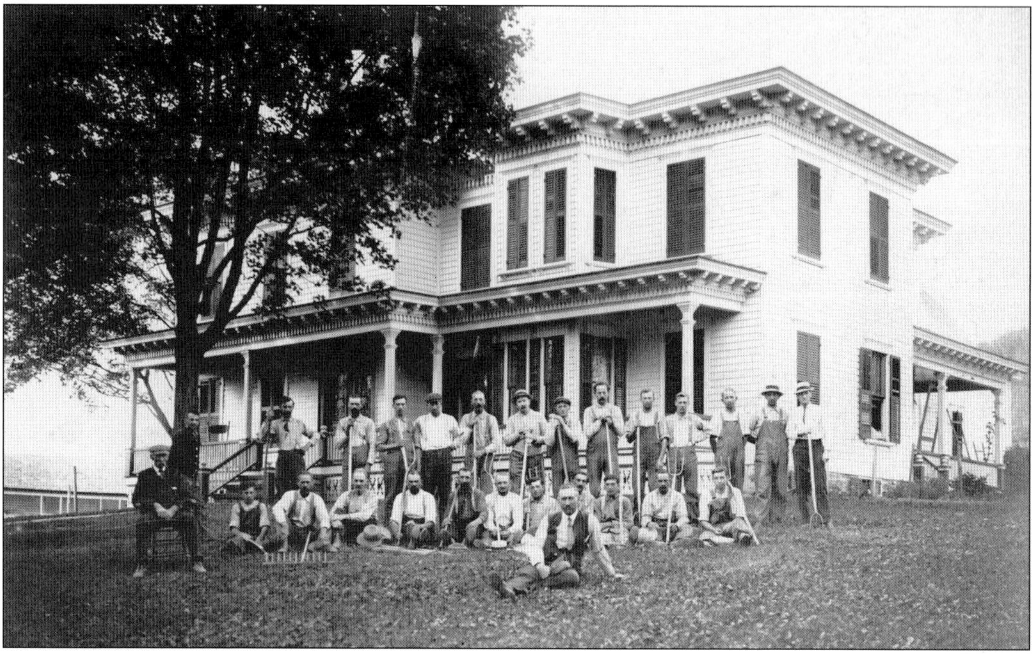

The Wyckoff House, Gilboa. Hired hands pose with Nathan Clinton Wyckoff (left) and his son Imer C. Wyckoff (seated, center) in front of the Wyckoff home around 1895. Nathan built this Victorian-style house in 1889 on the Wyckoff farm. The hired men have hay rakes and pitchforks for their work in bringing in the hay. (Courtesy of Kristen Wyckoff.)

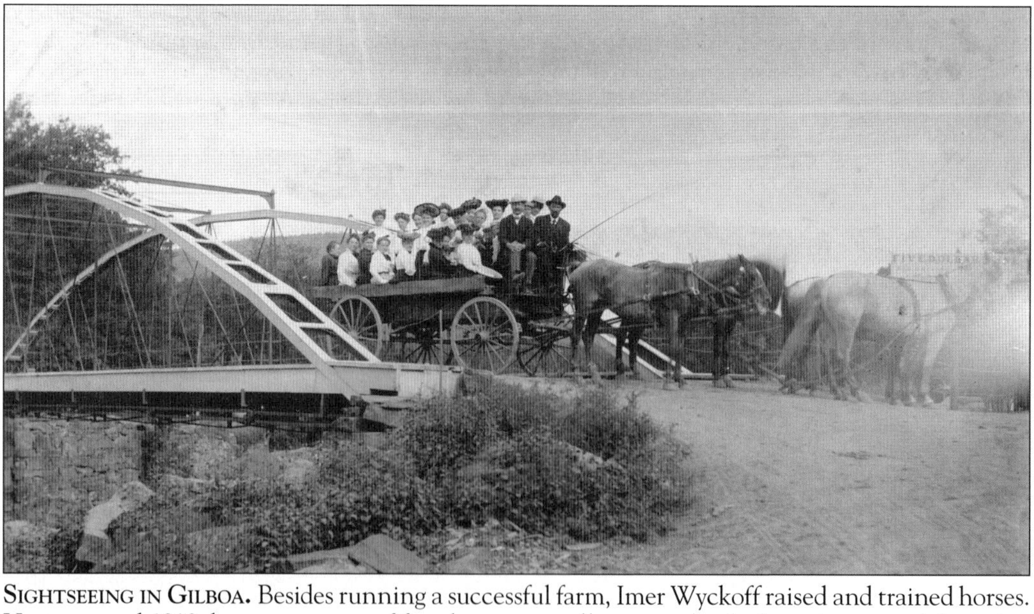

Sightseeing in Gilboa. Besides running a successful farm, Imer Wyckoff raised and trained horses. Here, around 1910, he uses a team of four horses to pull a wagonload of tourists on a sightseeing venture. They are crossing the lower bridge across the Schoharie Creek. Numerous visitors from the cities came to Gilboa for a summer vacation and stayed in the many boardinghouses. (Courtesy of Kristen Wyckoff.)

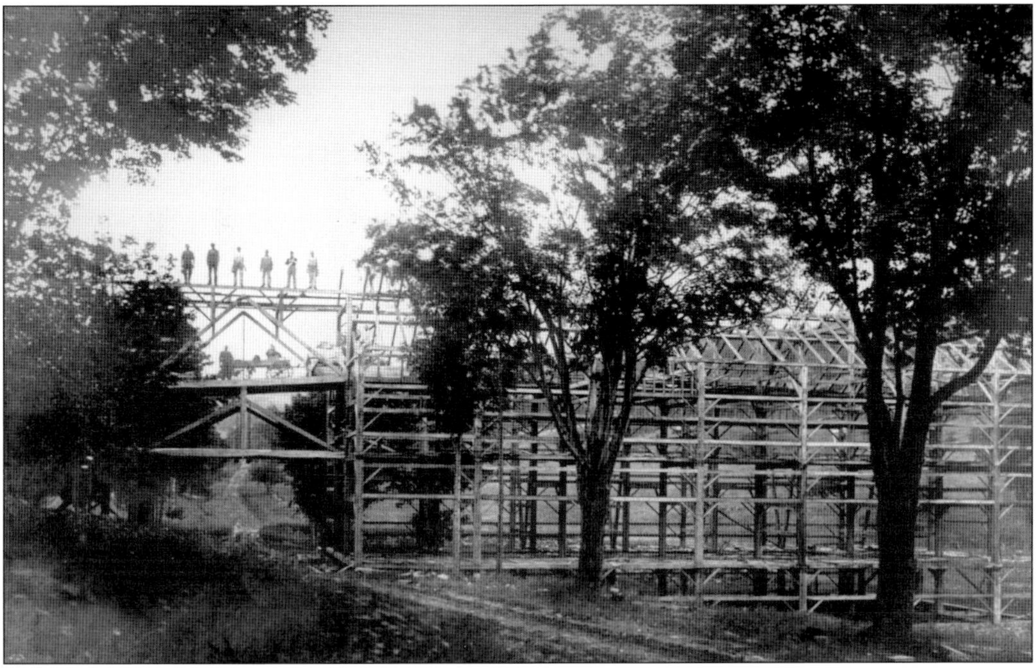

The Decker Barn, Gilboa, 1900. The Decker barn was built by William Henry Decker and completed in 1900. The barn has several unusual features. Loose hay was brought from the fields by horse and wagon to the fourth floor via a ramp that went over the road as shown here. The hay was off-loaded into a series of 10 haymows that reached to the ground floor. Cows were placed in stanchions in the basement level, and the hay was given to them through trap doors in the first floor. A team of horses bringing building supplies is visible on the ramp below the workers (above). The barn has recently been restored by Gregory Starheim. (Courtesy of the New York Power Authority.)

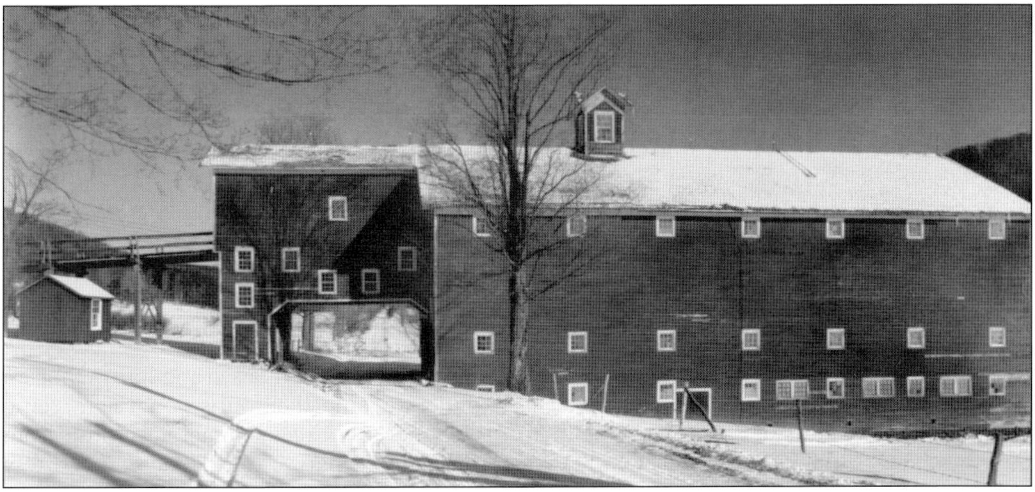

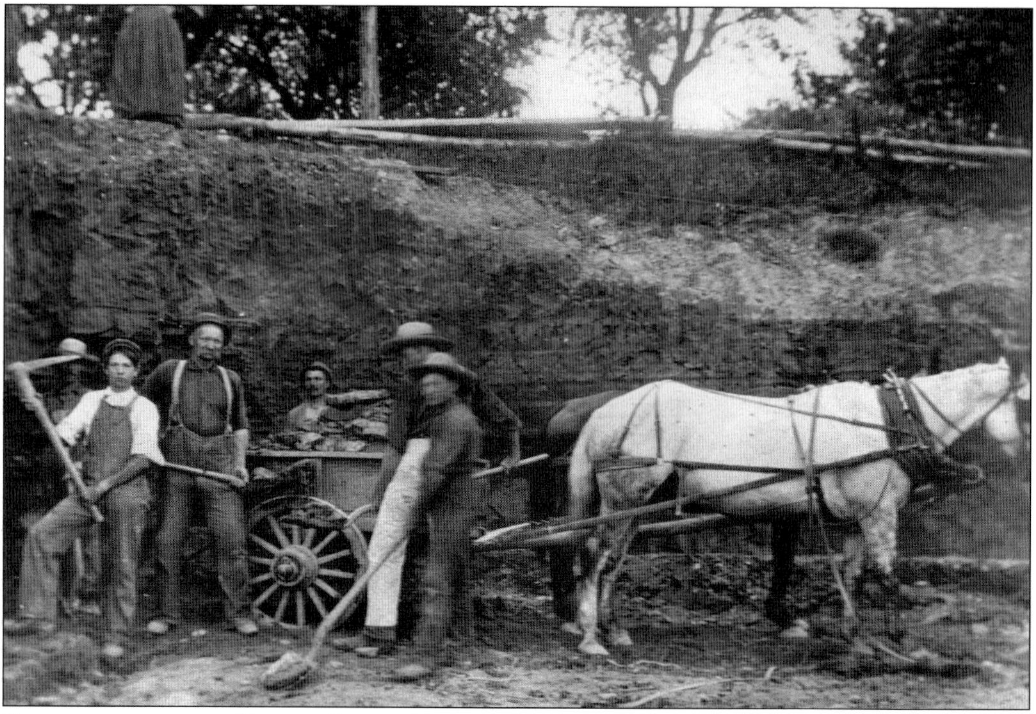

Excavating for the Decker Barn, Gilboa. The foundation of the barn had to be dug out by hand. Here, five men use picks and shovels to load a cart with rocks. The horse team consists of a white horse and a dark one, apparently a common combination in those days. (Courtesy of the New York Power Authority.)

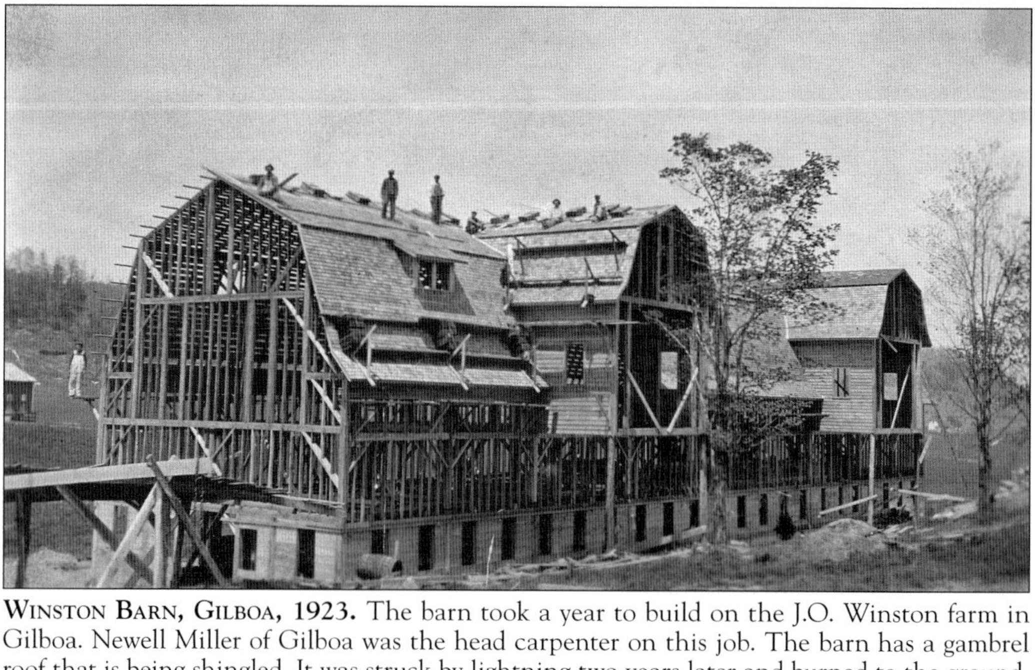

Winston Barn, Gilboa, 1923. The barn took a year to build on the J.O. Winston farm in Gilboa. Newell Miller of Gilboa was the head carpenter on this job. The barn has a gambrel roof that is being shingled. It was struck by lightning two years later and burned to the ground. (Courtesy of Rose Mace.)

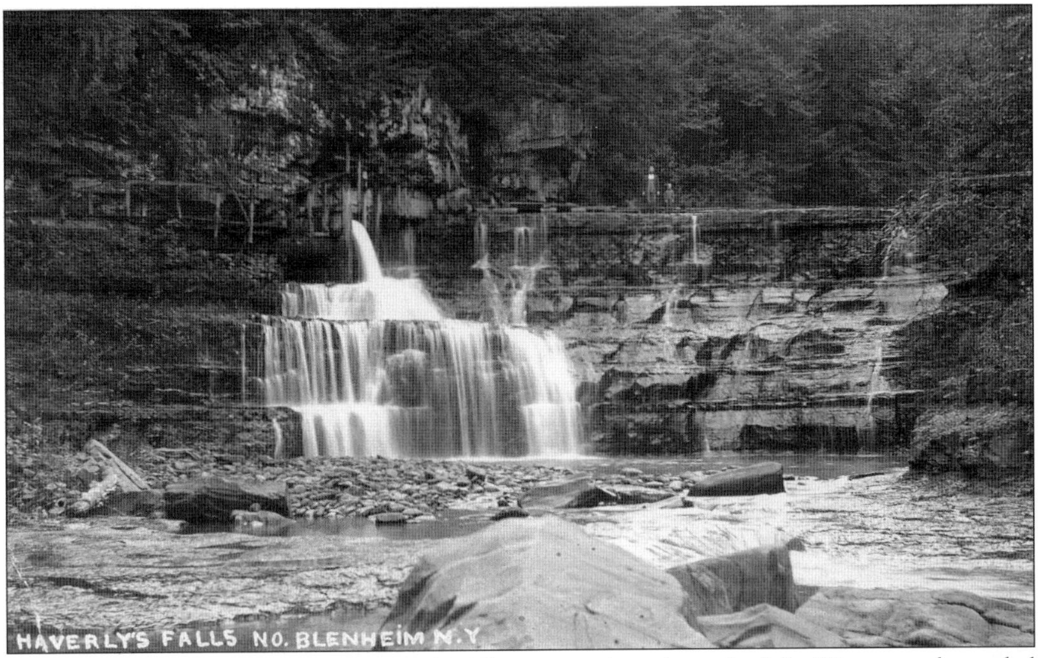

Haverly's Falls, North Blenheim, 1900. There was a dam above the falls. Water was channeled some 500 feet in a wooden pipe to drive a turbine and water wheel under Haverly's mill. The turbine was installed by Seneca Haverly around 1880 and used until 1928 when a gasoline-powered unit was installed. (Courtesy of OSFM.)

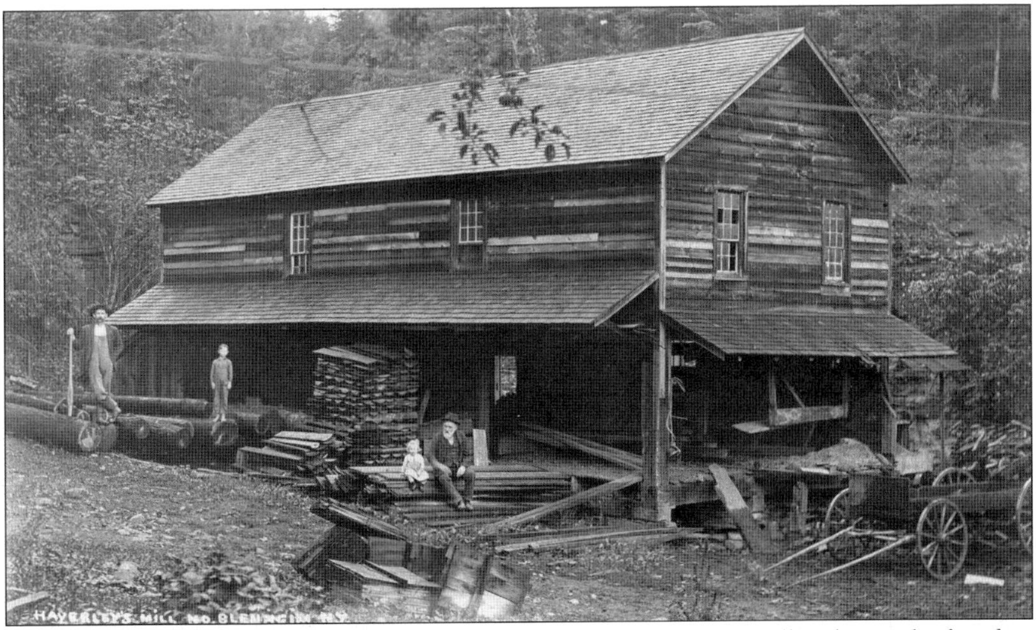

Haverly's Mill, North Blenheim. This 1900s view shows Haverly's mill with a stack of roofing shingles produced at the mill in the foreground. Seneca Haverly and granddaughter Estella Roth are seated (center). His son West is standing on the logs with a cant hook (used to roll logs). Virgil Weidman, a nephew, is standing near West. The mill operated from about 1880 until 1937. (Courtesy of OSFM.)

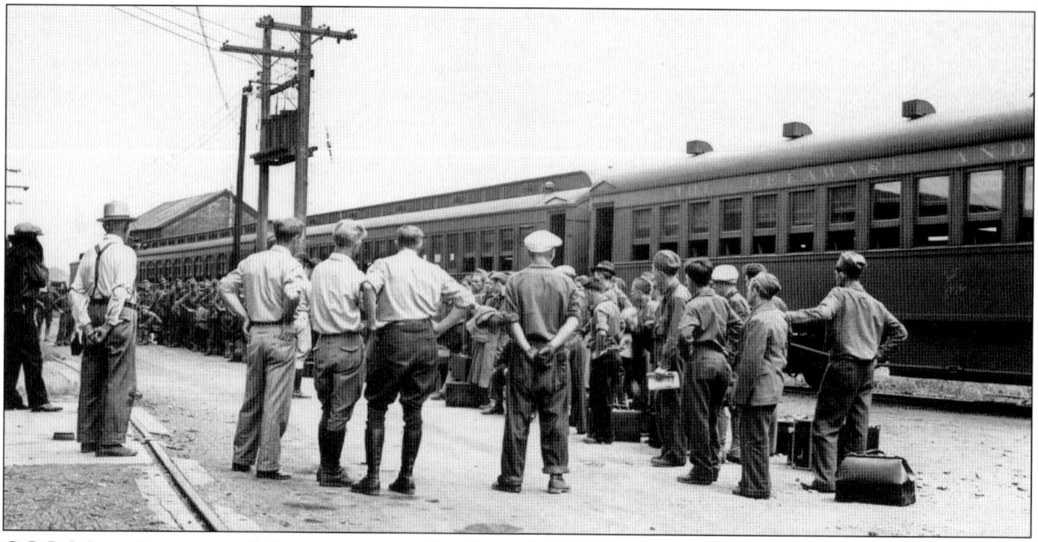

CCC Men Arrive in Middleburgh. Civilian Conservation Corps (CCC) members arrive at the Middleburgh depot in the 1930s en route to camps near Fultonham and Livingstonville. The corps was a public work-relief program and part of the New Deal. In the nine years of the corps' existence, 2.5 million young men participated. (Courtesy of MLHR.)

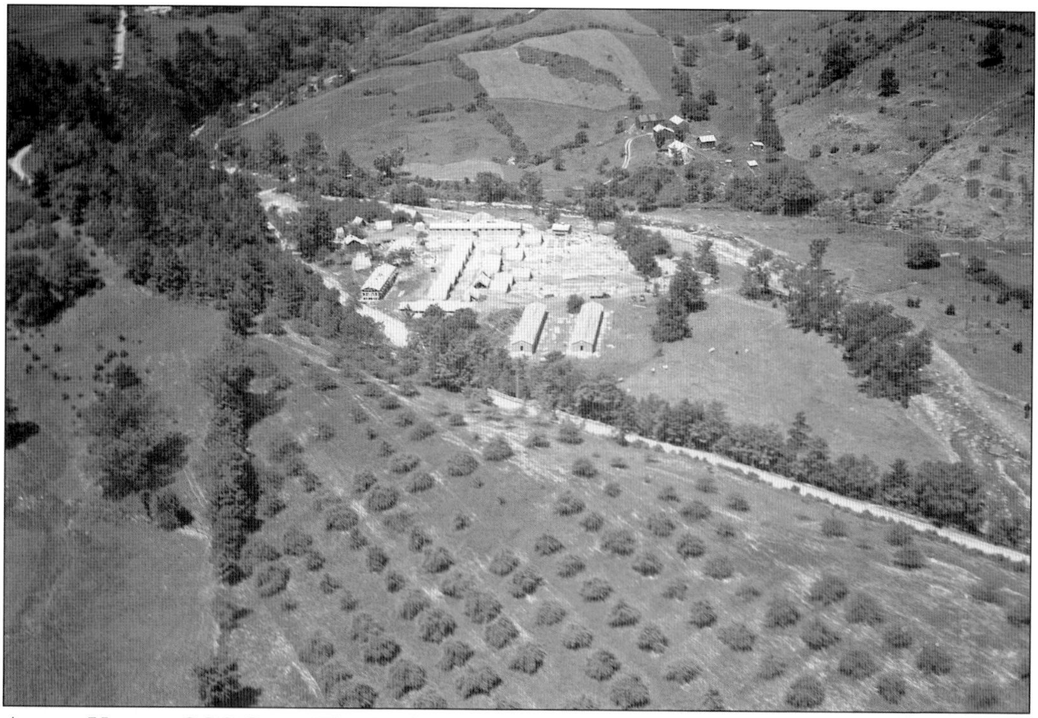

Aerial View of CCC Camp. The Civilian Conservation Corps camp in the town of Fulton along the West Fulton Road was used during the Depression (1935–1940) to house corps members who worked on conservation efforts in the area. They planted trees and worked to control erosion. (Courtesy of New York State Archives.)

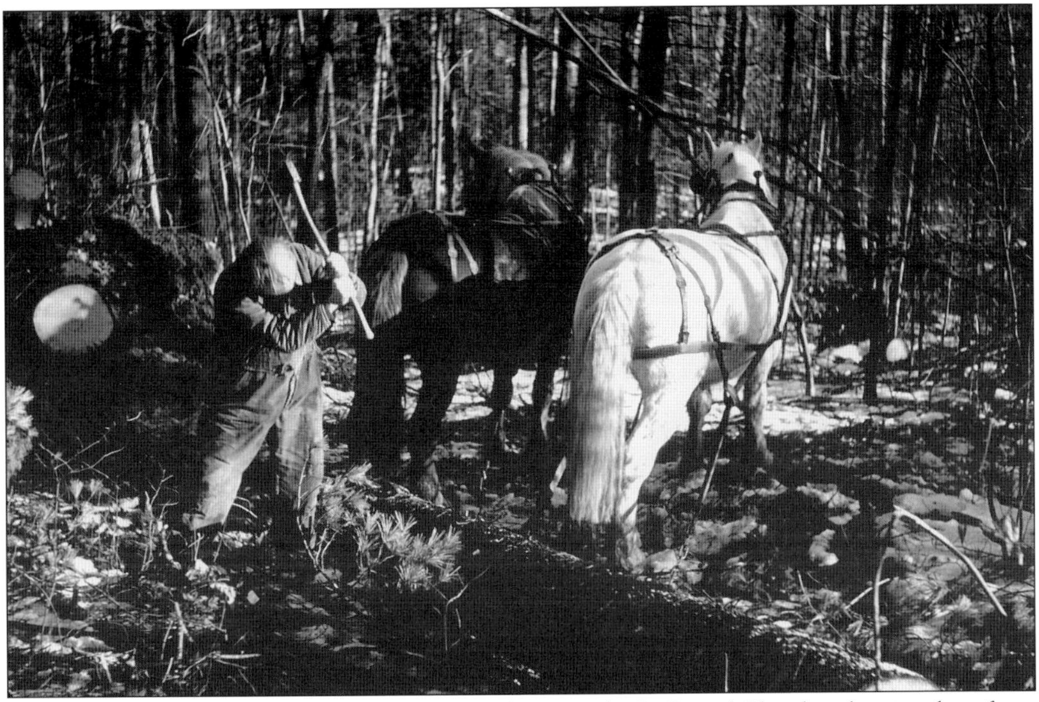

LOGGING WITH A TEAM. In this early-1940s photograph, LeGrand Shaul is drawing logs from the woods with a team of horses. One of the horses was blind, so it could only work as a team. Shaul is using the axe to place a spike into the log to attach a drawing chain to it. (Courtesy of the Shaul family.)

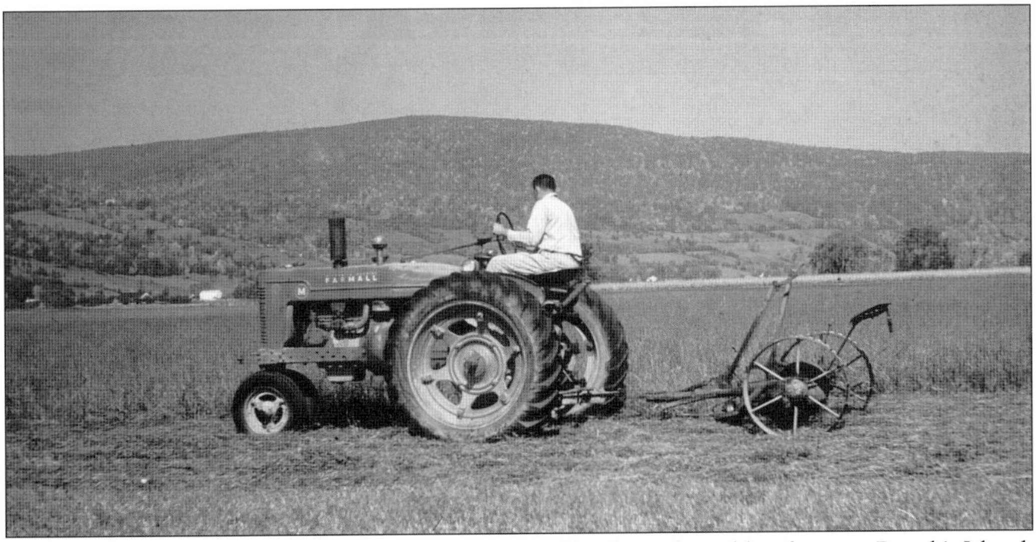

MOWING HAY ON THE SHAUL FARM. In 1940, Max Shaul purchased his farm on Bouck's Island, including the Gov. William C. Bouck house. The farm has grown to be one of the largest in the eastern United States. In this 1940s photograph, Shaul drives a 1939 Farmall M tractor to mow hay on the Fultonham flats. (Courtesy of the Shaul family.)

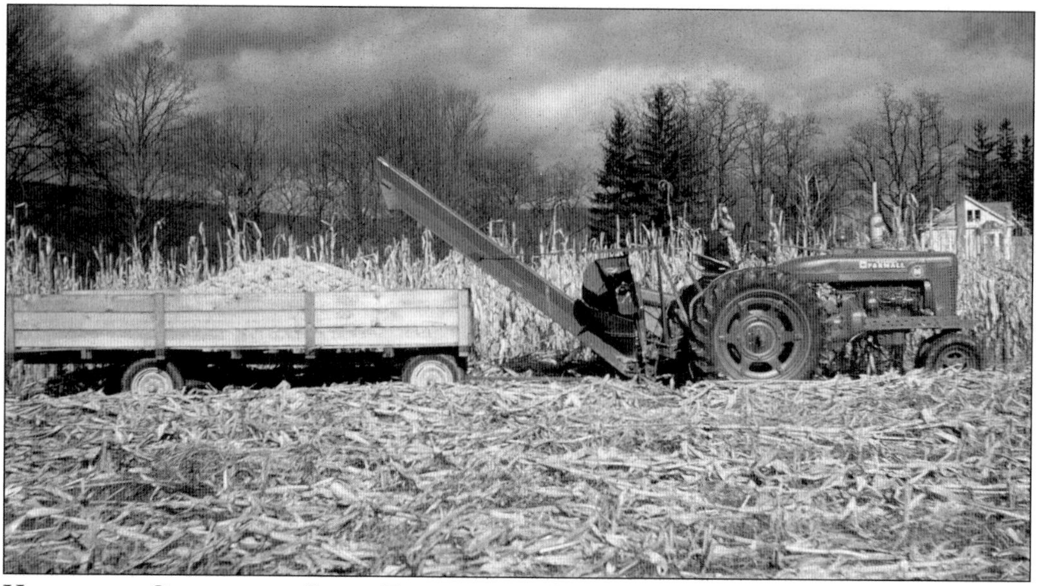

Harvesting Corn on the Shaul Farm, 1940. John Shaul poses on a 1939 Farmall M tractor, which is being used to harvest corn on the Bouck's Island farm. The Canady home is in the background. (Courtesy of the Shaul family.)

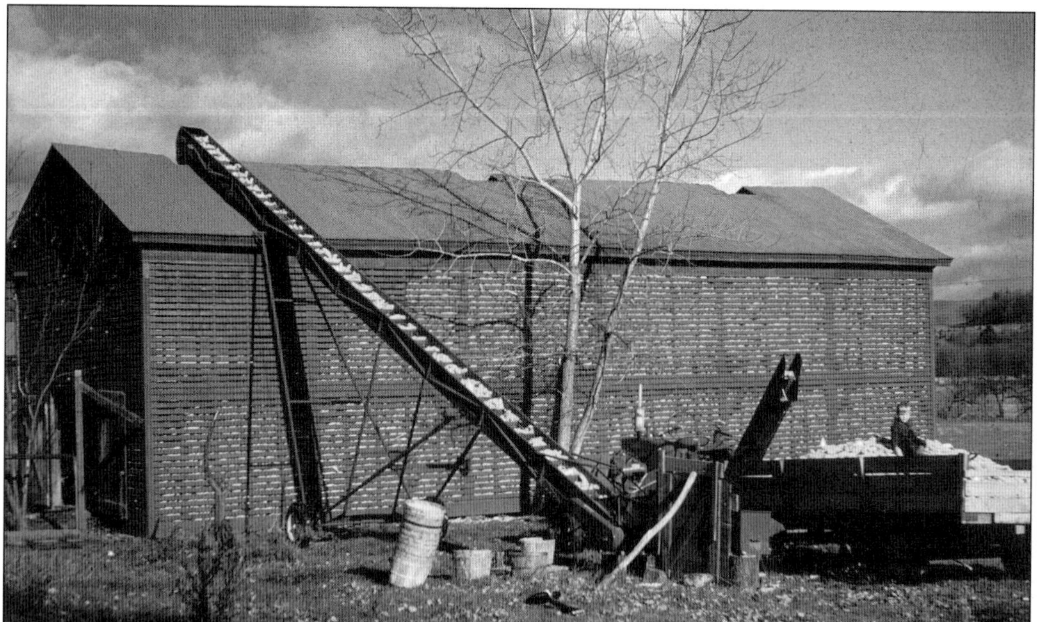

Loading Corn into the Corncrib, 1950. Corn is being loaded into the corncrib on the Shaul farm in Fultonham. The elevator moves the corn up into a hatch in the roof. The crib is made of slats of wood spaced to allow air circulation. (Courtesy of the Shaul family.)

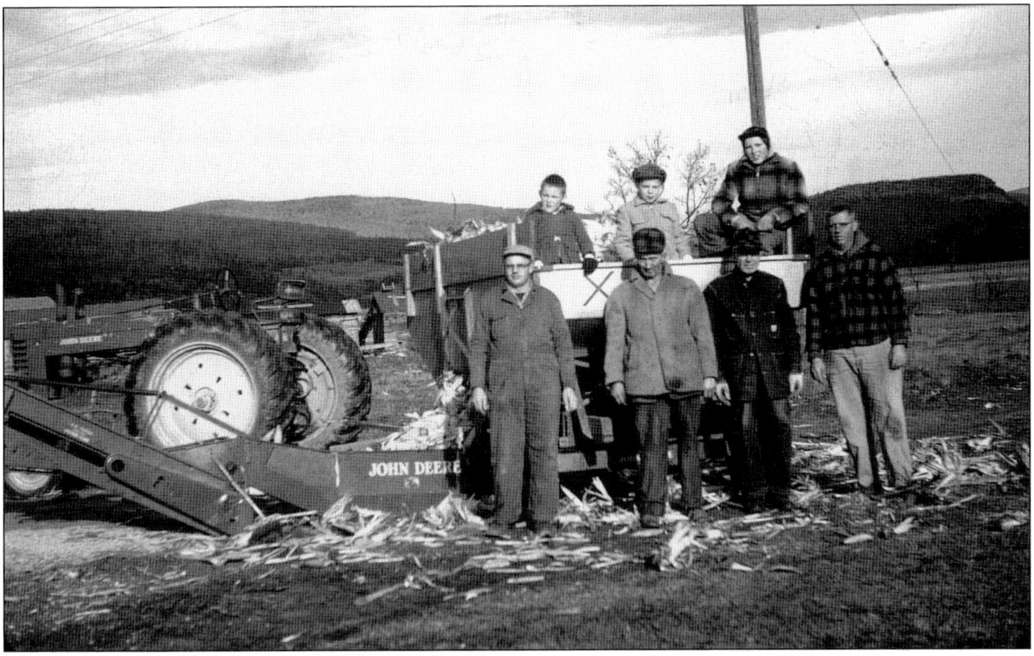

HARVESTING CORN ON THE SHAUL FARM, 1956. Using a John Deere A tractor, men are loading corn into corncribs on the Shaul farm in Fultonham. From left to right are (first row) Bob Shaul, Henry Goodrich, Ed Vroman, and Max Shaul; (second row) Charles, Dick, and John Shaul. Vroman's Nose is in the background (right). (Courtesy of the Shaul family.)

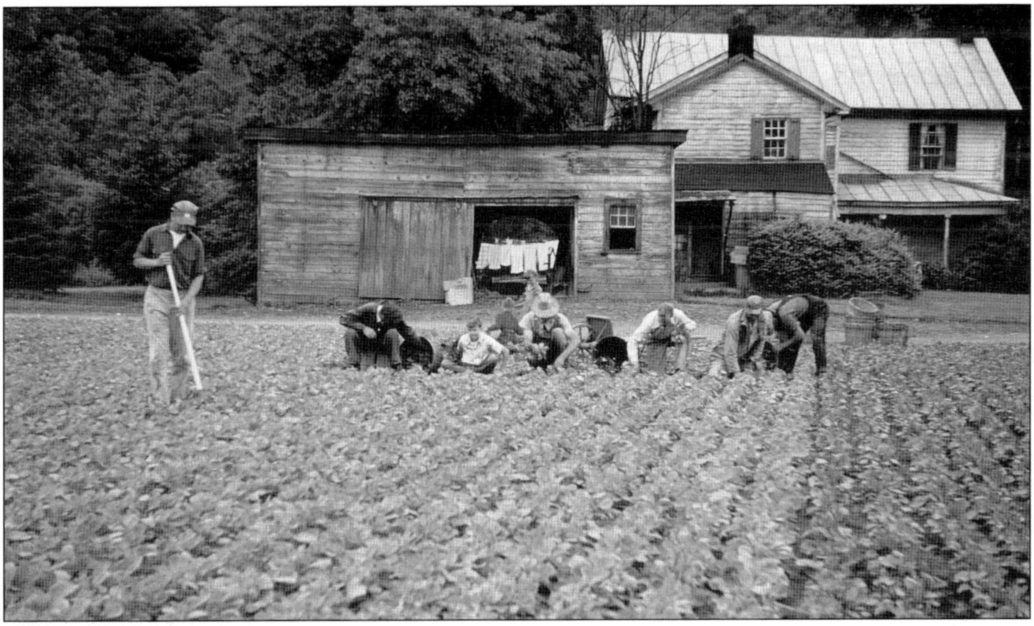

TRANSPLANTING SEEDLING CABBAGE PLANTS, 1948. This view is taken in a field behind the Shaul home on Bouck's Island. The Shauls had purchased the former Gov. William C. Bouck house, which was in a dilapidated state at the time. From left to right are Dick Otten, unidentified, Clarke Rhinehart, Ed Vroman, David Rhinehart, Milford Myers, and unidentified. The children in the back are John and Brownie Shaul. (Courtesy of the Shaul family.)

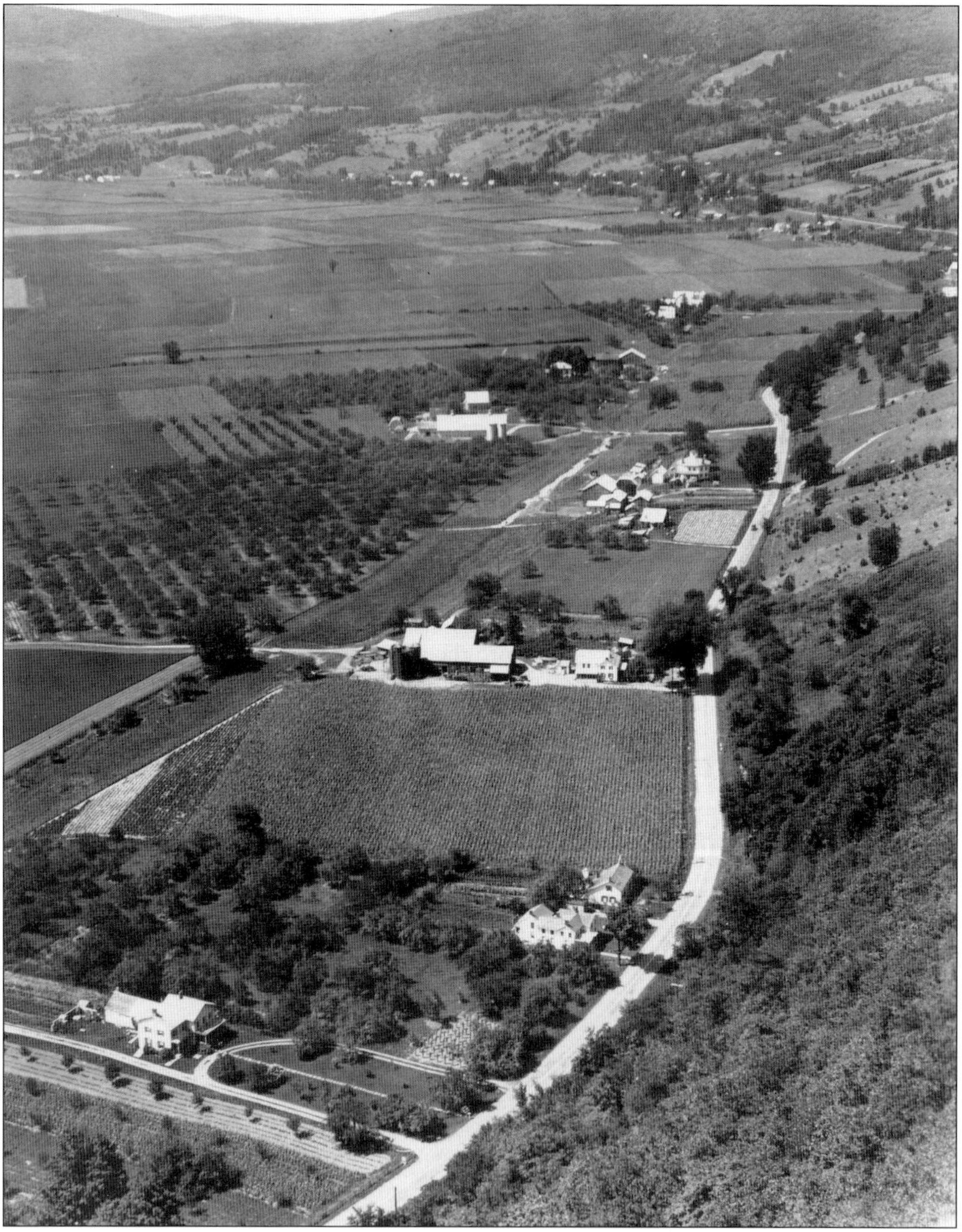

The Schoharie Valley in Fulton. This 1940s view from Vroman's Nose shows the fertile fields of the Schoharie Valley in the town of Fulton. Bohringer's fruit farm, then owned by Fred Bohringer and later by his son Robert, is at the lower left. The 1854 Octagon House is in the middle distance. The highway is State Route 30, known as the Timothy Murphy Trail. (Courtesy of OSFM.)

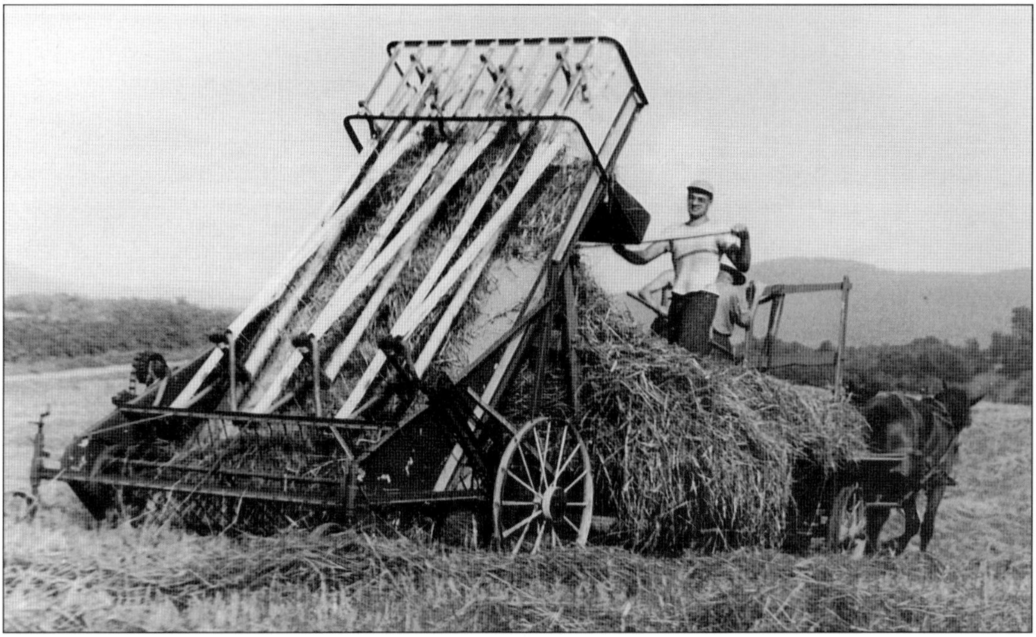

HAYING ON THE BARBER FARM. The Barber farm has been family owned since 1857. When Roger and Grace Barber took over the farm in 1948, it consisted of 85 acres and 30 head of dairy cows. Here, around 1950, Roger brings in the hay with the aid of a team of horses. The machine loads the hay from windrows and moves it into the wagon. (Courtesy of the Barber family.)

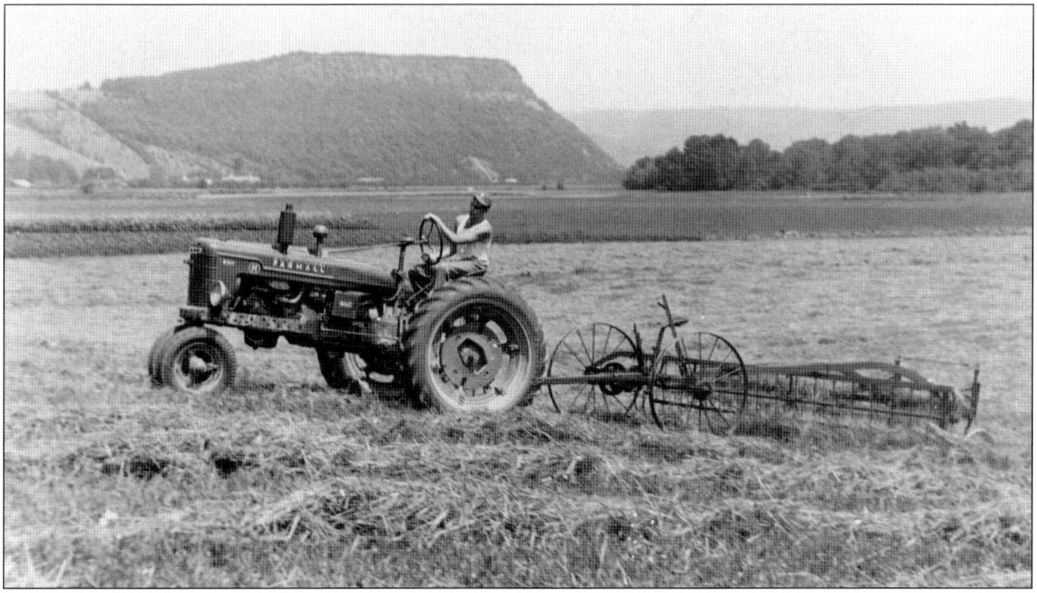

RAKING HAY ON THE BARBER FARM. Roger Barber uses a Farmall H tractor to rake hay around 1950. He expanded the farm to 580 acres and began the practice of selling vegetables from his roadside farm stand. The farm was named a Century Farm in 1970. Roger was New York State commissioner of agriculture from 1975 to 1983 and was active in many community organizations. Vroman's Nose is in the background. (Courtesy of the Barber family.)

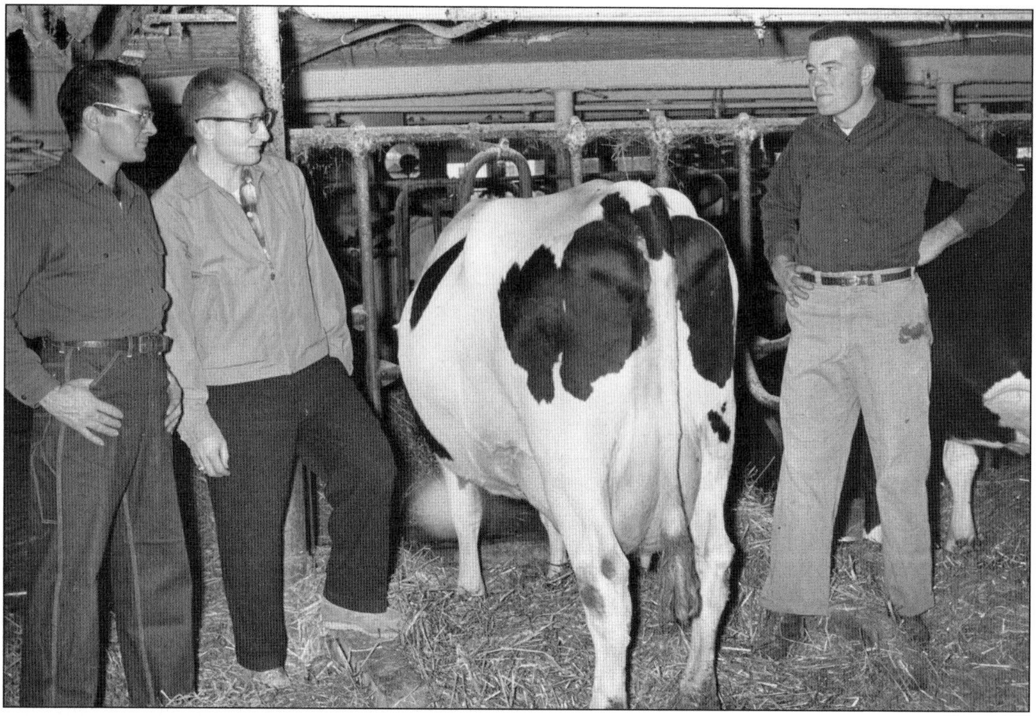

IN THE DAIRY BARN. Roger Barber (left) discusses the finer points of his Holstein cow in this photograph taken in the 1950s. His herd of registered Holsteins eventually reached over 300 head, producing more than 18,000 pounds of milk per cow annually. (Courtesy of the Barber family.)

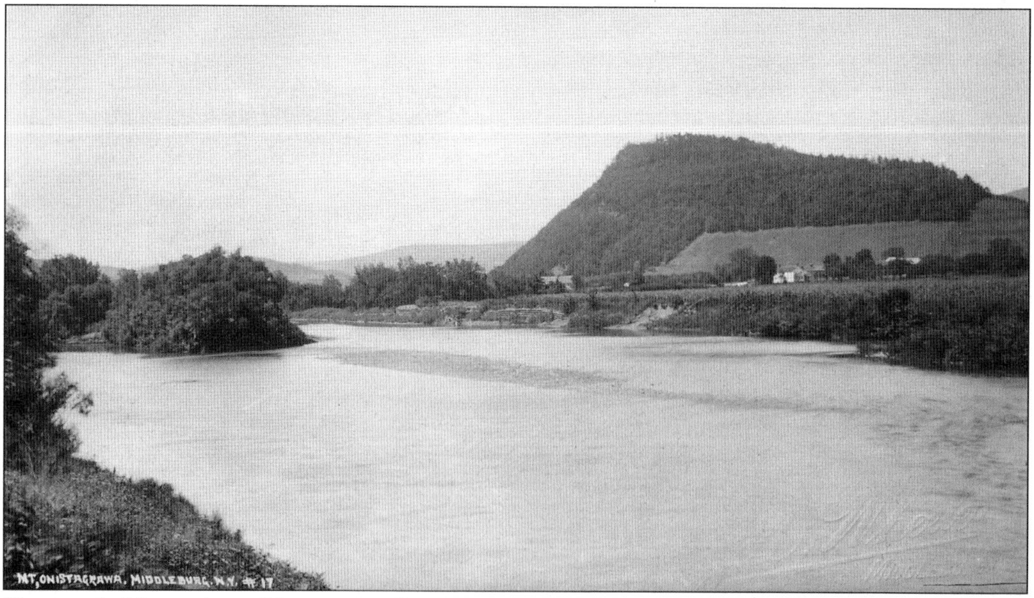

VROMAN'S NOSE, ALSO KNOWN AS ONISTAGRAWA. Vroman's Nose is one of the iconic images in the valley. The Indians called it Onistagrawa, meaning "Corn Mountain." Adam Vroman purchased some 1,000 acres of land below the mountain from the Indians in 1714. This 1900s scene shows the Schoharie Creek as it winds along the flats near Middleburgh. (Courtesy of OSFM, Robert Mahar collection.)

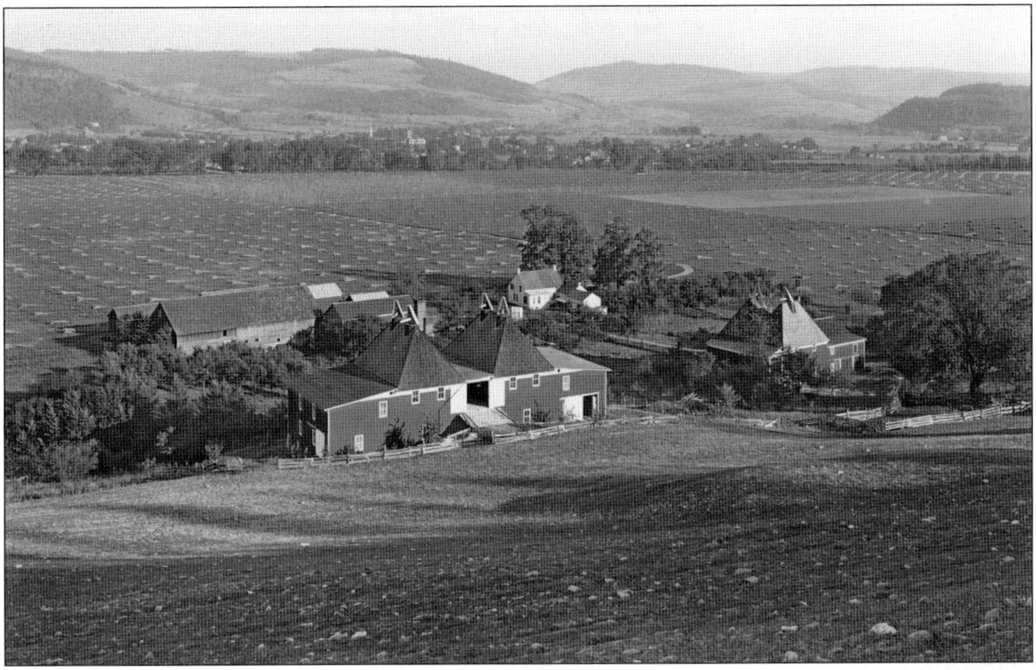

Pindar's Hop Farm, Middleburgh. The buildings with the peaked roofs are hop houses, where the hop flowers were heated to dry before packing and shipping. Visible in the distance are piles of hop poles, which, when erected, would hold the hop vines as they grew. This 1911 view was taken in the spring. (Courtesy of New York State Archives.)

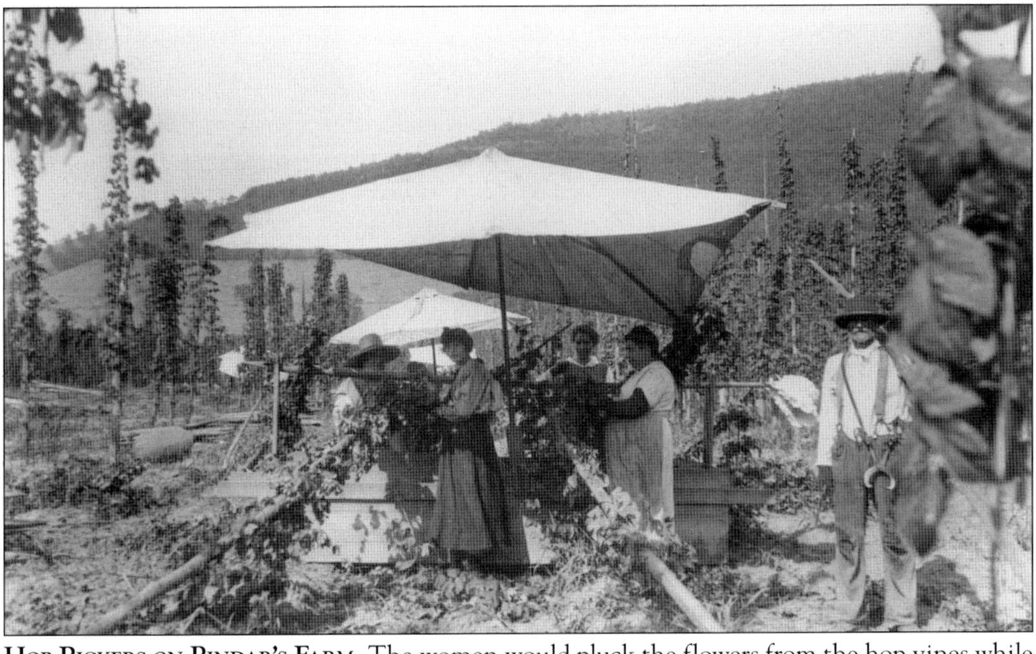

Hop Pickers on Pindar's Farm. The women would pluck the flowers from the hop vines while the men took down the poles with the vines on them and brought the hops to the pickers. The man on the right has a tool to pull the poles out of the ground. (Courtesy of Schoharie Colonial Heritage Association's Schoharie Valley Railroad Museum.)

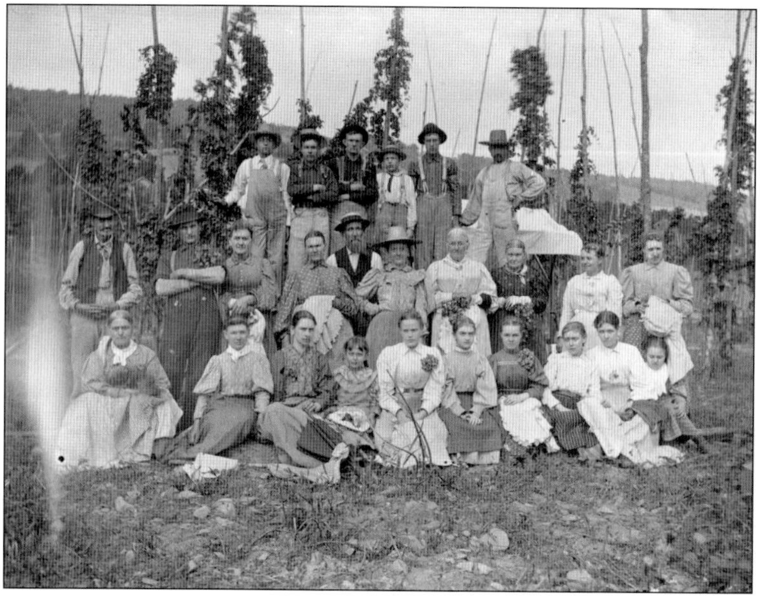

Hop Pickers. During the early 1900s, many Schoharie County farmers grew hops. The hop vine grows on the long poles seen in the background of this photograph. When the flowers were ready, hop pickers—men, women, and children—would harvest the hops. In 1855, a total of 440,750 pounds of hops were produced in the county, but production had virtually ceased by 1950. (Courtesy of OSFM.)

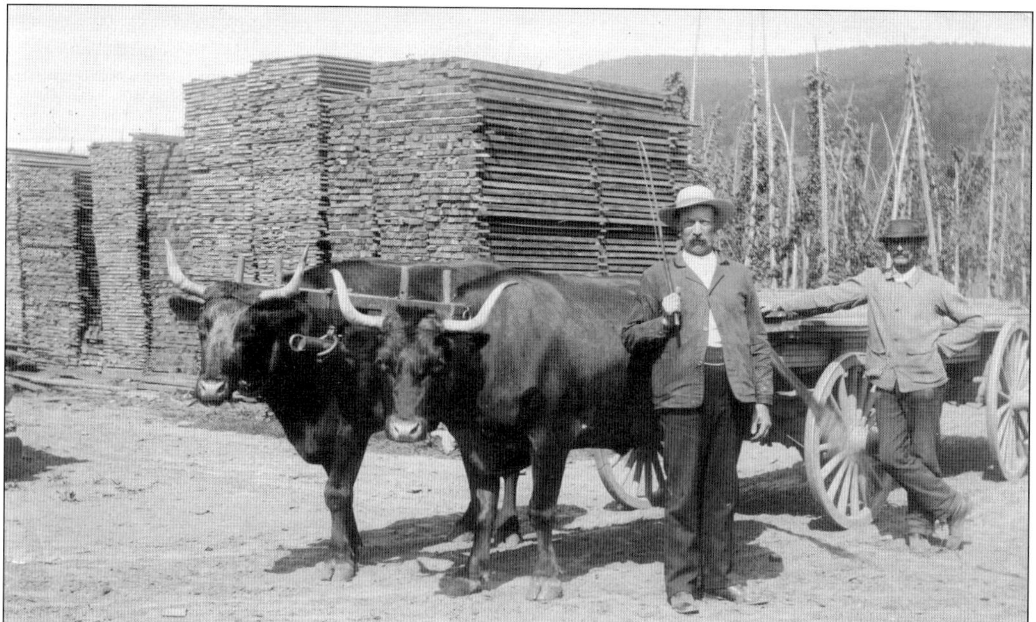

A Middleburgh Hop Yard. In James Borst's hop yard on Cliff Street in Middleburgh, Robert Gordon (left) and William Earles are pictured next to the oxen. The Creek Lumber Company owned the stacks of lumber in the background. Hop vines growing on poles can be seen to the right. (Courtesy of MLHR.)

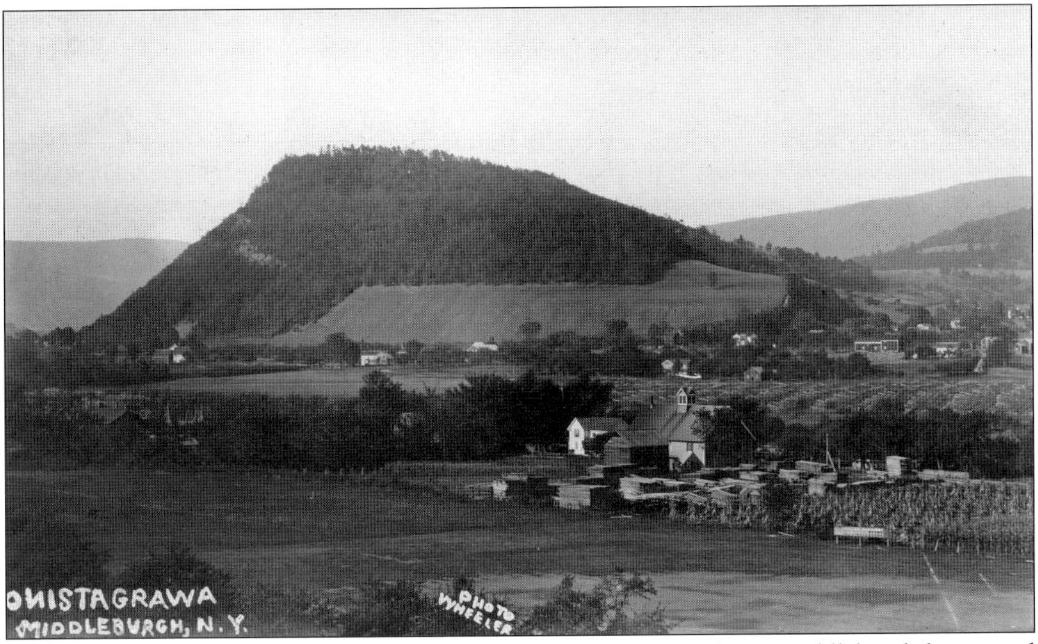

VROMAN'S NOSE AND MIDDLEBURGH FARMS. This 1900s scene shows Middleburgh barns and James Borst's hop fields, though the mountain lies in the town of Fulton. The open fields on the mountain are now treed, and the mountain itself is largely a protected nature preserve. (Courtesy of OSFM, Robert Mahar collection.)

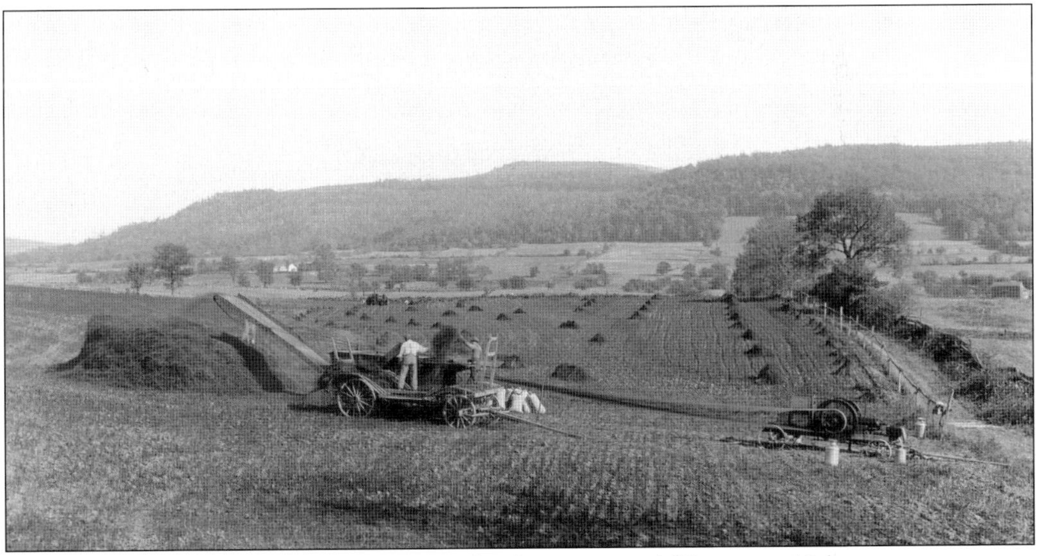

THRESHING NEAR MIDDLEBURGH, 1920. An International Harvester 10-horsepower tractor drives the thresher via a long belt. Cans are set near the tractor to provide cooling water. In the distance, a wagon team gathers the crop while another wagon is unloaded at the thresher. The grain drops into bags seen near the thresher while a large pile of chaff is created (left). (Courtesy of New York State Archives.)

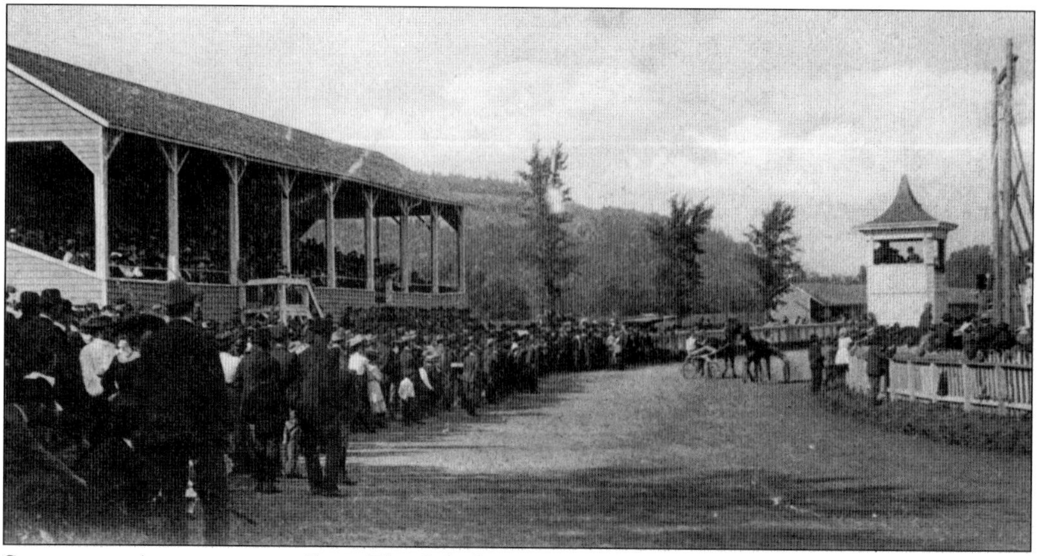

Schoharie Agricultural Fair. The Schoharie Agricultural Society was formed in 1843 with Gov. William C. Bouck as president. In 1844, the fair was held in Schoharie. Premiums were given for the best horse ($8 to Abraham Dietz), the best bull ($5 to George Manning), the best 100 pounds of cheese ($3 to Mrs. William Engle), and many others. Horse racing was popular, as shown in this c. 1905 view. The last fair in Schoharie was in 1917. (Courtesy of MLHR.)

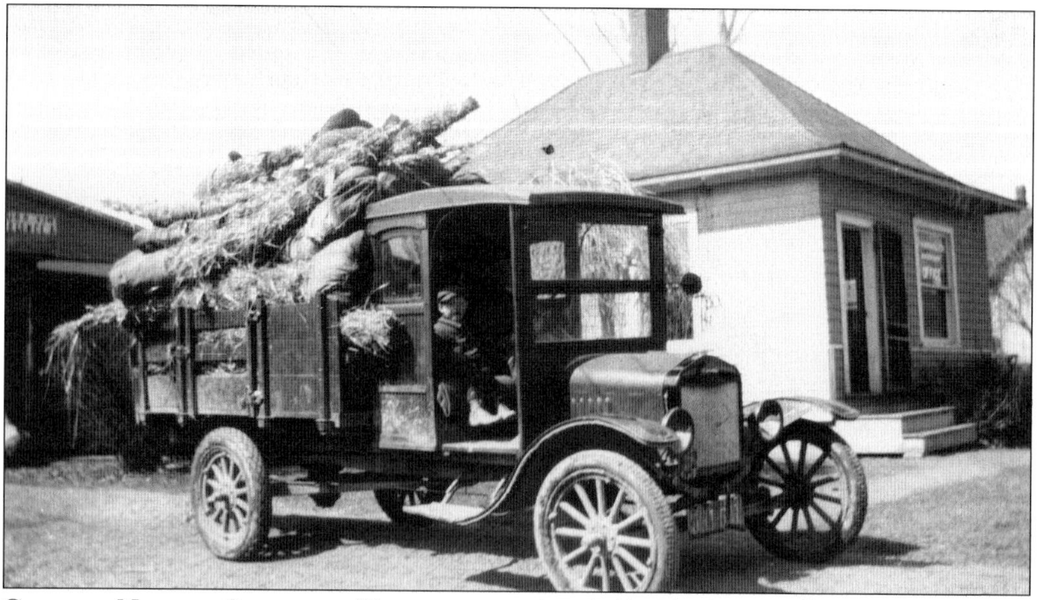

Guernsey Nursery, Schoharie. The nursery was founded by Floyd A. Guernsey around 1890. At first, it was on the south side of Bridge Street. When the Schoharie Agricultural Fair was disbanded in 1917, the Guernseys bought the fairgrounds and expanded. Today, the nursery continues as a four-generation family business. In this 1920s photograph, a boy waits in a Ford Model T one-ton truck loaded with bundled trees for delivery. (Courtesy of Skip Edmonds.)

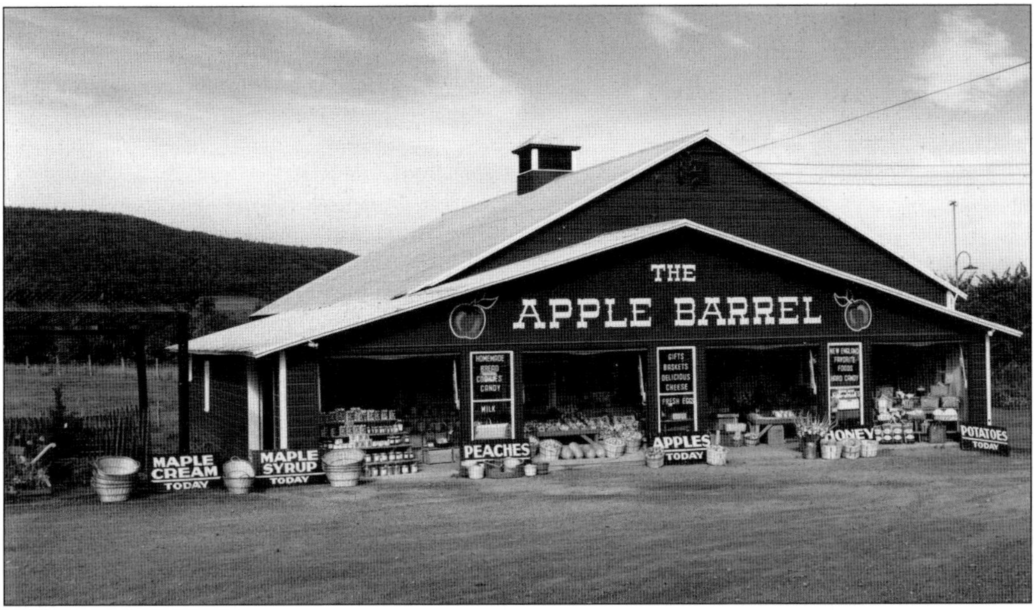

The Apple Barrel, Schoharie. The Apple Barrel was built in the 1940s as an outlet for Edwin and Helen Vedder's orchard on Terrace Mountain. Willis and Ruth Vedder Truax bought the outlet in 1965 and named it the Apple Barrel. They sold seasonal produce, including apples, peaches, potatoes, and maple products. Robert and Sue Loden have owned the Apple Barrel since 1983 and have converted it to a full-line country store and café. (Courtesy of Willis Truax Jr.)

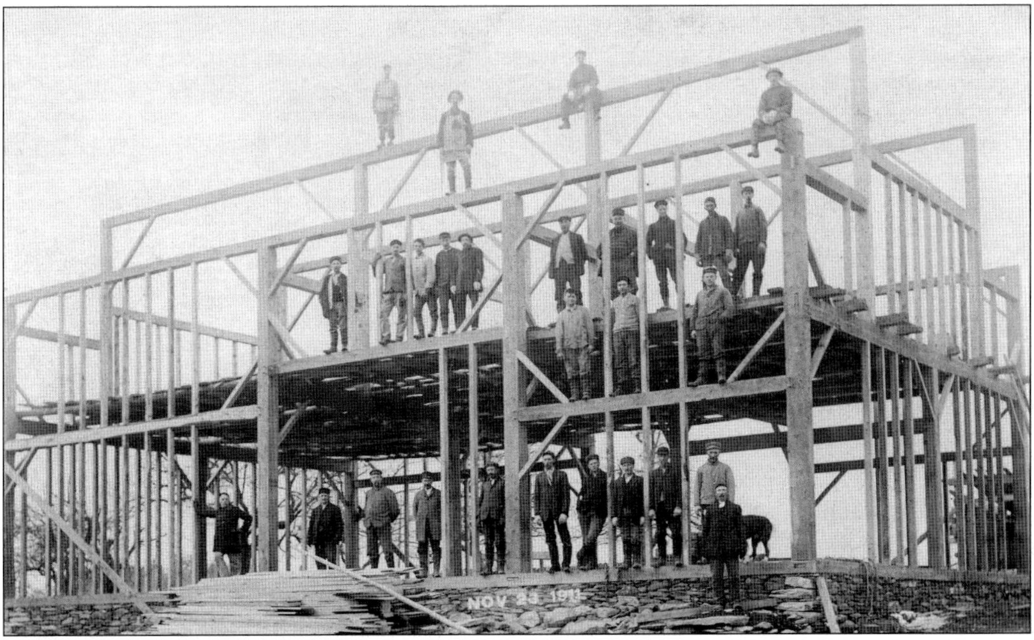

Gallupville Barn Raising. Here, 28 men and a dog participate in the raising of the Ed French barn on November 23, 1911. According to Chester Zimmer, "This was about the end of the post and beam mortise type of barn construction. All the material was laid out and made ready ahead of time. Alvin Manchester, one of the carpenters, then 22 years old, stands on the top." (Courtesy of OSFM, Chester Zimmer collection.)

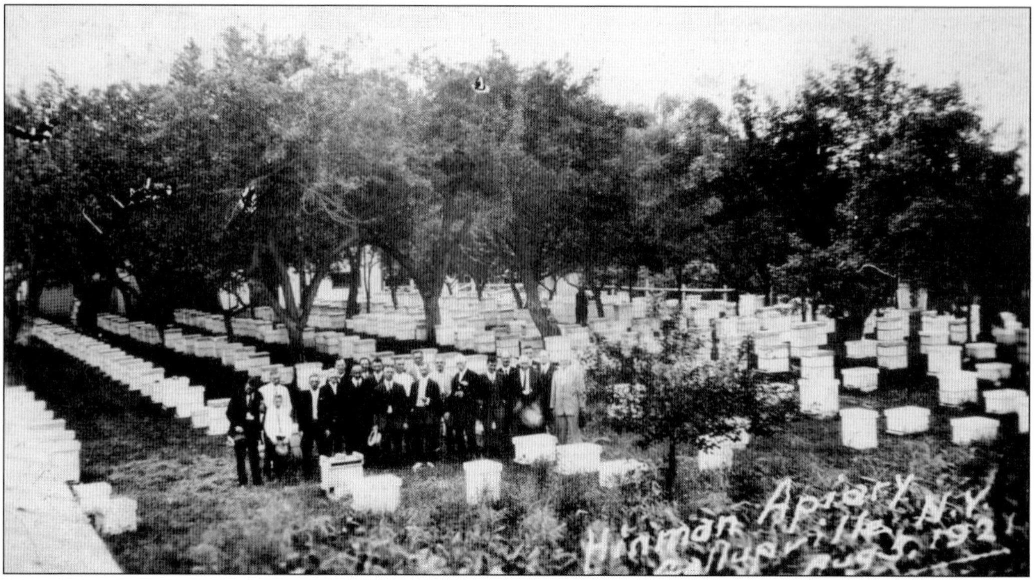

BEEKEEPERS' OUTING, GALLUPVILLE. Beekeepers assemble for a photograph during their outing at the Frank Hinman and Wallace Stahlman apiary in Gallupville, on August 5, 1921. Here, more than 250 beehives are visible. In the 1920s, honey was sold locally in five-pound aluminum pails—not in jars as today. Barrels of honey were shipped to New York City and even to Germany, where metheglin, a spicy mead, was made from the fermented honey. (Courtesy of Naomi Zimmer Wikane.)

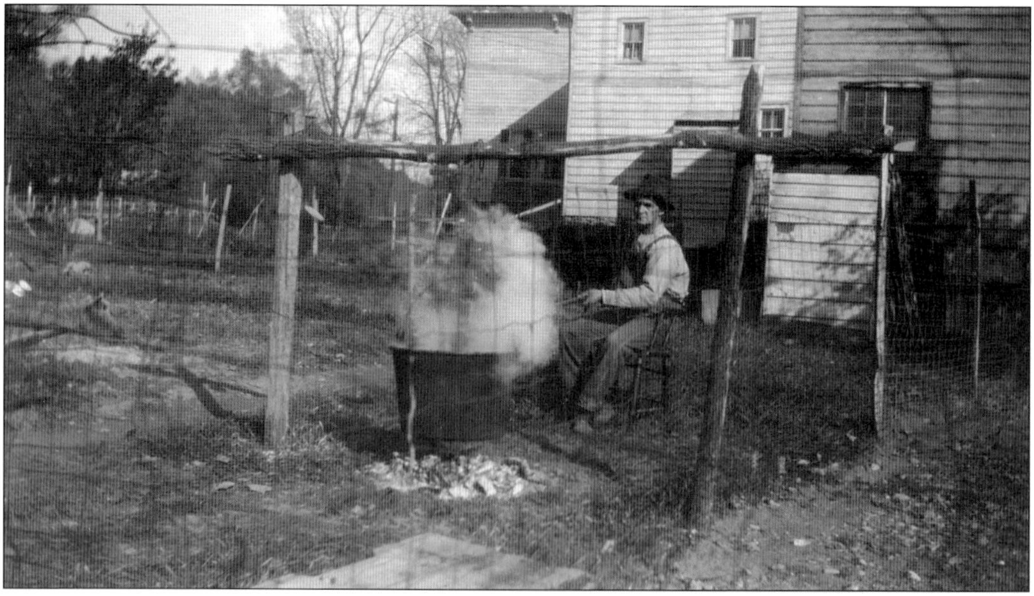

HOMEMADE APPLE BUTTER. In the 1940s, many people made their own foodstuffs. Wallace Stahlman of Gallupville is making apple butter in a large cauldron. He has lit a fire underneath the pot to slowly boil away the water from the apples. Pectin from the cores and peels helped in making a smooth, butter-like consistency. Apple butter was canned for the winter or sold to neighbors. (Courtesy Naomi Zimmer Wikane.)

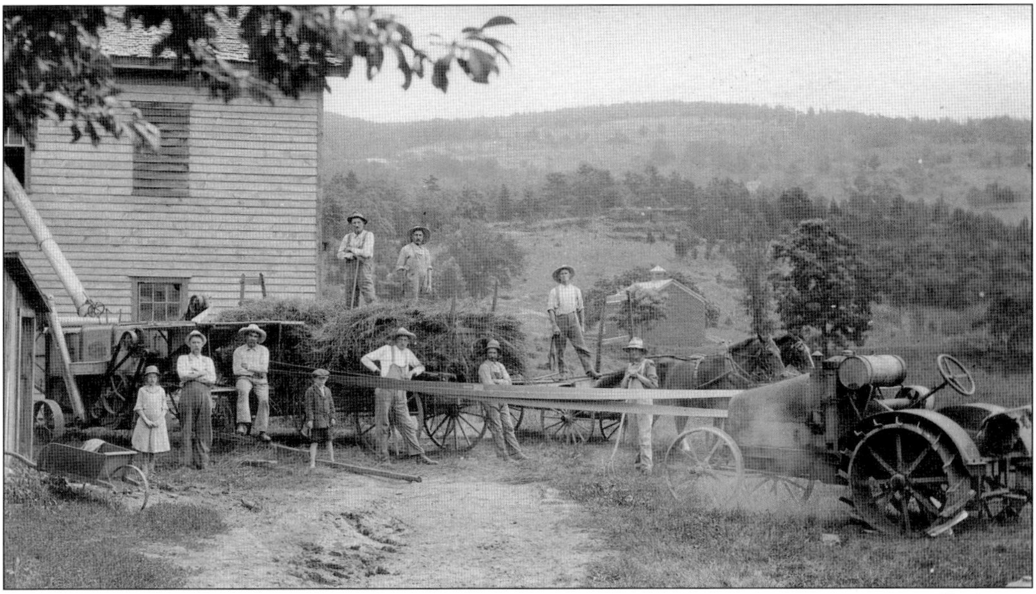

Harvesting, Gallupville. During the 1920s, new methods of farming were continually being developed. Here, on a farm near Gallupville, an International Harvester tractor is used to provide power to a Case thresher that also delivers the straw into the barn. The horse and wagon were still used to bring in the harvest from the fields. (Courtesy of OSFM, Chester Zimmer collection.)

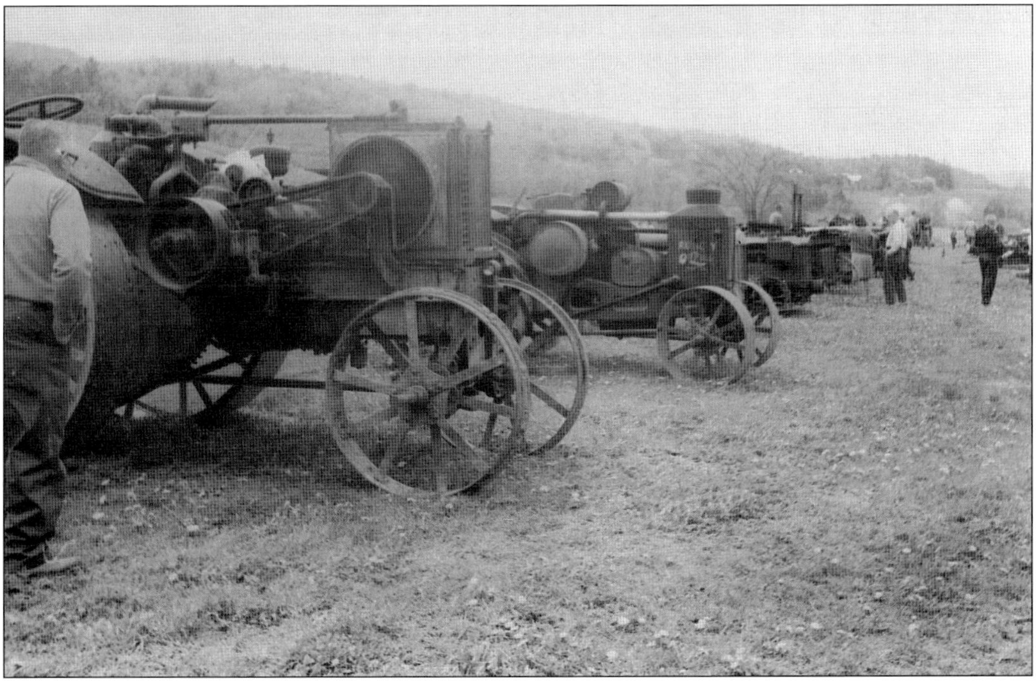

The Gas Up, Shutters Corners, 1968. The idea of the Gas Up originated in 1967 with Fritz Rolfe, his sons Ron and Todd, and local collectors of antique tractors. The first Gas Up show at Shutters Corners near Gallupville was in 1968. The 1968 photograph shows a tractor lineup with a 1921 International Harvester Titan tractor (left) followed by a 1923 Rumley Oil Pull tractor. (Courtesy of Todd Rolfe.)

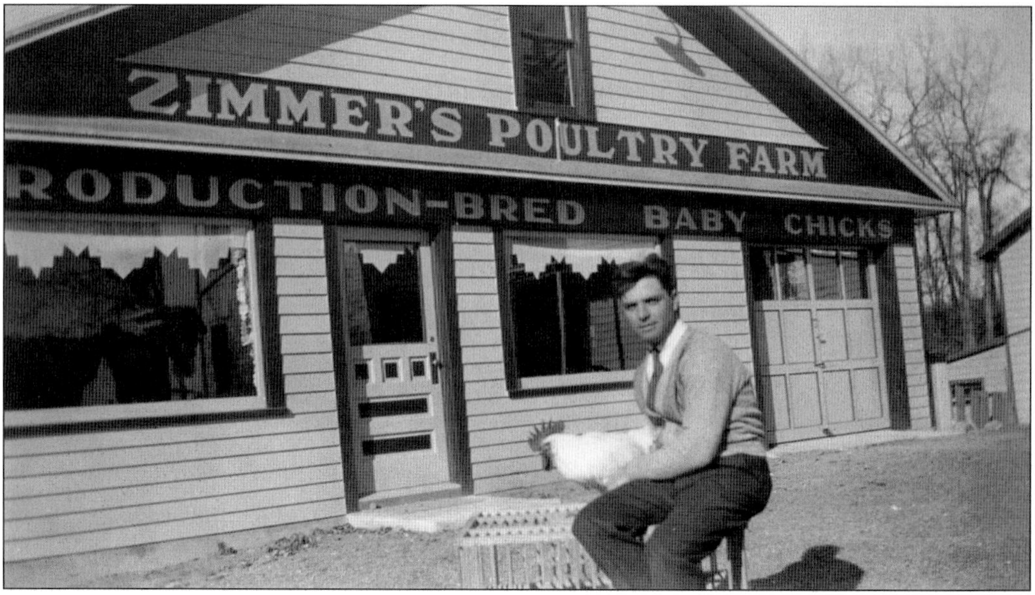

Zimmer Hatchery, Gallupville. Chester Zimmer holds a white leghorn chicken in front of the Zimmer Poultry Farm hatchery in Gallupville in 1940. Chester began the poultry business in 1934, and the farm was one of the most up-to-date in the state by 1949. Within 10 years, however, the poultry industry had completely changed. Zimmer quit the hatchery business in 1959, but he kept other parts of the poultry business until 1972. (Courtesy of Naomi Zimmer Wikane.)

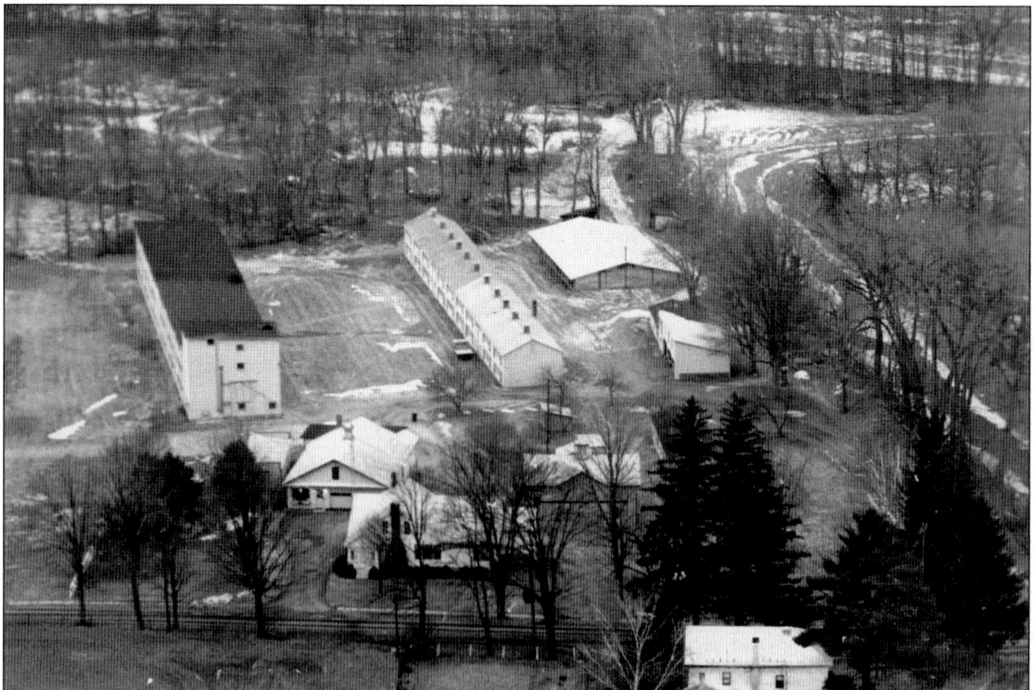

Aerial View, Zimmer Poultry Farm. This 1962 aerial view shows the Zimmer residence, bottom center, the hatchery behind the house, and the two- and three-story henhouses in the rear. King's Creek is on the right. (Courtesy of Naomi Zimmer Wikane.)

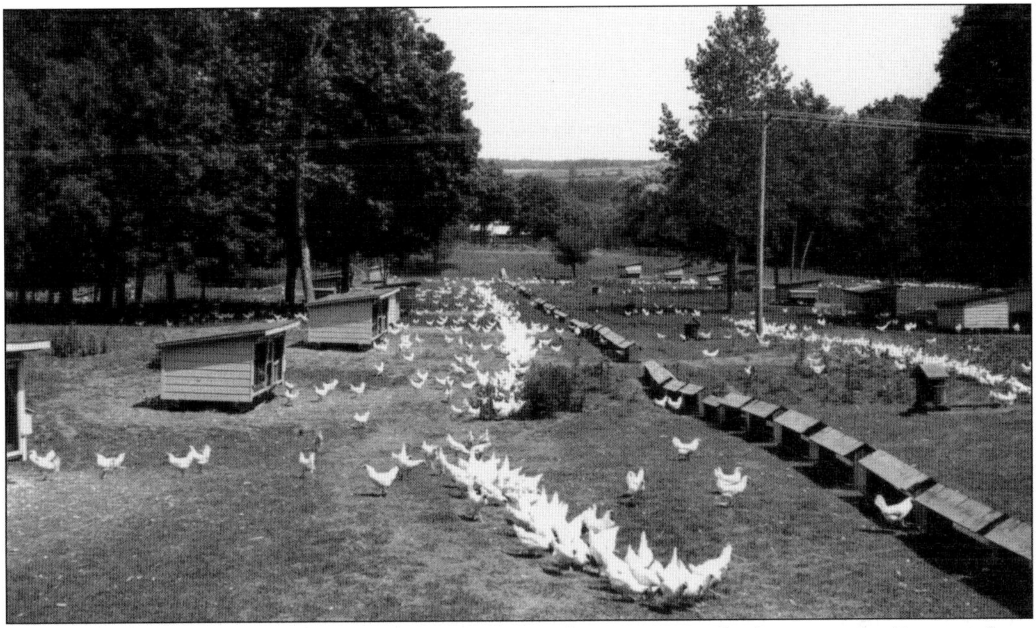

Free-Range Chickens on the Zimmer Farm. In the summers, chickens on the Zimmer farm were placed in free range. Here, white leghorns are being fed on the ground. The small houses on the left are night coops, where the chickens were safely locked up for the night. The little structures on the right are feeders. (Courtesy of Naomi Zimmer Wikane.)

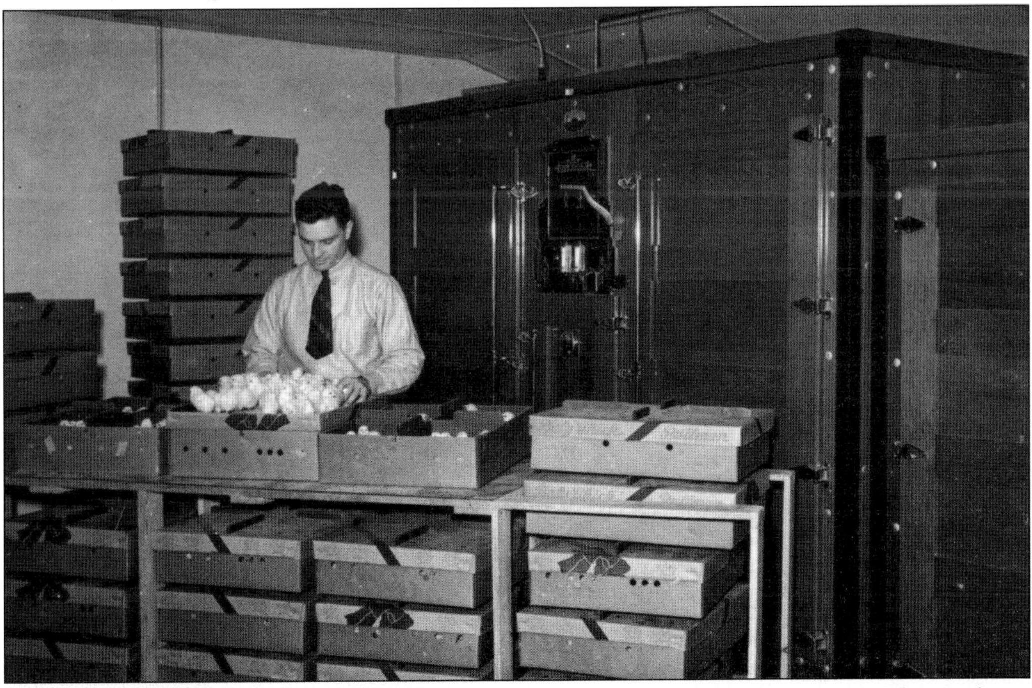

Packing Chicks. Chester Zimmer packs chicks into boxes for delivery to customers. The incubator is behind Chester. The chicks have just hatched out of the incubator and are being packed 100 to a box—25 chicks in each quarter section. In a peak year, 250,000 chicks were sold within a 50-mile radius. (Courtesy of Naomi Zimmer Wikane.)

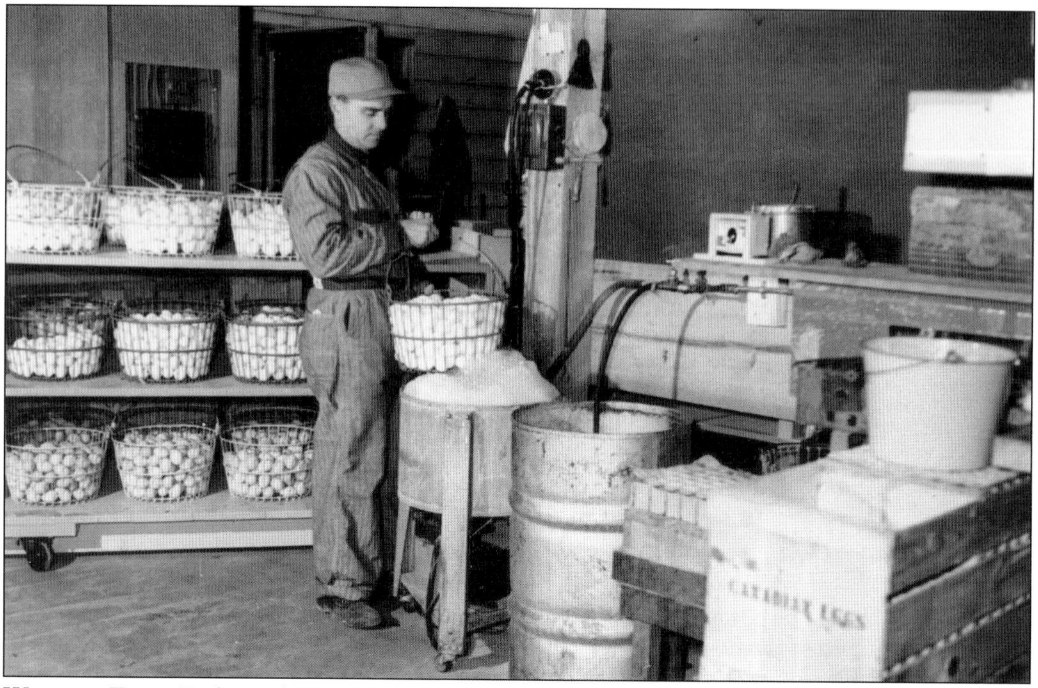

WASHING EGGS. Baskets of eggs were brought from the Zimmer henhouses. The eggs were washed in the egg washer, then candled, graded by size (extra large, large, medium, and small), and crated 30 dozen to a crate for sale direct to stores, restaurants, and bakeries in Schenectady. At peak, 15,000 layers could produce 10,000 eggs in a day. Some eggs went to the incubator to produce chicks for sale. (Courtesy of Naomi Zimmer Wikane.)

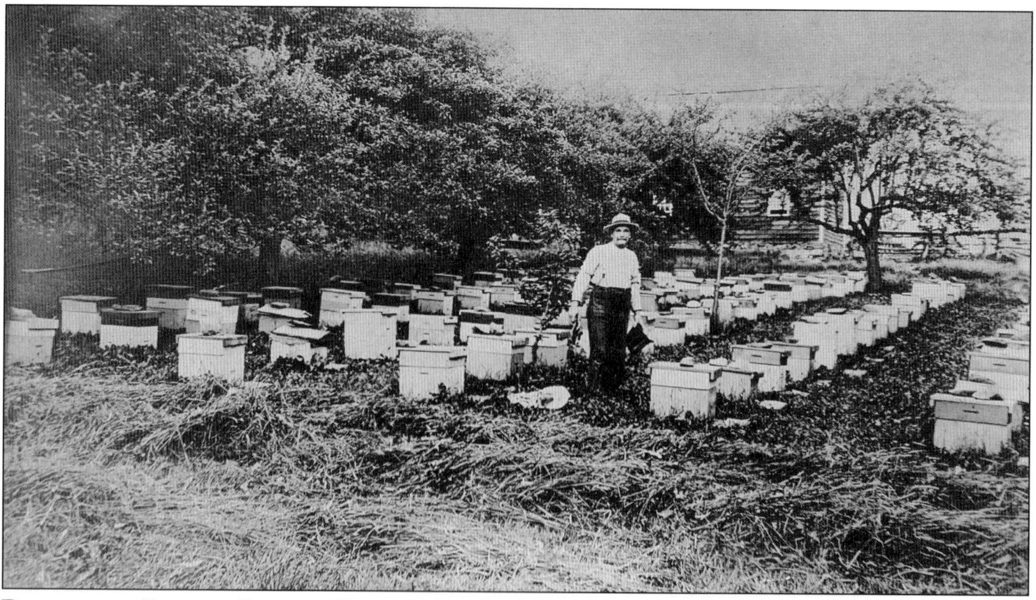

BEEKEEPING, CENTRAL BRIDGE. Clinton Munck of Central Bridge works among over 80 beehives in this c. 1915 photograph. He holds a smoker to calm the bees before he inspects the hive. Though Clinton is not described as a beekeeper in the census, his neighbor Reuben Cox is so described. (Courtesy of Robert Holt.)

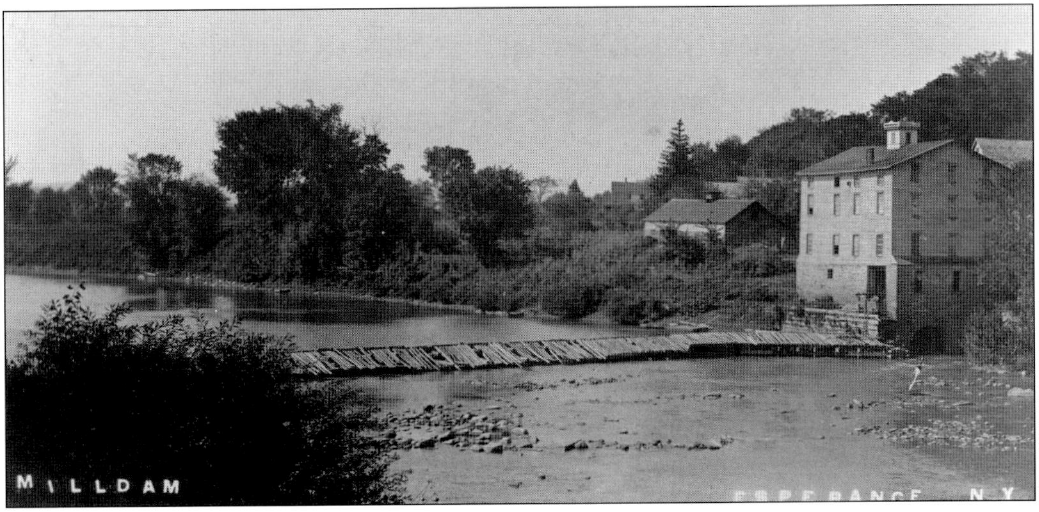

Esperance Mill. The mill was built in 1868 and run by Hanes and Isham. They milled wheat, rye, and buckwheat flour. At the lower left in the photograph below, there was a sawmill. Next door was a flax mill. The power was provided by water secured by a dam, which had to be replaced periodically because of the flooding of the Schoharie Creek. The mill was removed in the 1930s. (Courtesy of OSFM.)

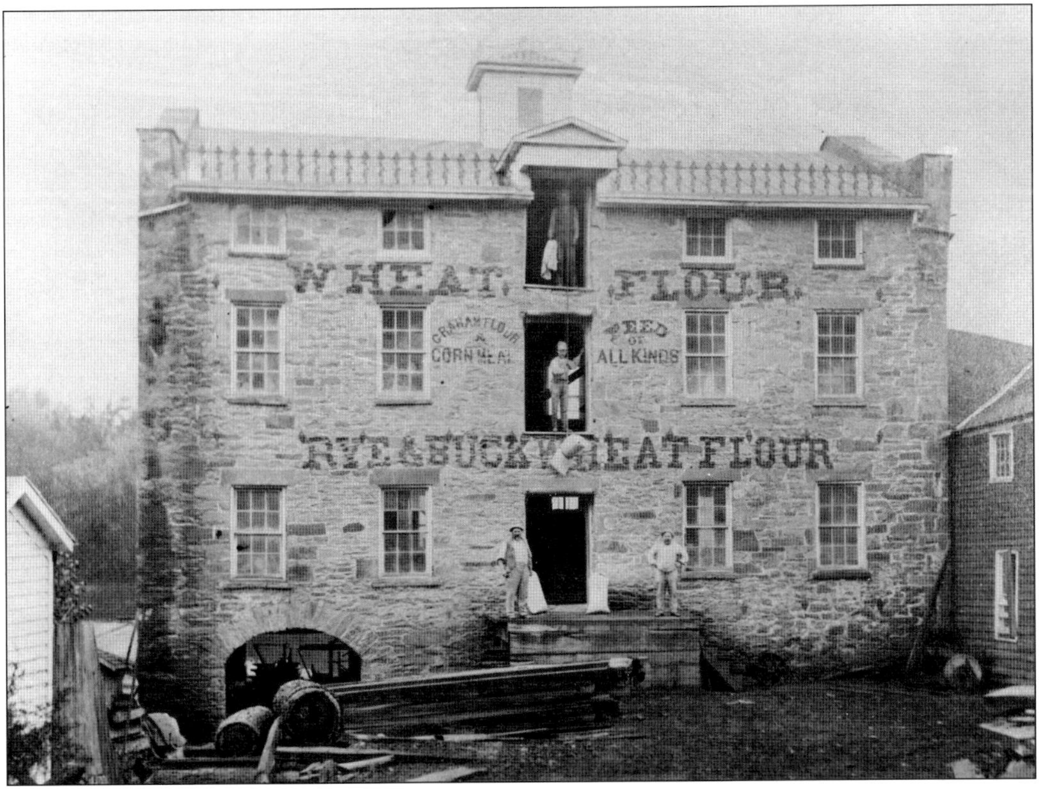

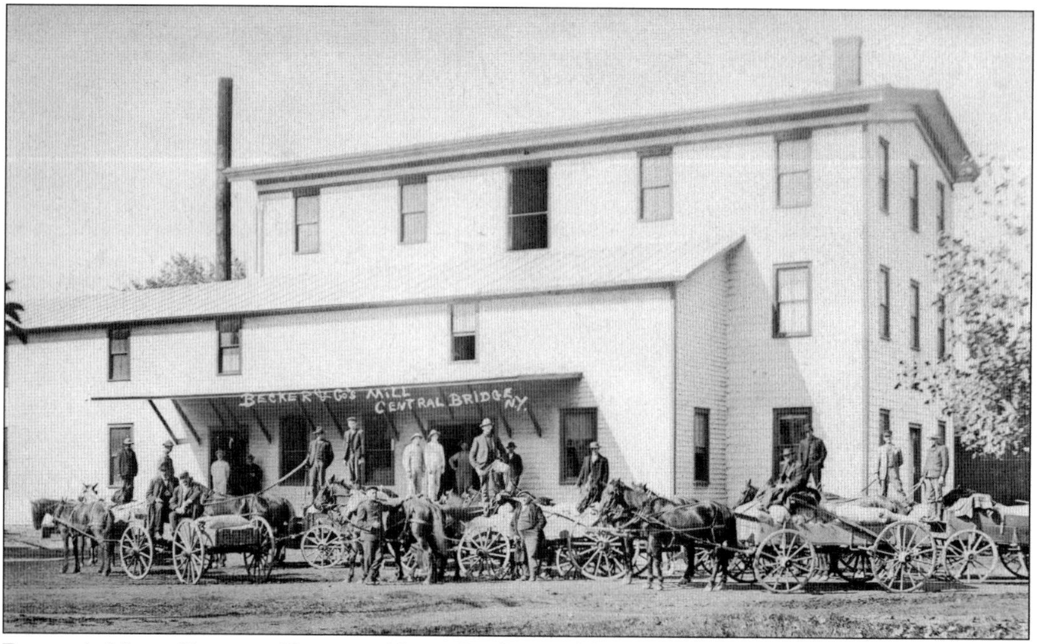

BECKER'S MILL, CENTRAL BRIDGE. Abram Becker and his son Wellington ran the mill from the 1880s until around 1930. Here, around 1910, farmers are bringing bags of grain to be milled into flour. The mill burned and was rebuilt several times. Ernest A. Howard, Beacon Feeds, and Richer Feeds occupied the same site for many years. (Courtesy of Robert Holt.)

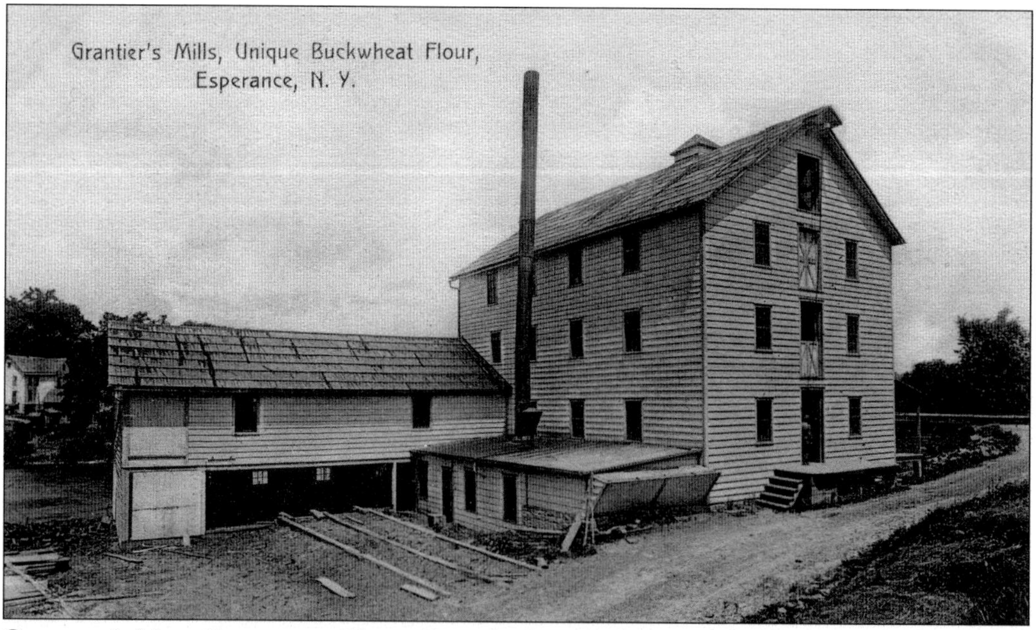

GRANTIER'S MILL, ESPERANCE. The mill was built around 1903. Unlike earlier mills that relied on water-driven turbines to provide power, this one used a diesel engine. Bert Grantier advertised "a new process for stone-ground, absolutely pure buckwheat flour." Buckwheat was widely grown in the Schoharie Valley in the early to mid-1900s. In the 1940s, the mill processed animal feeds. The building was torn down in the 1970s. (Courtesy of OSFM, Robert Mahar collection.)

Two

GILBOA

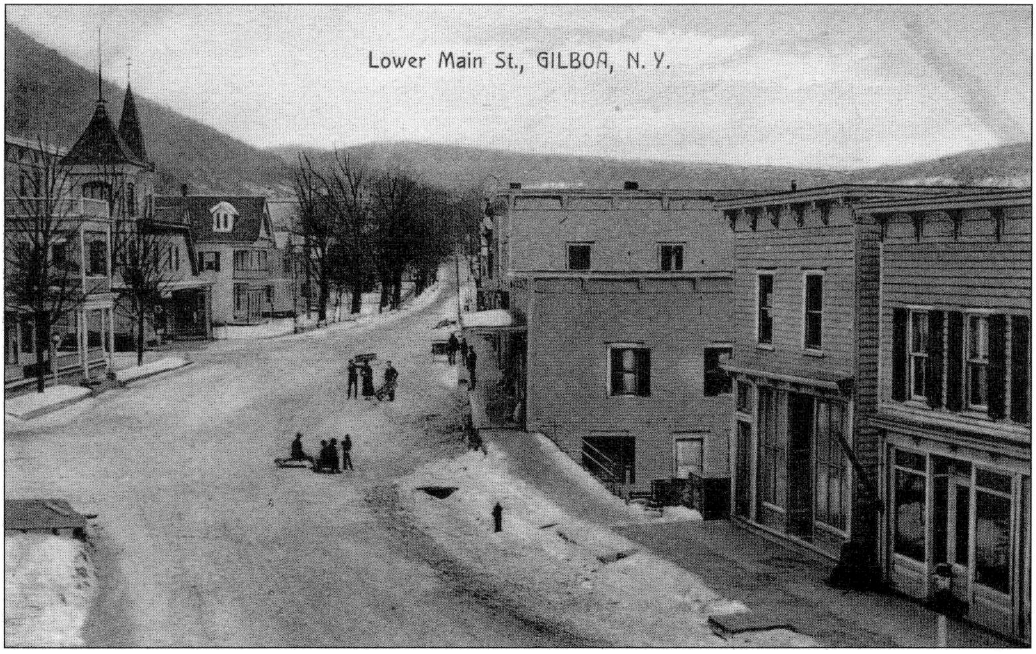

THE VILLAGE OF GILBOA, EARLY 1900S. This winter view of Main Street shows a peaked roof and a steeple (left). The first is a hardware store, while the second is the Methodist church. On the left is the Gilboa House hotel. On the right are Van Loan's meat market and the George Ira Case store. Case sold jewelry and was a gunsmith. (Courtesy of OSFM, Robert Mahar collection.)

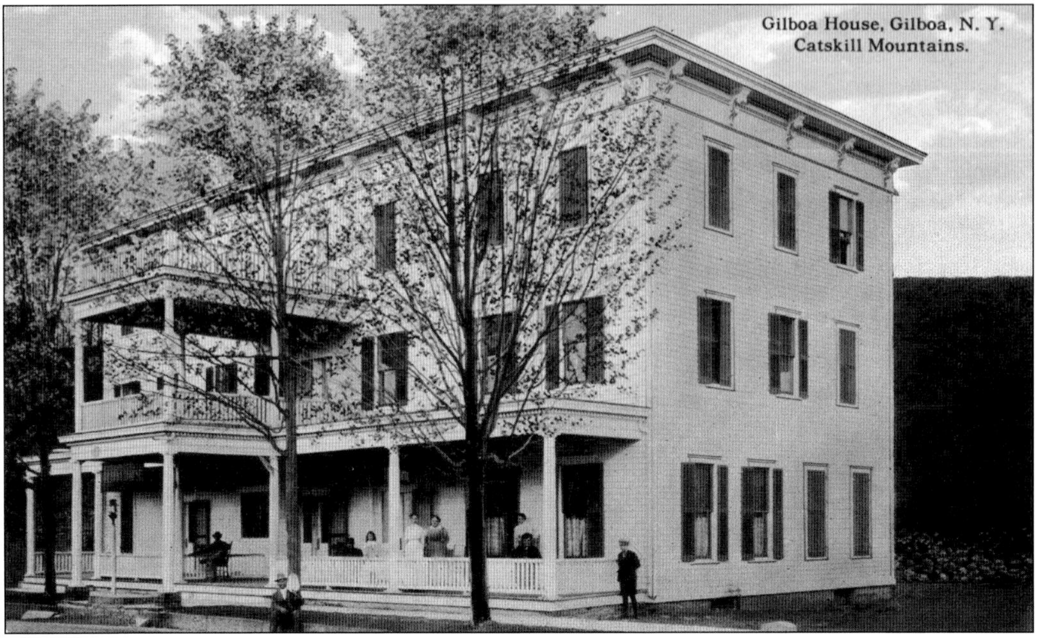

GILBOA HOUSE. George A. Peters was the proprietor of this hotel and boardinghouse in the early 1900s. This was one of the largest hotels in the center of the old village. It too was lost when the dam was constructed. Workmen from the dam no doubt inhabited the hotel during the construction years. (Courtesy of author's collection.)

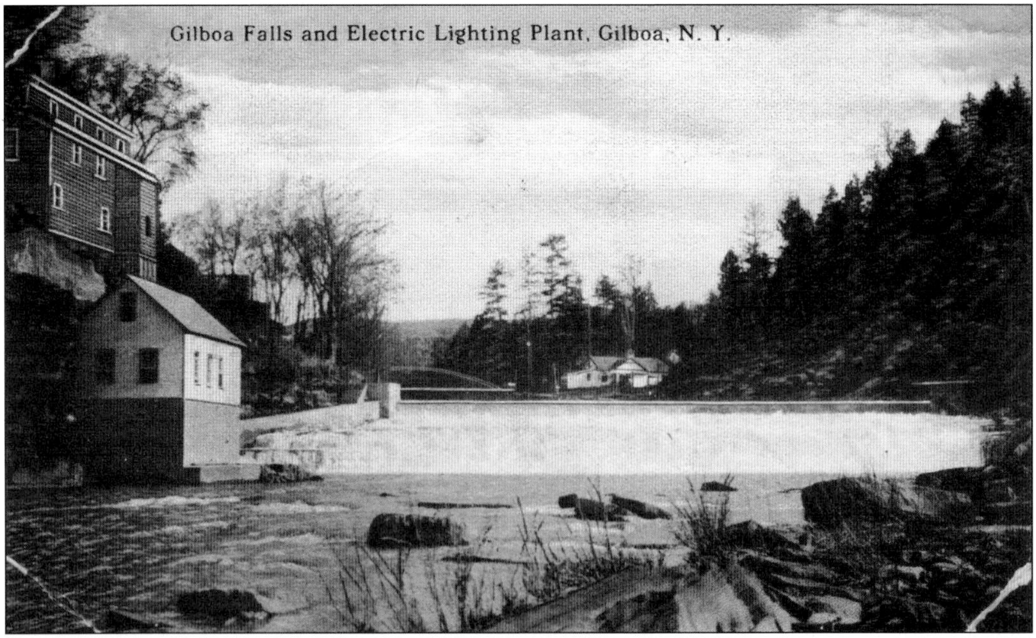

GILBOA FALLS AND THE ELECTRIC PLANT, 1910S. The falls are shown in the middle of the photograph, and they provided power for the electric plant. The Tri-County Power and Light plant is the building on the lower left. Above it is an old cotton mill, which was closed in 1869. Cotton would be brought in from the south and woven into cloth. (Courtesy of Edwin Truax.)

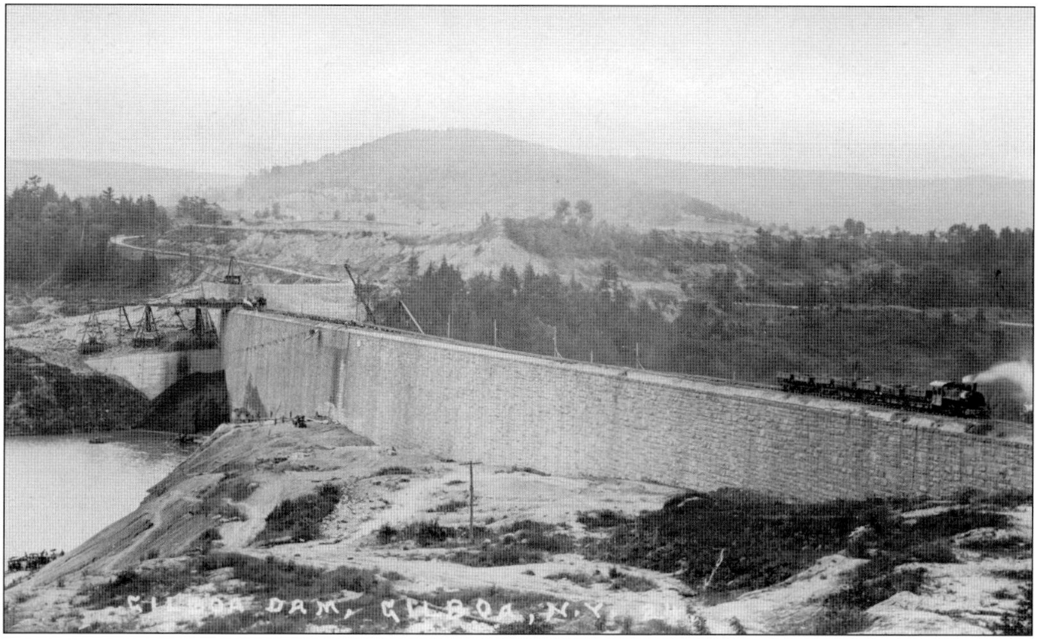

DAM CONSTRUCTION, GILBOA, 1920S. As early as 1897, New York City began looking for more sources of water. Surveys in the Gilboa area began in 1916, and construction of the Gilboa Dam started in 1917. Residents were required to move from the "taken" areas, but most remained until the dam was nearly completed in 1927. A train loaded with material is visible on the dam wall. (Courtesy of OSFM.)

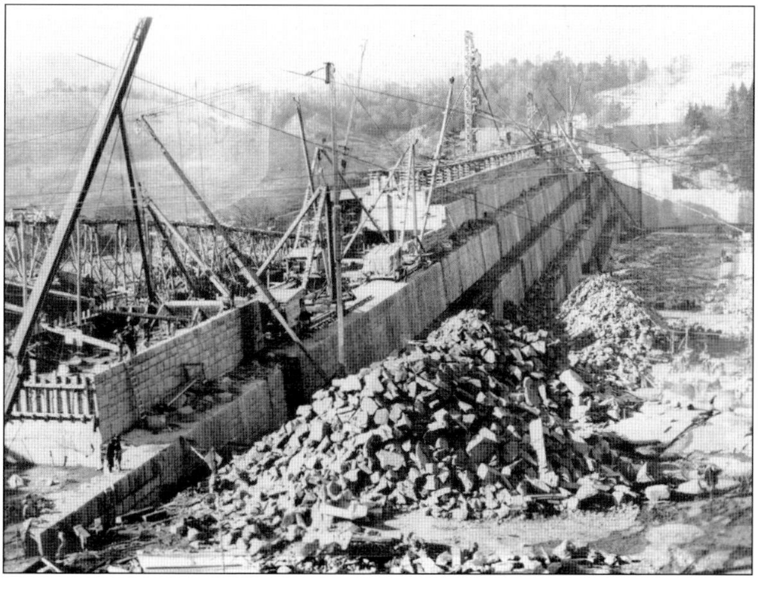

A CLOSER VIEW OF THE DAM CONSTRUCTION. This c. 1925 view of the construction of the Gilboa Dam shows the derricks used to haul material to the top of the dam. Workmen came from far and wide (even from Europe) and lived in the village boardinghouses. Many stayed in the area after the dam was completed. (Courtesy of Kenneth Clark.)

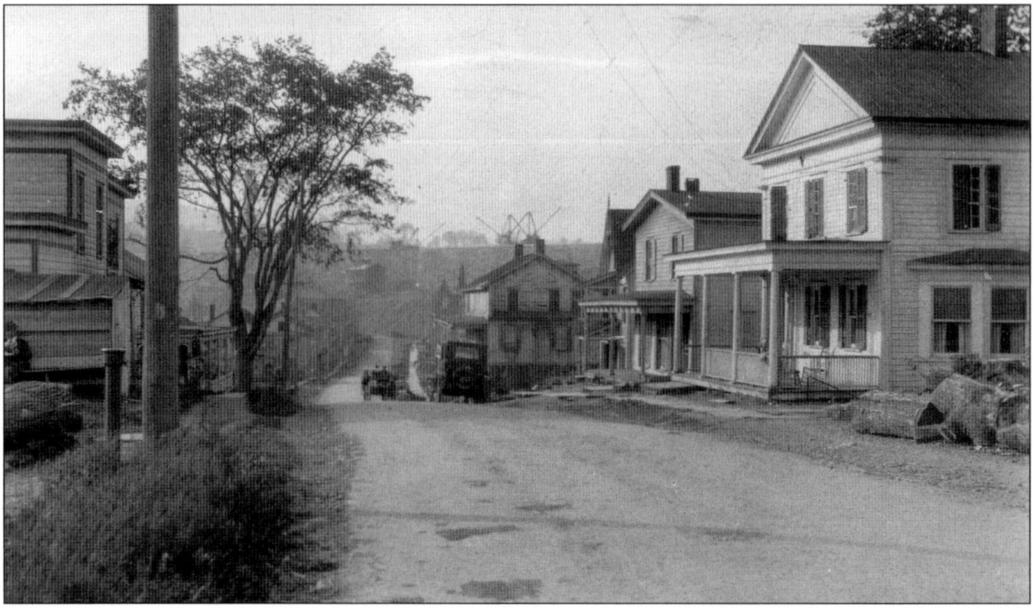

Gilboa Village View, 1920s. This image was taken during the construction of the Gilboa Dam. The construction derricks can be seen on the skyline. Many trees have already been cut down. The Methodist church is in the middle distance. The building on the left belonged to the Dickinson family while the one on the right was the Van Palmer residence. (Courtesy of OSFM.)

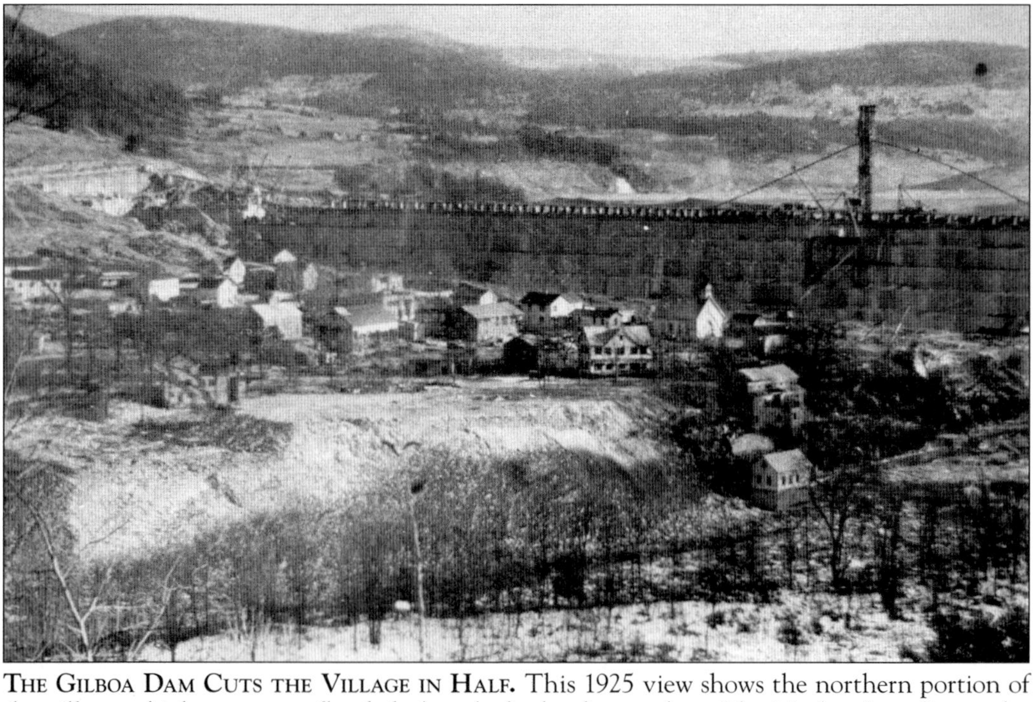

The Gilboa Dam Cuts the Village in Half. This 1925 view shows the northern portion of the village, which was never flooded, though the land was taken. The Mackey farm lies to the left. To the right is the school with its bell tower. The Tri-County Power and Light plant is to the lower right. All the buildings were demolished by the time the dam was completed. (Courtesy of Kenneth Clark.)

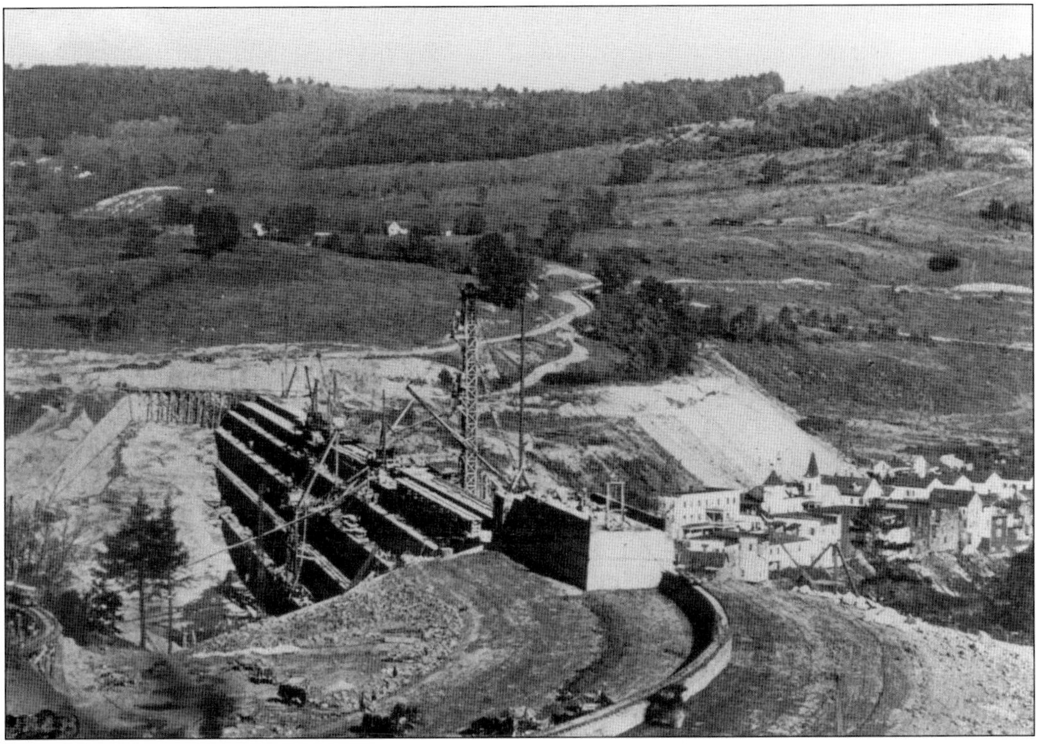

The Dam Dwarfs Gilboa Village. The southern portion of the village of Gilboa is shown in miniature below the dam construction. The old Methodist church with its steeple, the hardware store, and the Gilboa House are plainly visible. In all, 430 buildings were eventually razed or burned and seven cemeteries were removed from the "taken" areas. More than 350 people lost their homes. (Courtesy of Beatrice Mattice.)

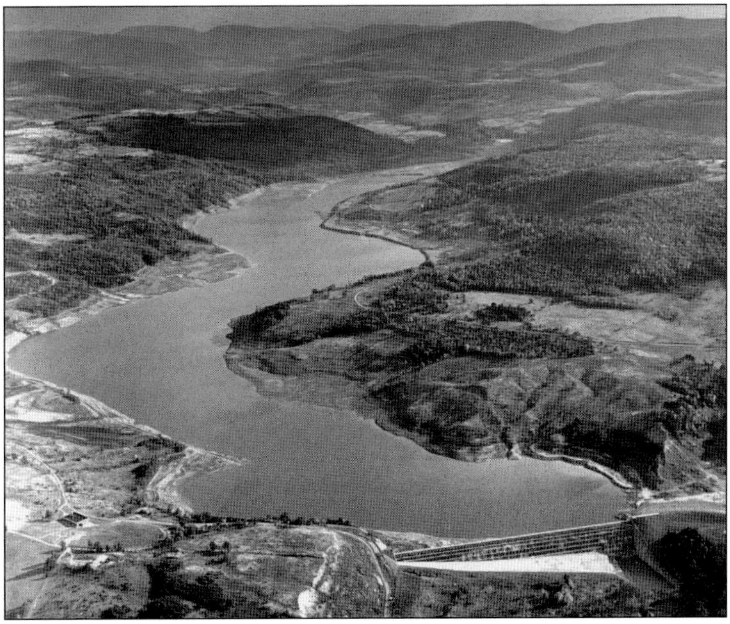

The Schoharie Reservoir. This 1930s aerial view shows the six-mile-long Schoharie Reservoir with the Gilboa Dam at the lower right. The dam was impounded in July 1926, and the reservoir was filled by October 1927. Water from the Schoharie Reservoir flows through the 18-mile-long Shandaken Tunnel, emptying into the Esopus Creek, then moving to the Ashokan Reservoir, and finally into the New York City aqueducts. (Courtesy of New York State Archives.)

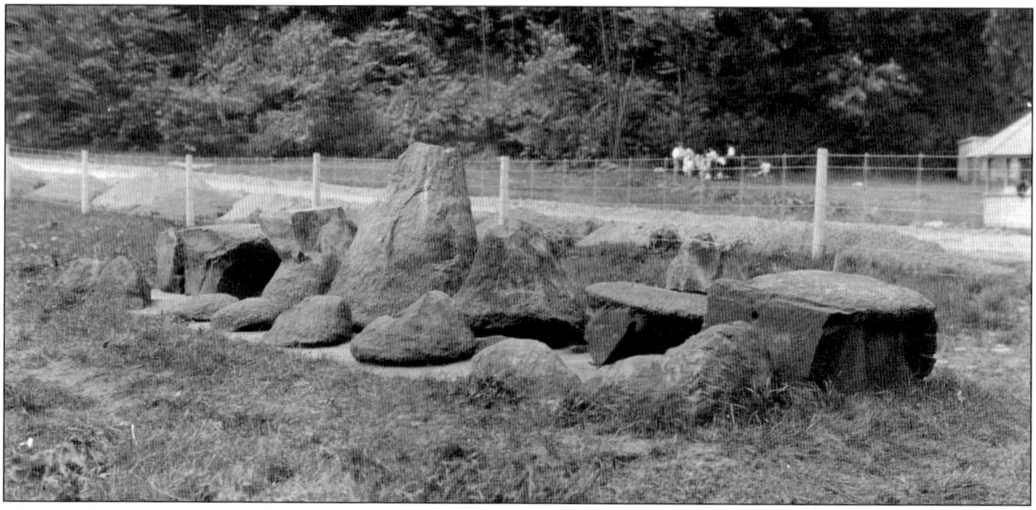

Gilboa Fossils. During the construction of the Gilboa Dam, fossilized tree stumps were discovered. They are from the early Devonian period and are some 385 million years old—the oldest known. The Eospermatopteris, as the trees are known, were 40-feet-tall, fern-like trees producing spores. During this epoch, the climate was warm, and there were no mammals or birds, though fish-like creatures abounded. The Gilboa Museum now has an exhibit on the fossils and life in old Gilboa. (Courtesy of OSFM.)

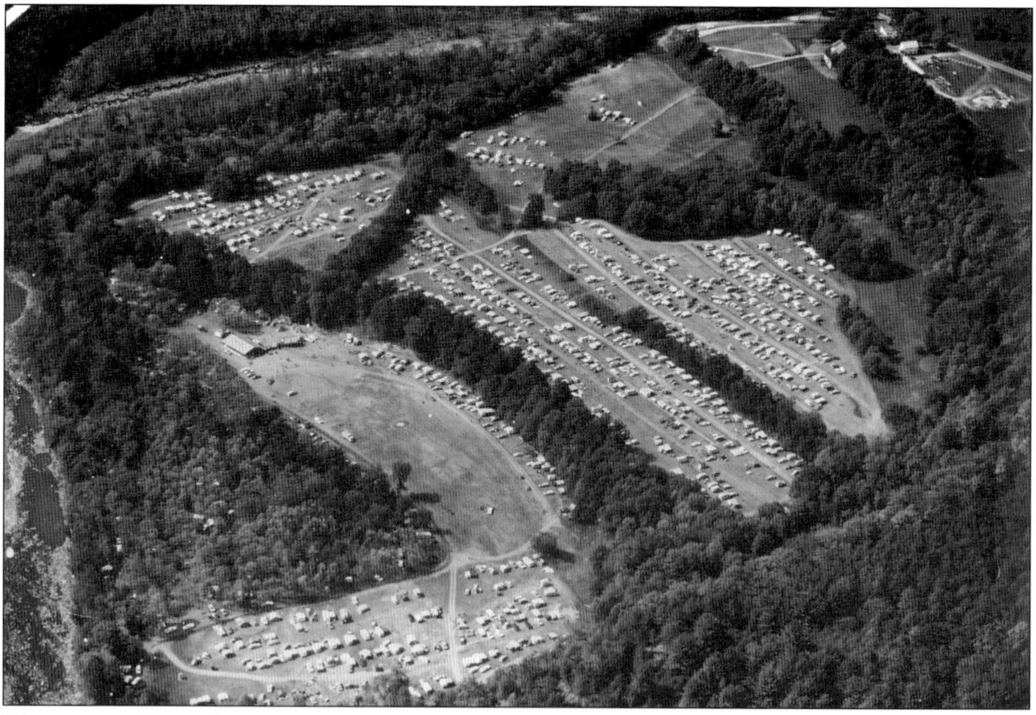

Nickerson Park Campground. Frank and Arvilla Nickerson owned the Nickerson Park Campground in Gilboa. The land was once a farm and was gradually turned into a large campground. Here, in May 1964, the New York State Campers and Hikers convention is in full swing. The Schoharie Creek borders the campground on two sides (top and left). The campgrounds are now owned by Doug and Donna Brown. (Courtesy of OSFM.)

Three

Blenheim, Breakabeen, and Fultonham

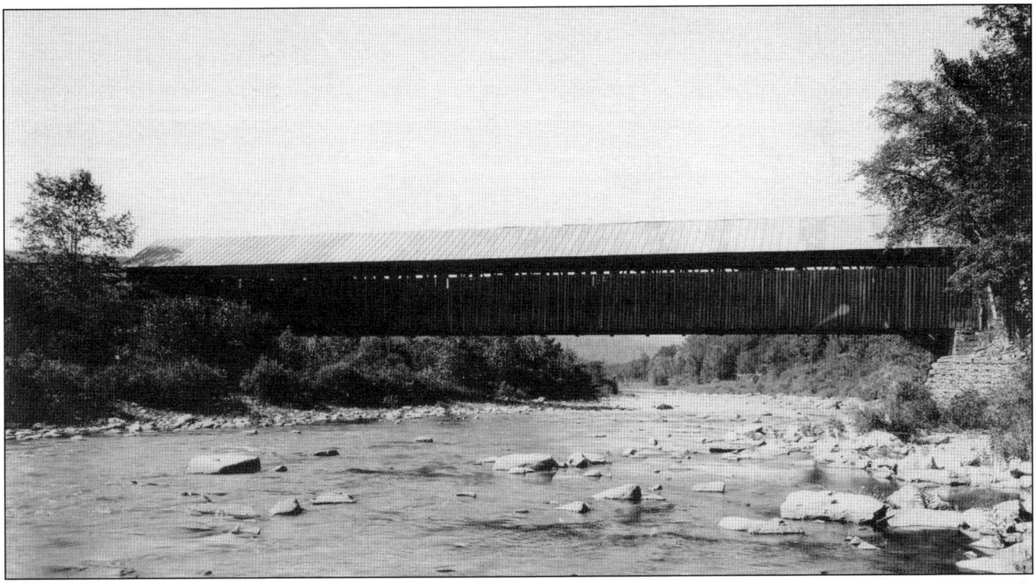

The Blenheim Covered Bridge. The covered bridge across the Schoharie Creek at North Blenheim was once the world's longest, single-span, wooden covered bridge. It was built in 1855 by Nicholas Powers of Pittsford, Vermont. The bridge was supported by a single massive wooden arch. The span between abutments was 210 feet, and the covered portion was 238 feet long. The bridge was retired in 1931. It was destroyed in the flood of 2011. (Courtesy of Edwin Truax.)

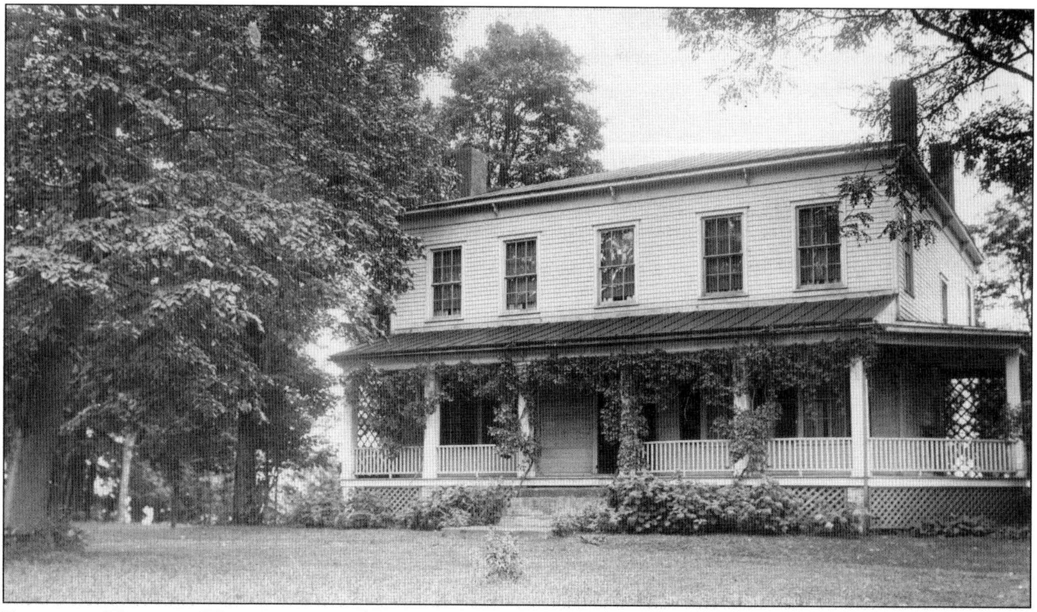

LANSING MANOR. The manor in the town of Blenheim was built by John Lansing in 1819 for his daughter and son-in-law. Lansing was speaker of the New York State Assembly (1788–1789), chief justice of the New York State Supreme Court (1798–1801), and chancellor (1801–1814). The manor house, now a museum decorated in the period style, is operated by the New York Power Authority in cooperation with the Schoharie County Historical Society. (Courtesy of OSFM.)

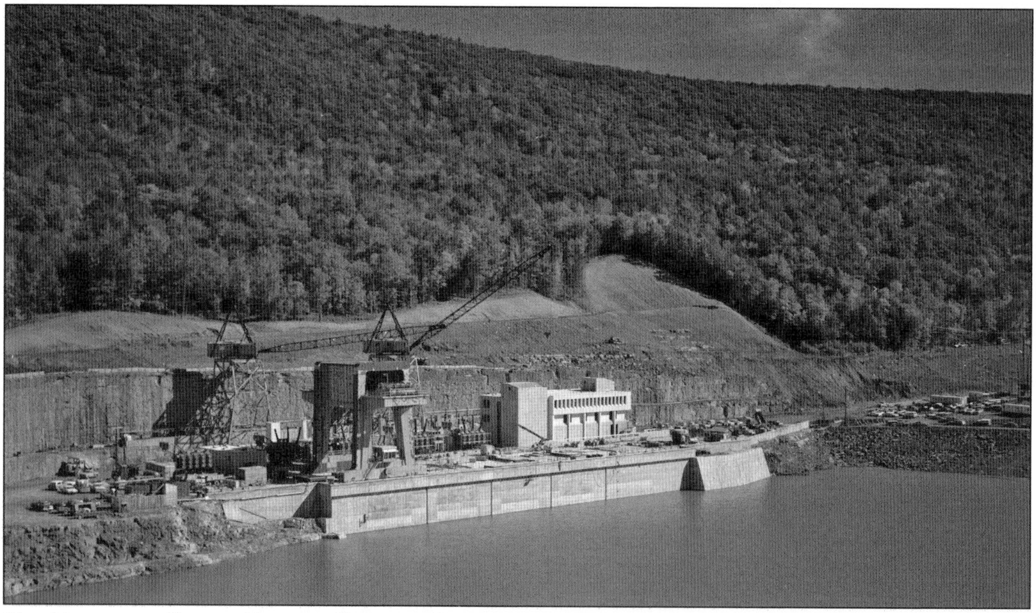

THE BLENHEIM-GILBOA PUMPED STORAGE PROJECT. Construction started in 1969 and was completed by July 1973. This project required damming the Schoharie Creek at North Blenheim. The project is used to provide peak electrical power as it is needed. The plant has a 1,160-megawatt capacity. Water from an upper reservoir on Brown Mountain falls 1,000 feet to drive turbine generators. This 1970s photograph shows the construction as it nears completion. (Courtesy of the New York Power Authority.)

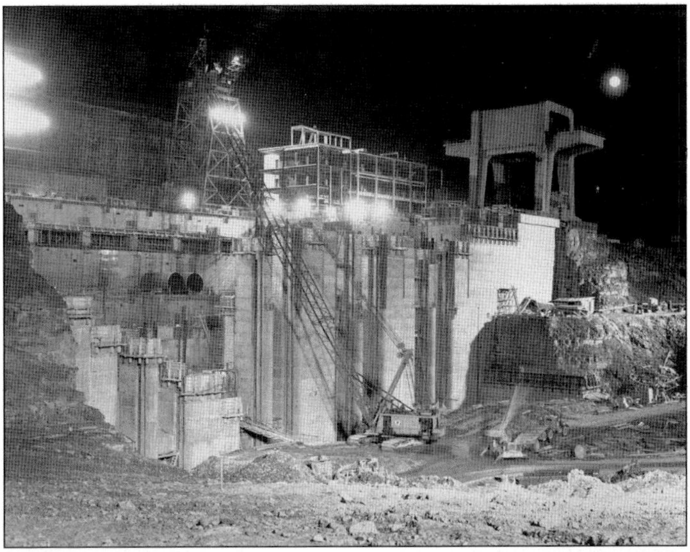

Project Construction, 1971. Construction continued day and night as the power plant was built and the tunnel up to Brown Mountain was created. Here, cranes are at work on the outside of the plant. The water of the reservoir would be near the level of the lights when the project was completed. (Courtesy of the New York Power Authority.)

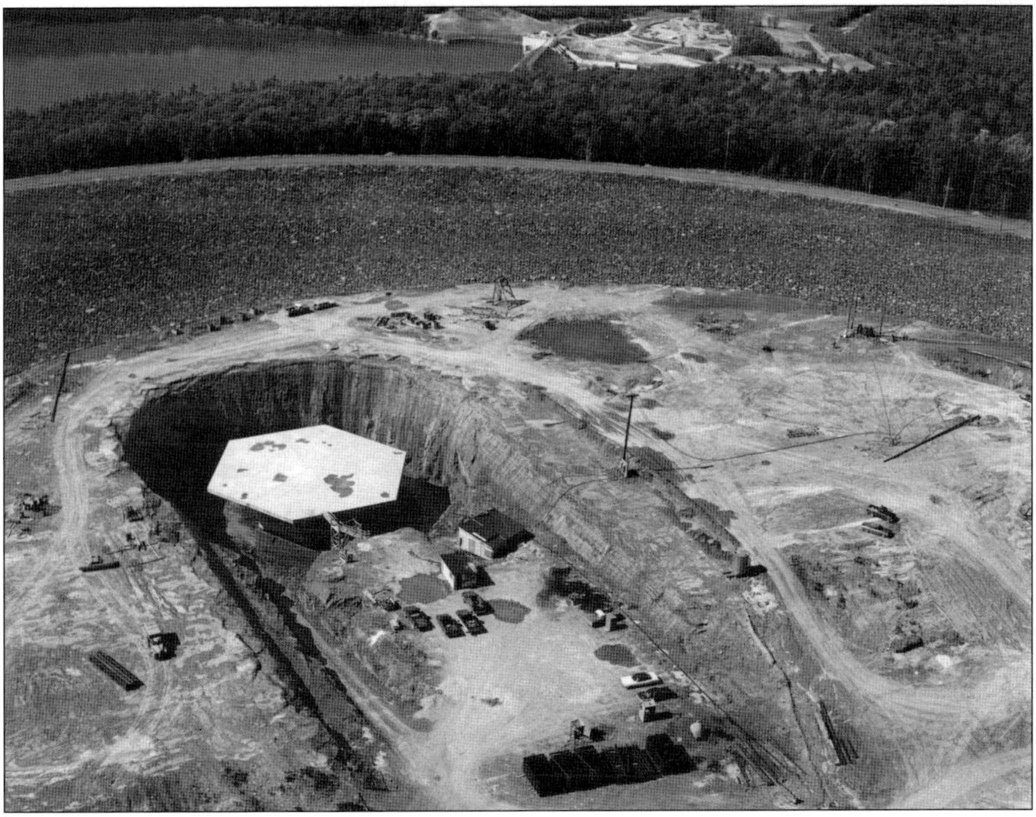

The Brown Mountain Upper Reservoir, 1970. When completed, this area was filled with water. When peak power is needed (generally during the daytime), water falls 1,000 feet into the turbine generators below. These produce the required electricity. The process is reversed at night when electricity demand is low, and water is returned from the lower reservoir to the upper one. Here, the water intake cover is visible. The dam and lower reservoir are at the upper right. (Courtesy of the New York Power Authority.)

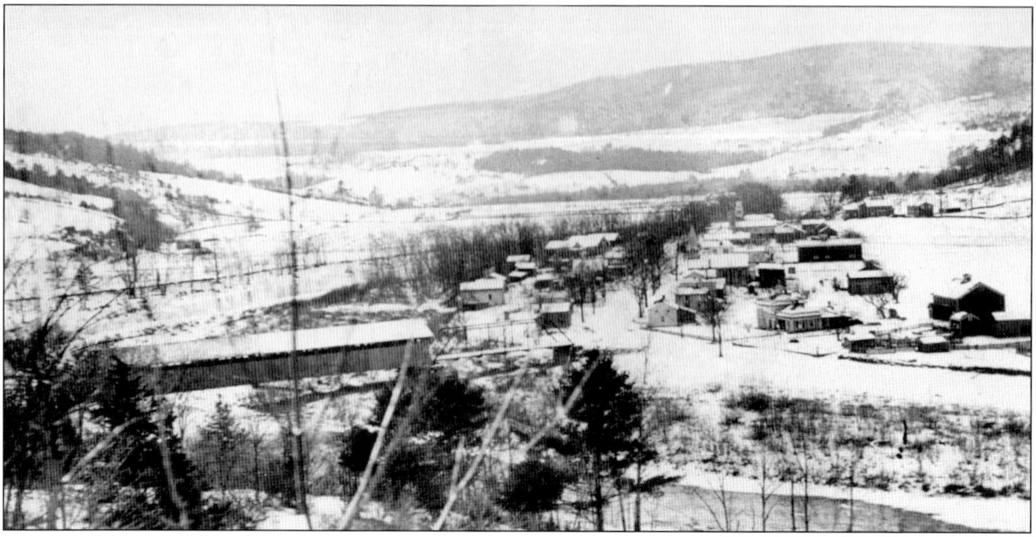

North Blenheim, around 1920. This winter scene shows the hamlet of North Blenheim and the Schoharie Valley beyond. The Schoharie Creek curls around the hamlet. The Blenheim covered bridge is visible. It has an extension made necessary by a flood that cut off the covered bridge from the hamlet. (Courtesy of the New York Power Authority.)

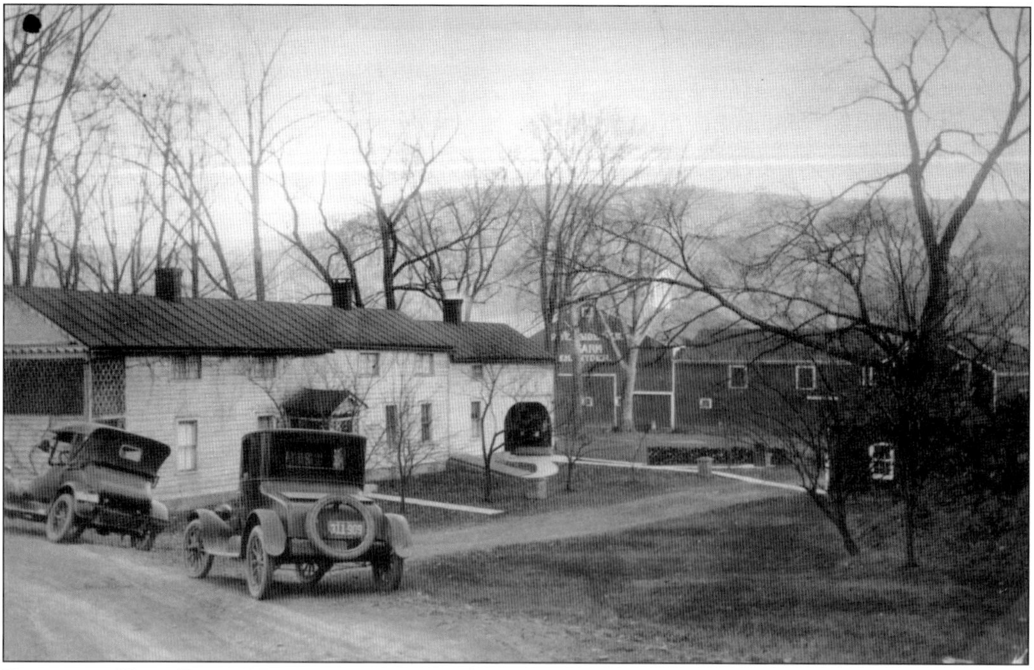

Riverside View Farm, North Blenheim. This 1920s view of Riverside View Farm shows the barn (which was damaged in the 2011 flood) at the edge of the Schoharie Creek in North Blenheim. At the time, the farm was owned by S.H. Snyder. The white house on the left no longer stands. (Courtesy of the New York Power Authority.)

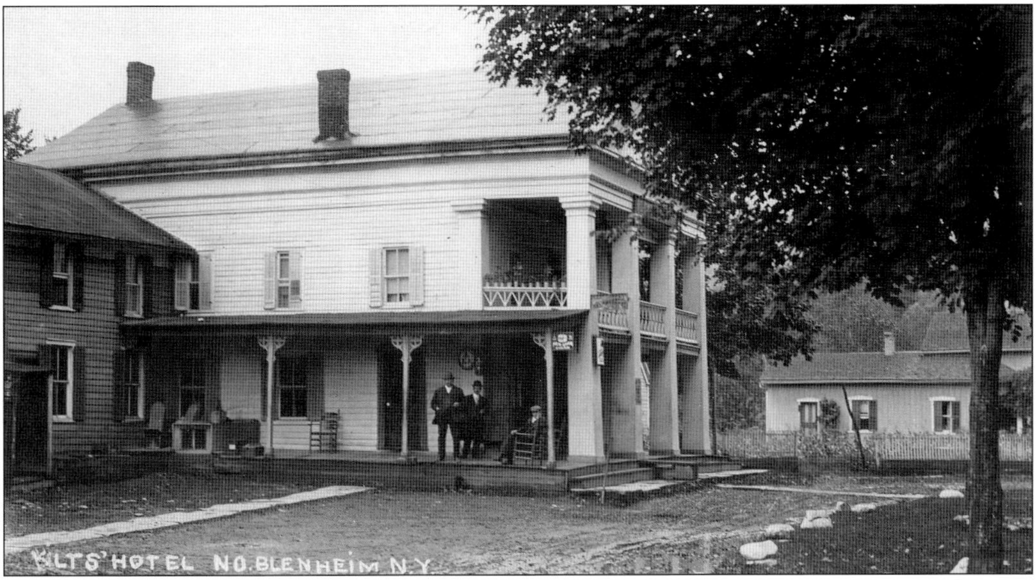

BLENHEIM HOUSE. The hotel was owned successively by George Mattice, Melvin Wright, and Joseph Cottone. It burned on March 18, 1938. There were many such hotels in the hamlets of the Schoharie Valley. This one shows the influence of the Greek Revival architectural style with its four handsome porch columns. (Courtesy of MLHR.)

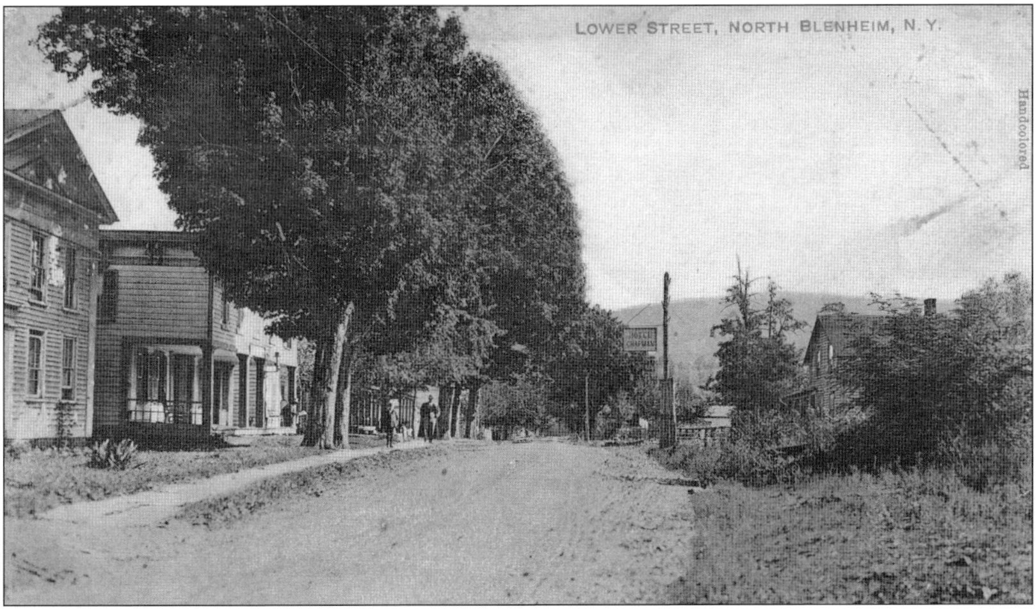

LOWER STREET, NORTH BLENHEIM. The hamlet of North Blenheim is divided into two parts by the course of the Schoharie Creek—the lower and the upper. This view shows Lower Street (now State Route 30), which is north of the upper hamlet and on the lower part of the creek. Chapman House, an inn for many years, is the Greek Revival building on the right. (Courtesy of author's collection.)

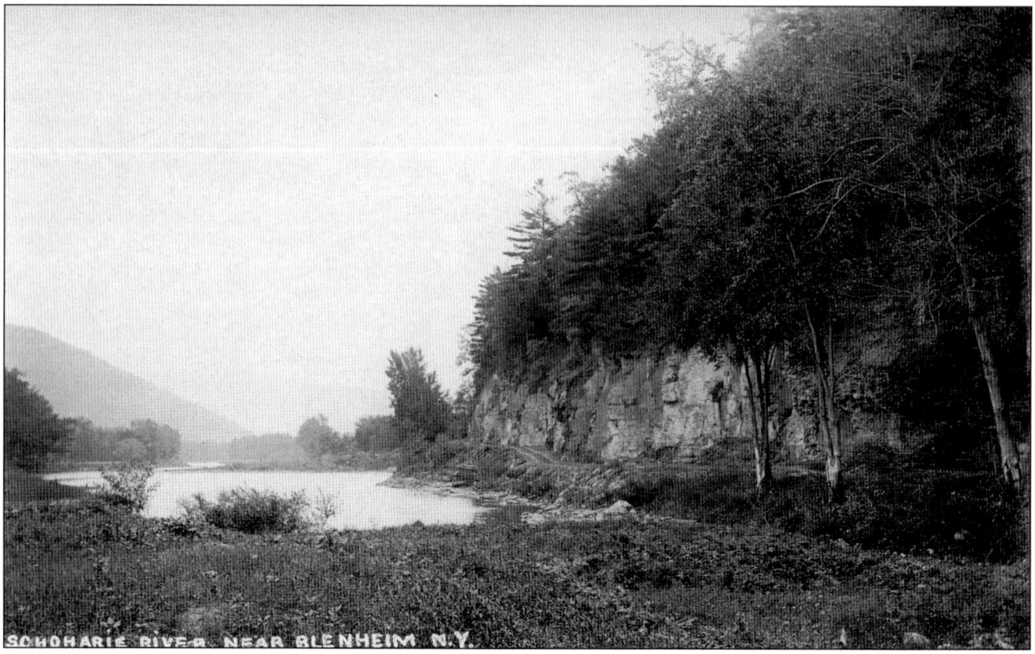

The Schoharie Creek near North Blenheim. This c. 1910 view shows that travel was not easy in those days. The dirt road under the cliff was rather narrow and probably subject to flooding. Today, this is State Route 30, and even now, the roadway is quite narrow at this point. (Courtesy of OSFM, Chester Zimmer collection.)

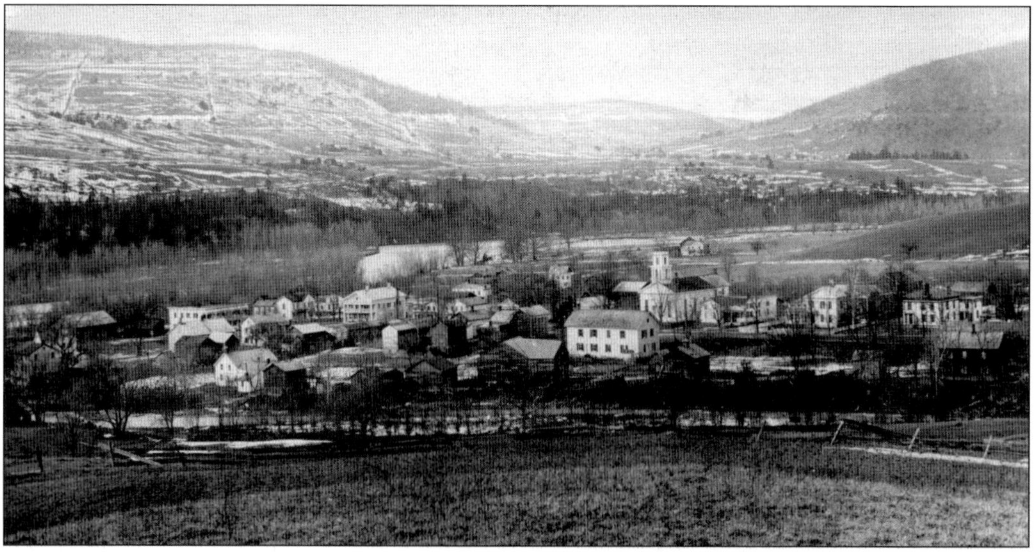

The Hamlet of Breakabeen. The hamlet was listed in the National Register of Historic Places in 1974. Most of the 33 contributing buildings, including the general store and the Presbyterian church, are of the Greek Revival style and were built before 1870. The Keyserkill Creek is in the foreground and flows into the Schoharie Creek. The name *Breakabeen* was given by the Dutch settlers after a species of fern, or bracken, that covered the flats here. (Courtesy of OSFM, Robert Mahar collection.)

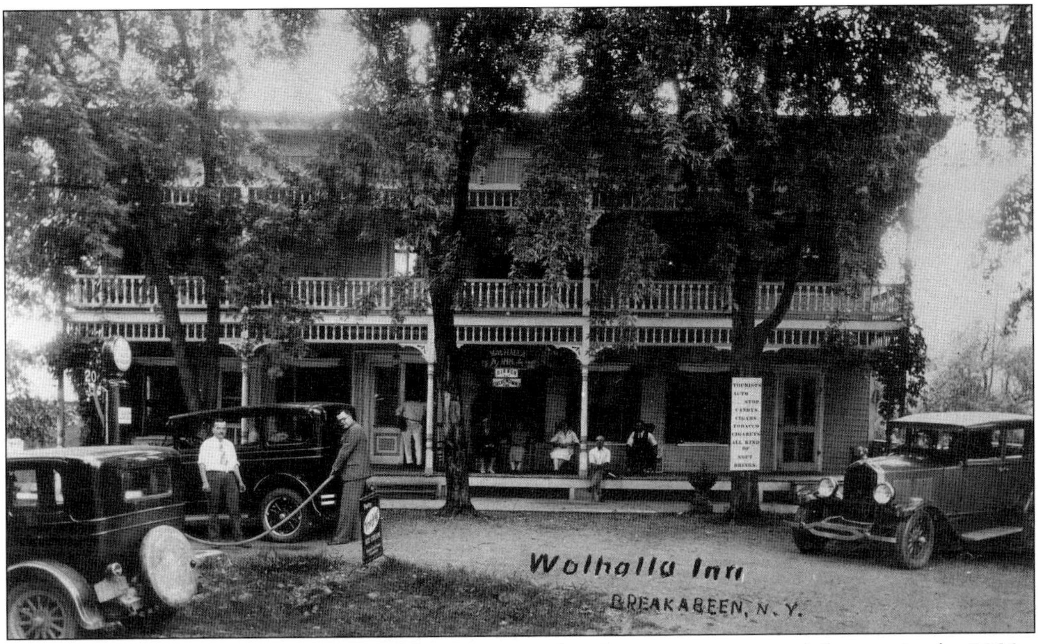

The Walhalla Inn, Breakabeen. The inn was a familiar tourist automobile stop in the 1920s. The cost of gasoline was 20¢ a gallon, and the sign says that tourists could get "candys, cigars, tobacco, cigarets, and all kinds of soft drinks." FroJoy ice cream was available. Chicken dinners were $1 while regular dinners cost 75¢. The inn burned on February 4, 1974. (Courtesy of author's collection.)

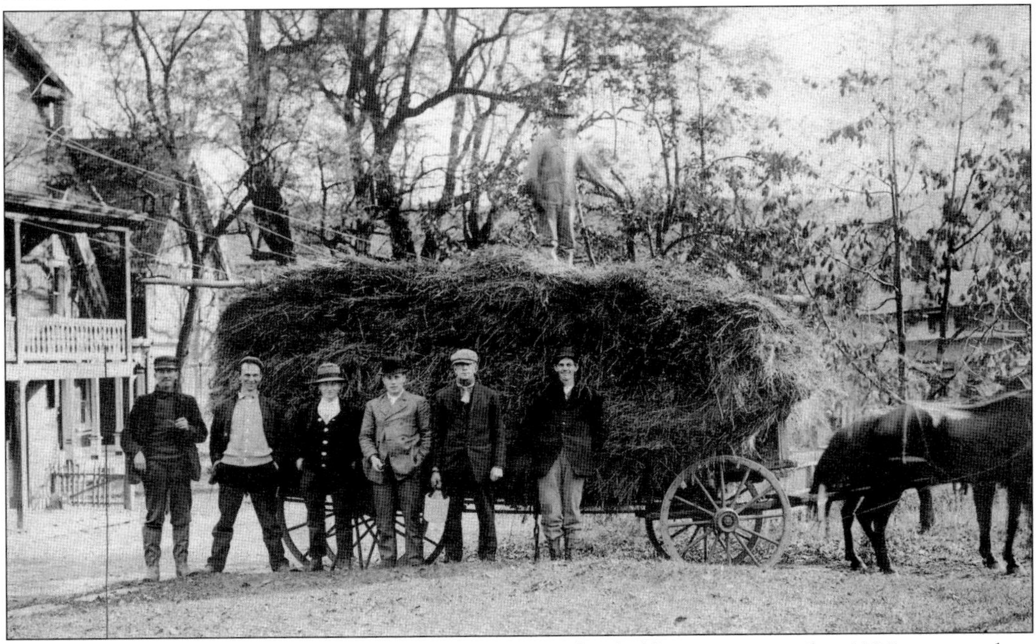

Breakabeen Boys. Six young men stand in front of a loaded hay wagon in this 1920s scene taken in the hamlet of Breakabeen. From left to right are Steve Nelson, Homer Nelson, Frank Becker, Dewitt Rosecrans, Clyde Becker, and Ben Bergh. Brainard White is on the wagon holding the horse's reins. (Courtesy of Rose Mace.)

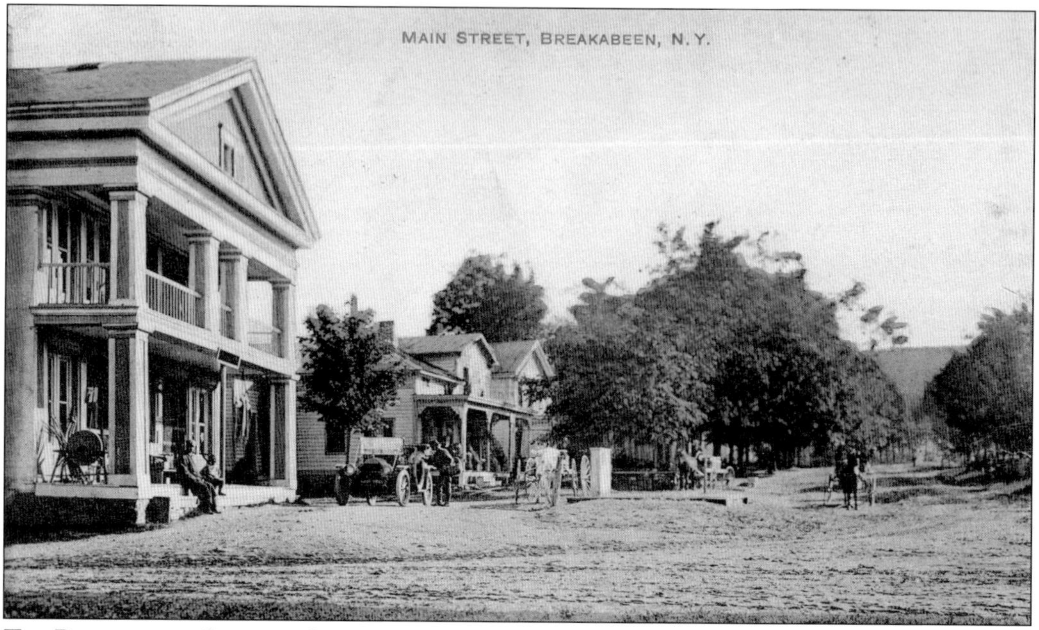

THE BREAKABEEN GENERAL STORE, AROUND 1905. The store was originally owned by John and Mary Mayham in 1856. Irwin Kling purchased the store and operated it until his death in 1927 when the store passed successively to Howard Kling, the Starks, and the Birsens. The store is now owned by James and June Corcoran. (Courtesy of OSFM, Robert Mahar collection.)

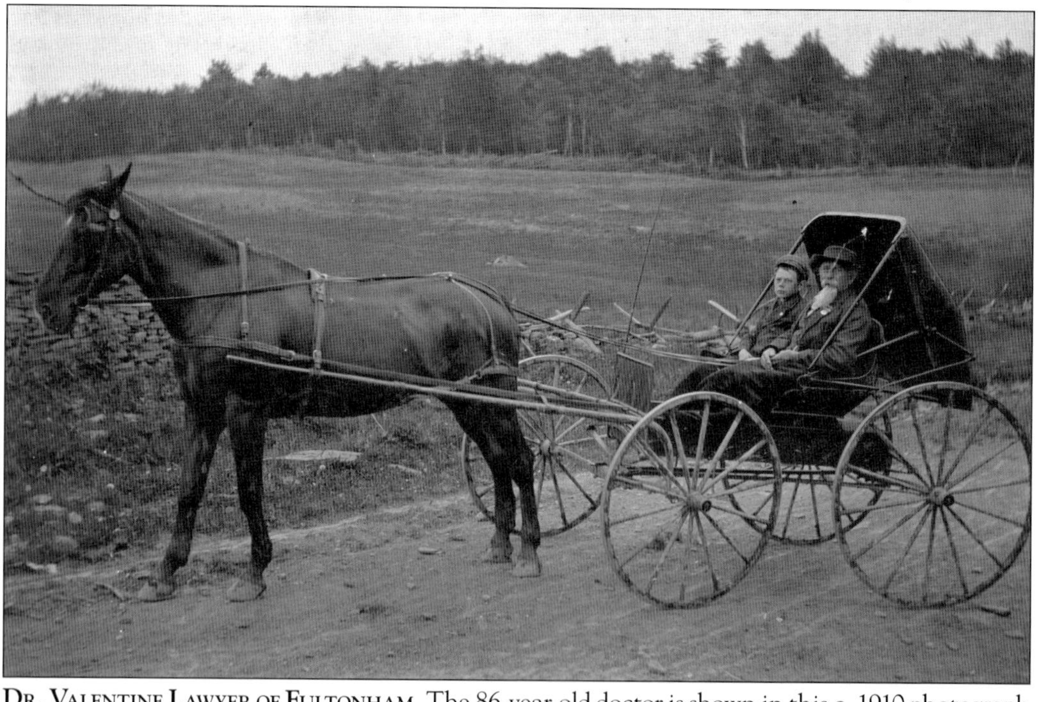

DR. VALENTINE LAWYER OF FULTONHAM. The 86-year-old doctor is shown in this c. 1910 photograph by Philip Messer, a 22-year-old photographer, of Middleburgh. In those days, country doctors visited their patients by day and by night in horse-drawn buggies like this one. (Courtesy of author's collection.)

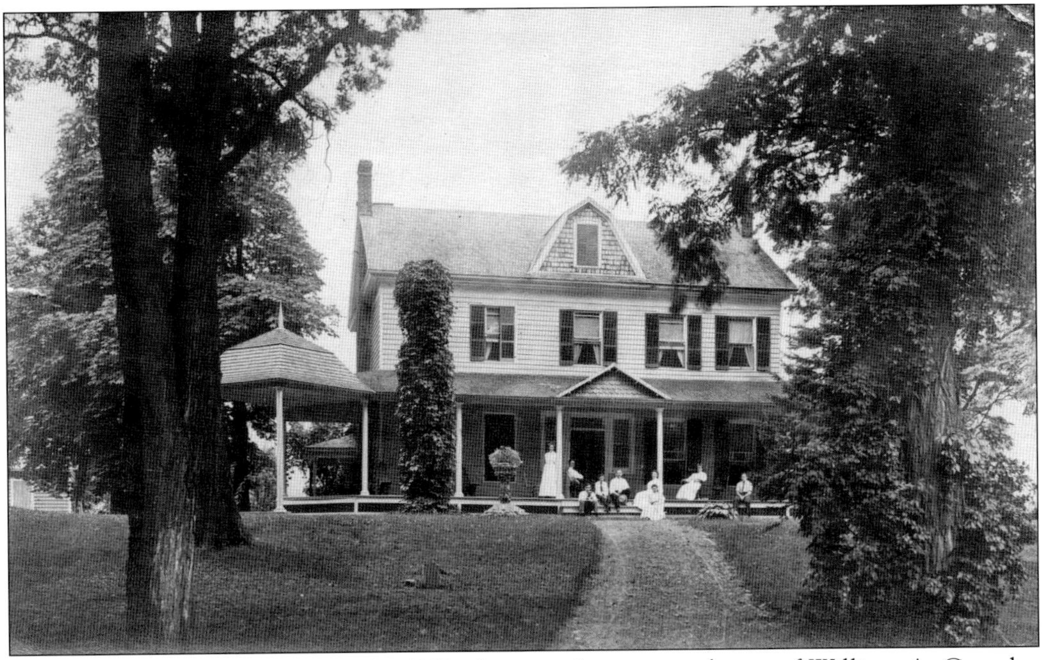

A FULTONHAM SUMMER HOME. In 1910, this was the summer home of William A. Canaday and family of Albany, New York. The house was built on Bouck's Island before the American Revolution. Bouck's Island stands between two branches of the Schoharie Creek. Of the three pre-Revolutionary houses on Bouck's Island, this is the only one still standing. The other two were burned during the British raid on the Schoharie Valley in 1780. The home is now owned by the Harry Ricker family. (Courtesy of author's collection.)

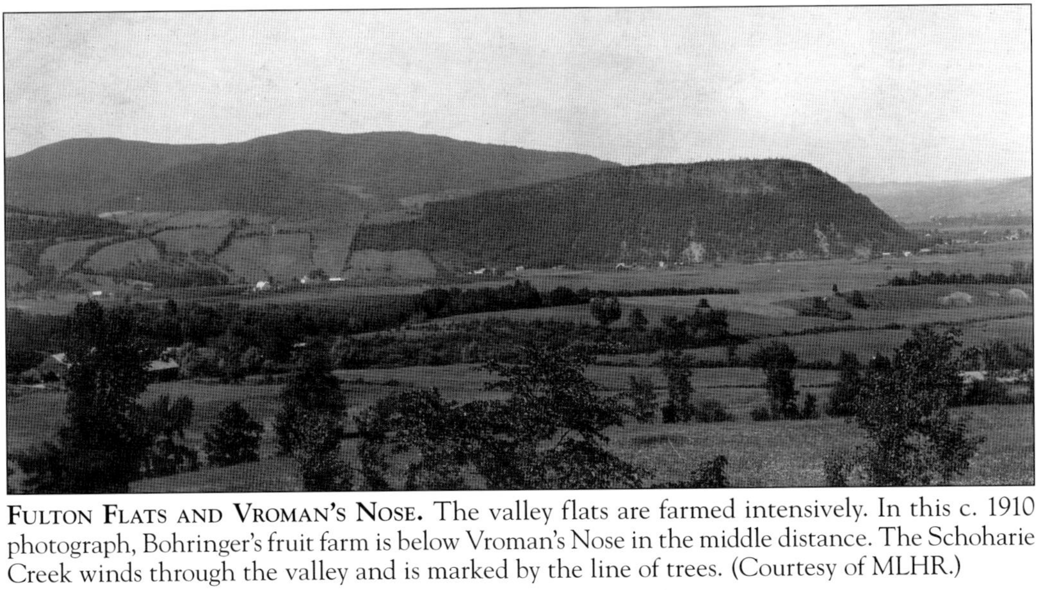

FULTON FLATS AND VROMAN'S NOSE. The valley flats are farmed intensively. In this c. 1910 photograph, Bohringer's fruit farm is below Vroman's Nose in the middle distance. The Schoharie Creek winds through the valley and is marked by the line of trees. (Courtesy of MLHR.)

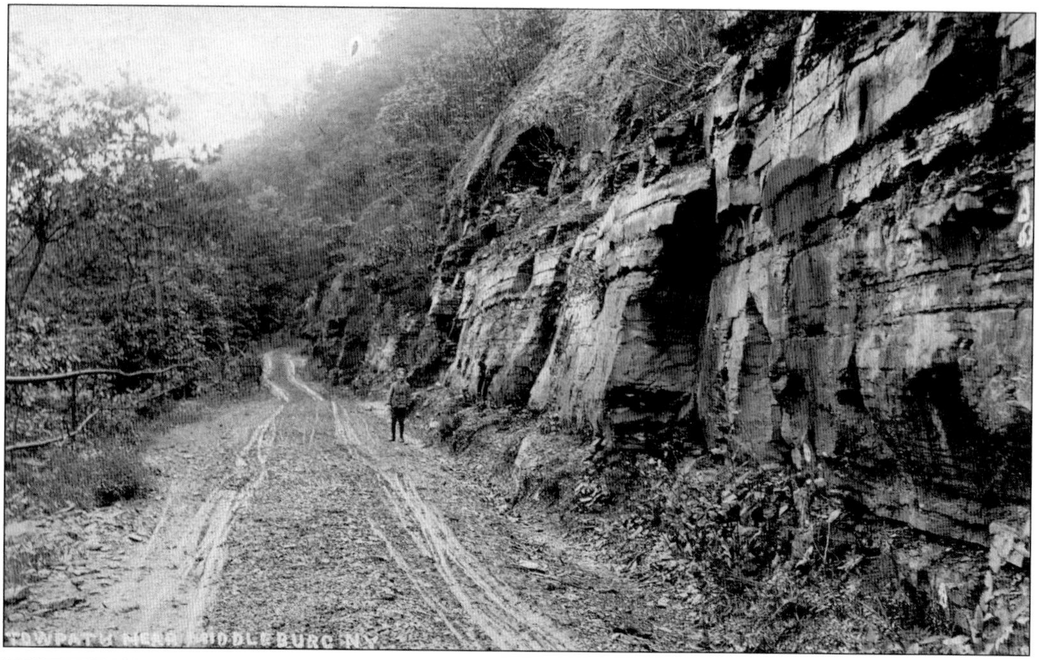

Toe Path, Fulton. The main road from Middleburgh to Fultonham once followed an old Indian path along the steep western side of the Schoharie Valley. This 1900s view shows the part of the road that was known as the Toe Path. This road was improved, and State Route 30 followed it until it was relocated onto Bouck's Island in the 1960s. (Courtesy of OSFM, Chester Zimmer collection.)

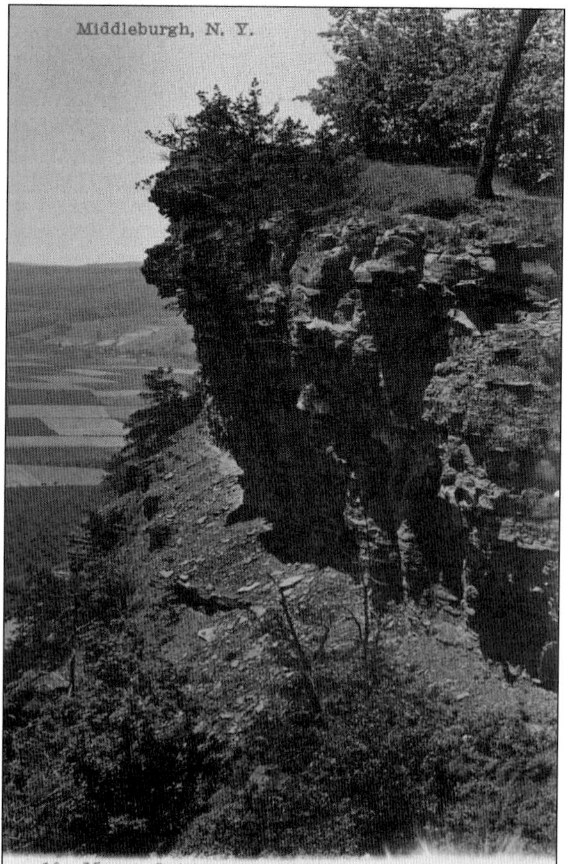

Vroman's Nose Nature Preserve. The preserve was dedicated in 1984. It has hiking trails and from the summit, spectacular views of the valley fields. During the glacial times, the ice was a mile thick here and covered Vroman's Nose. The rocks on the bottom of the glacier ground polished the rock of Vroman's Nose where the glacial scratches on the summit are still visible. (Courtesy of OSFM, Robert Mahar collection.)

Four

Middleburgh

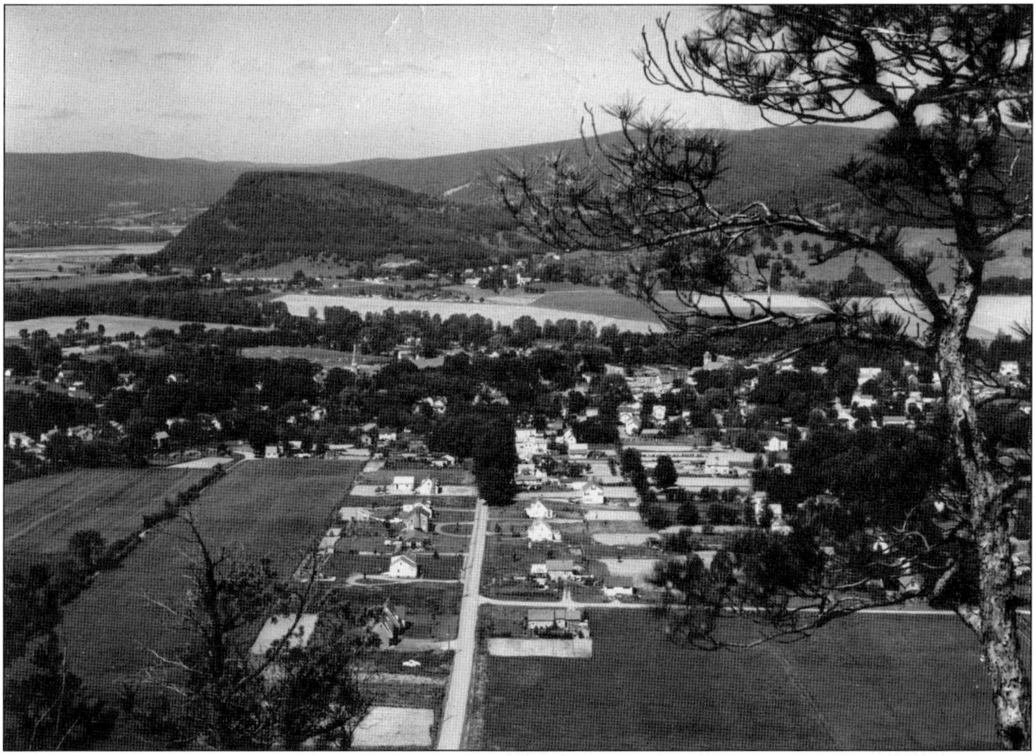

View of Middleburgh. This view was taken from the cliff above the village and shows Middleburgh as it was in the 1950s. Vroman's Nose is in the distance. The Schoharie Creek is marked by the tree line in the center of the photograph. The steeples of St. Mark's Evangelical Lutheran Church and the Methodist church are also visible. (Courtesy of MLHR.)

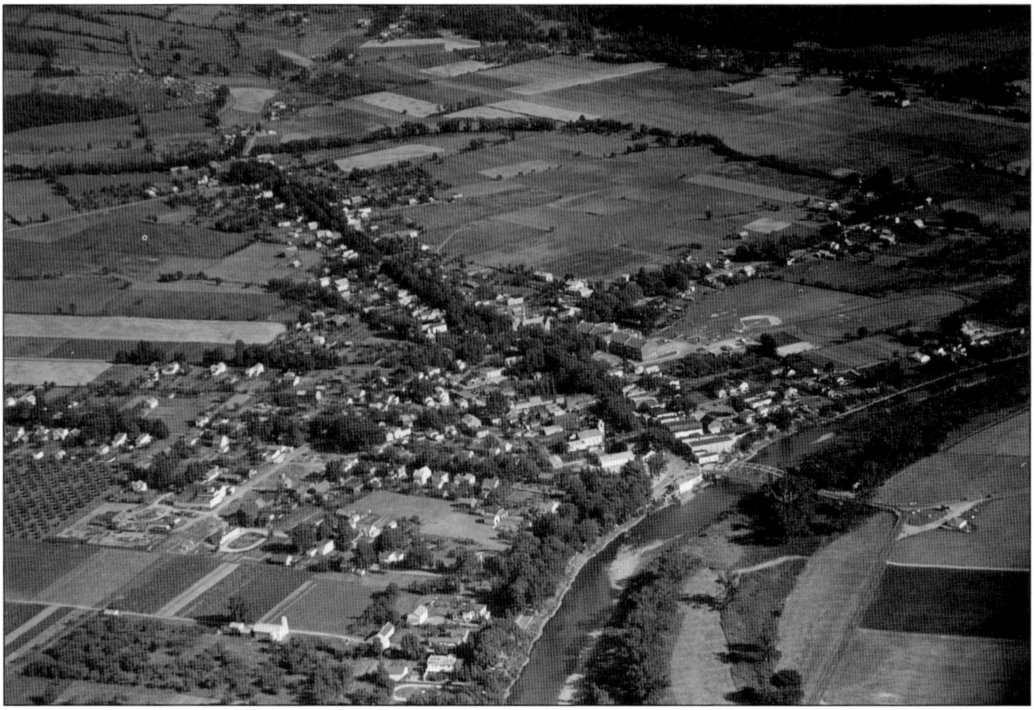

AERIAL VIEW OF MIDDLEBURGH, 1960S. At lower right is the old iron bridge across the Schoharie Creek. The treed road going diagonally is Main Street, and River Street runs along the creek. The Middleburgh Cemetery is visible at the upper left. At that time, there was an orchard in the village, shown at left. (Courtesy of MLHR.)

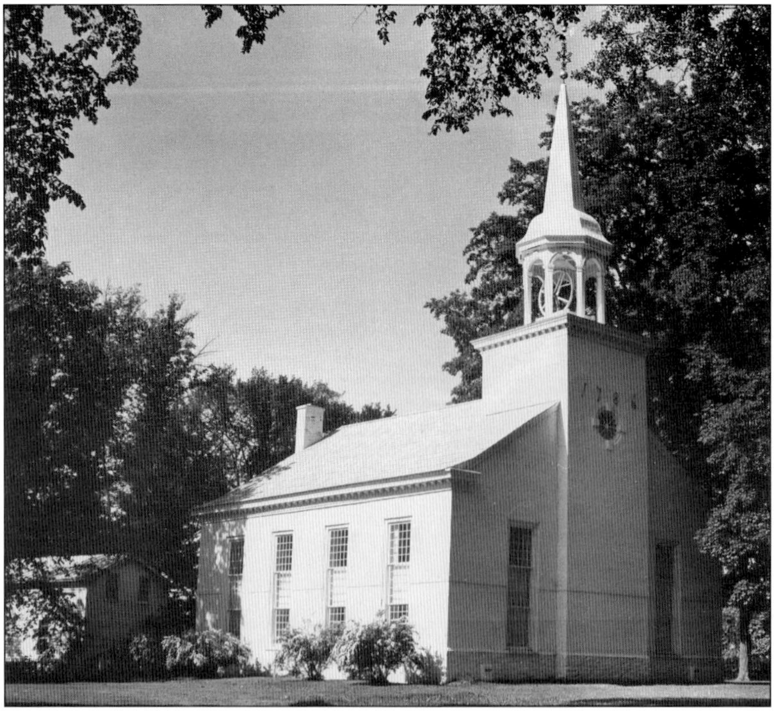

THE MIDDLEBURGH REFORMED CHURCH. The church building was erected in 1786 after British and Indian raiders burned its predecessor in 1780, during the American Revolution. The numerals on the tower were wrought by Ludwig Schneider at that time. The first minister in the area was Johann Jacob Ehle, who arrived from Heidelberg, Germany, in 1722. The church shared pastors with the Schoharie Reformed Church until 1790. (Courtesy of MLHR.)

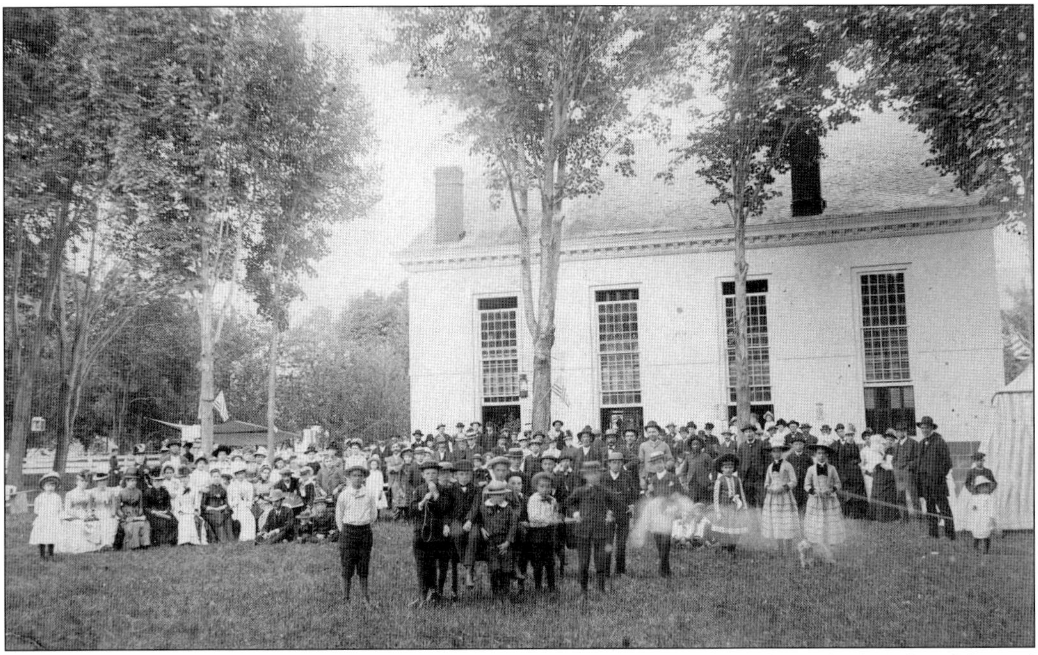

THE 100-YEAR CELEBRATION. The congregation of the Middleburgh Reformed Church celebrated the centennial of the church building on August 19, 1886. Here, a group of youngsters is in the foreground while the adults stand to the back. A tent is at the right, no doubt to serve refreshments. (Courtesy of MLHR.)

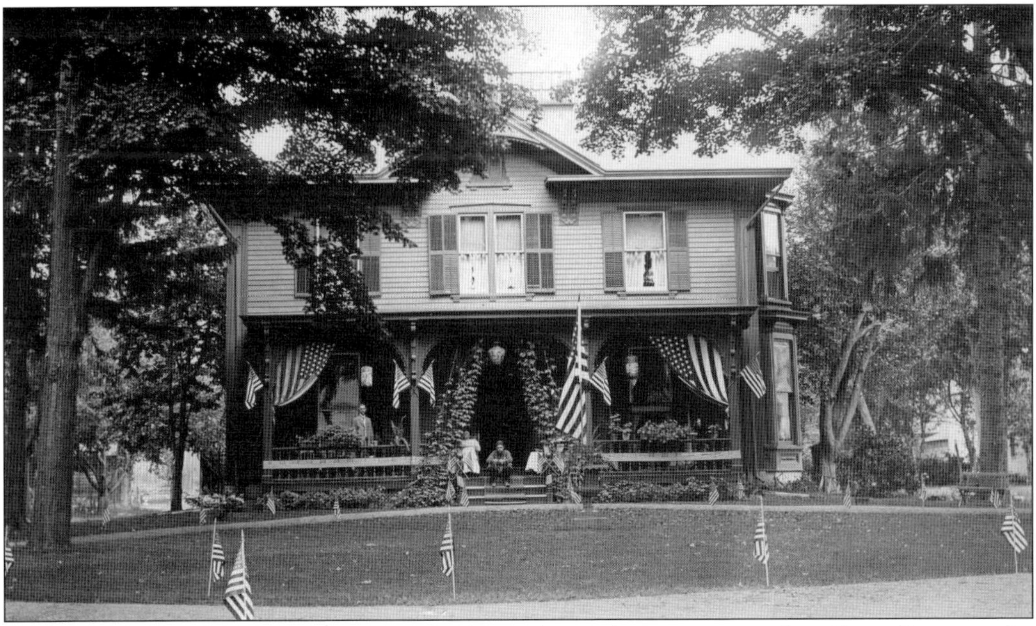

BEEKMAN HOUSE, MIDDLEBURGH, 1912. The Beekman house is situated on River Street in the village of Middleburgh. Here, it is decorated for a celebration, possibly part of the 1912 Old Home Week. The house is but one of many mansions that line River Street, a signal of past wealth generated by hop farming in the area. The owner Dow Beekman was a prominent judge, speaker, and writer. (Courtesy of MLHR.)

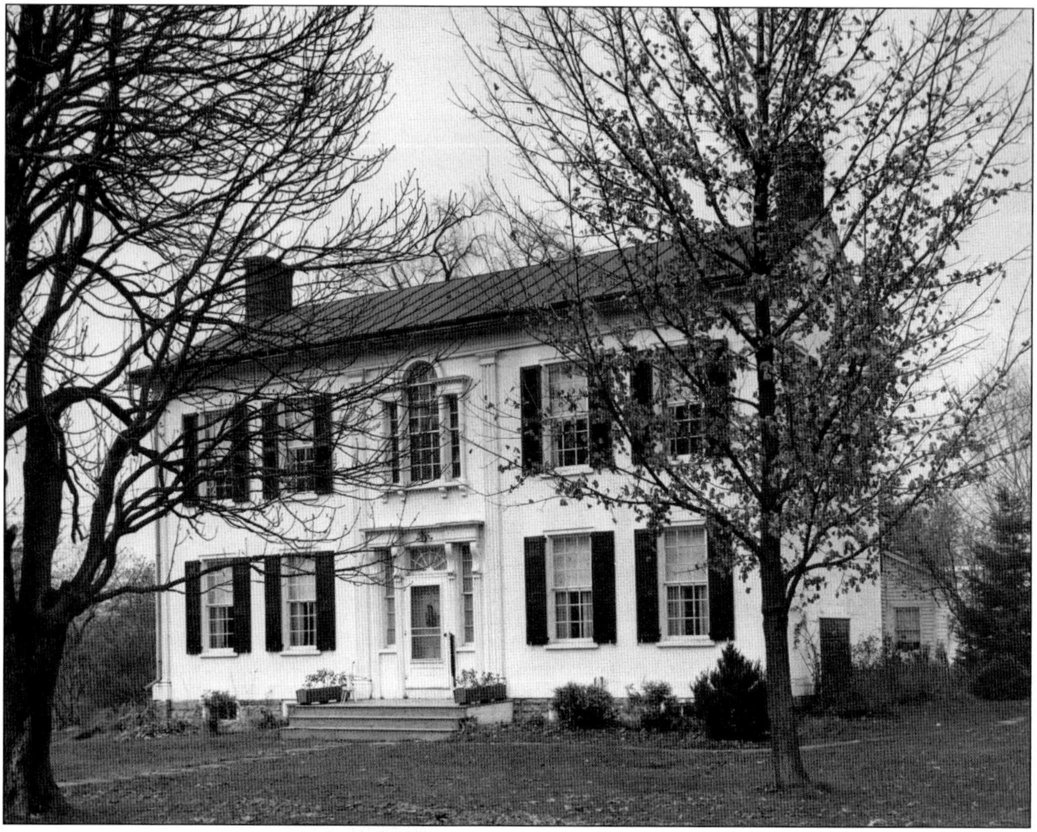

STANTON HALL, MIDDLEBURGH. Located on Clauverwie in Middleburgh, Stanton Hall was built shortly after the American Revolution and was owned by Freeman Stanton in 1818. Stanton was a prosperous merchant, a member of the legislature in 1824, and assistant to Gov. William C. Bouck. Of note is the beautiful Palladian window above the entrance. (Courtesy of MLHR.)

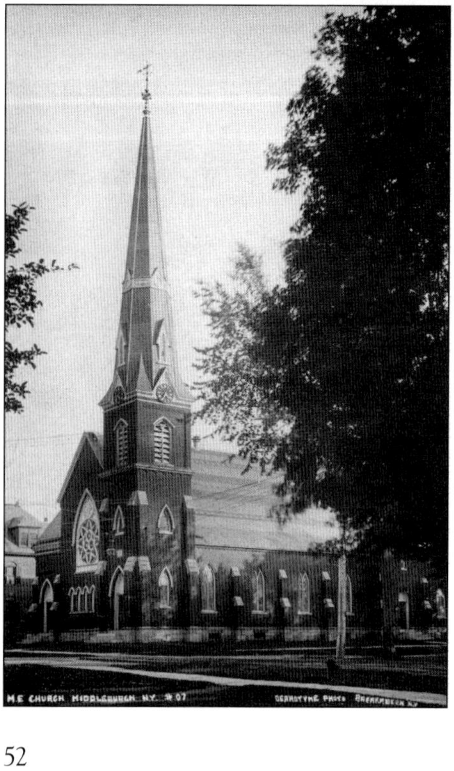

THE MIDDLEBURGH METHODIST EPISCOPAL CHURCH. With its distinctive spire, the church was built in 1874 and dedicated May 20, 1875. To raise funds, seats were sold at public auction in 1875 for between $10 and $35, bringing in a total of $1,208. L.W. Clemens was the minister at that time. In 1902, a new large organ was installed, and all mortgage notes were burned in 1910. (Courtesy of MLHR.)

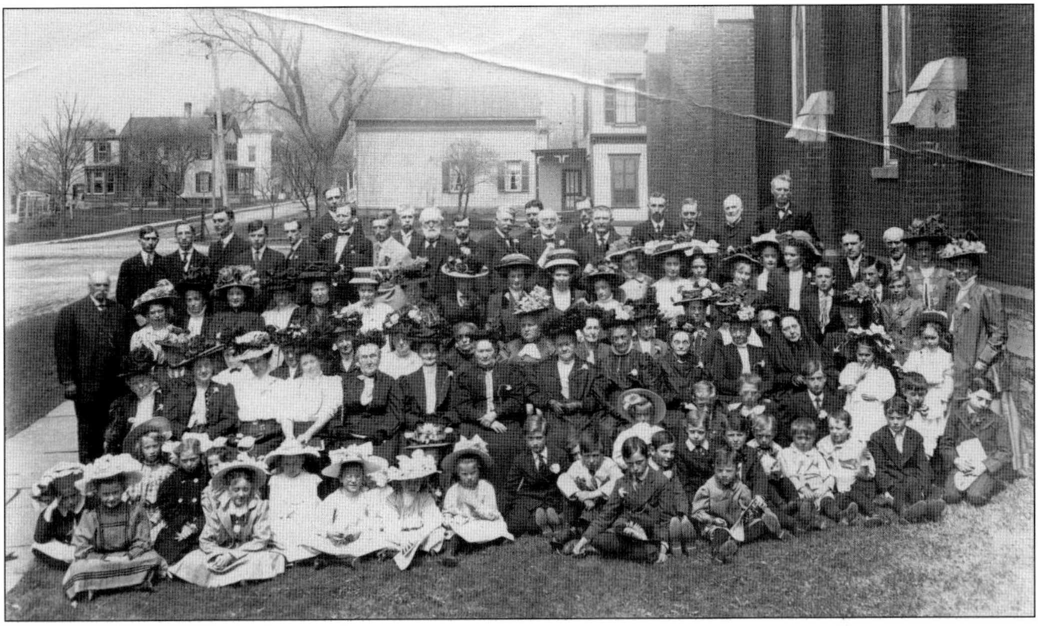

MOTHER'S DAY, 1909. The Methodist Church congregation gathered for this photograph on Mother's Day, May 9, 1909. The ladies and young girls wore special flowered hats for the occasion. Many of the gentlemen wore carnations in their lapels. The minister was Rev. B.L. Crapo. William Albro, Elias Dutton, G.W. Vroman, Harvey Borst, and George E. Borst were trustees. (Courtesy of OSFM.)

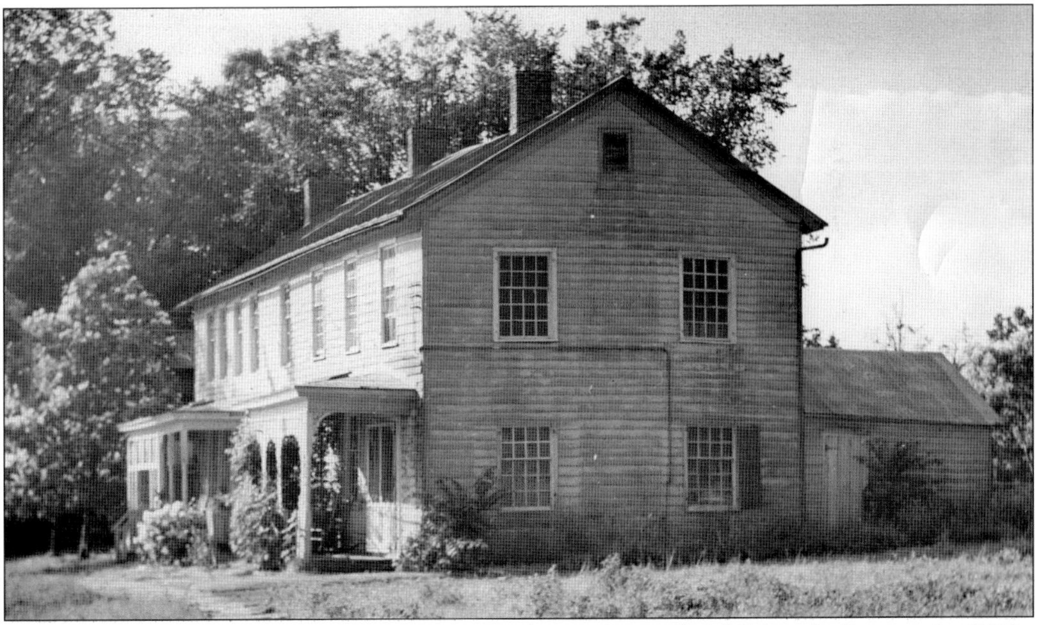

THE BULL'S HEAD TAVERN. The tavern was on the outskirts of Middleburgh. During the 1800s, drovers took cattle from upstate New York and drove them down the turnpikes to New York City. The Bull's Head tavern had a large sign with a bull's head on it. The drovers could immediately tell that this was a place to stay the night. Today, the drovers are gone, and so is the tavern. It was located where the school administrative offices are now. (Courtesy of OSFM.)

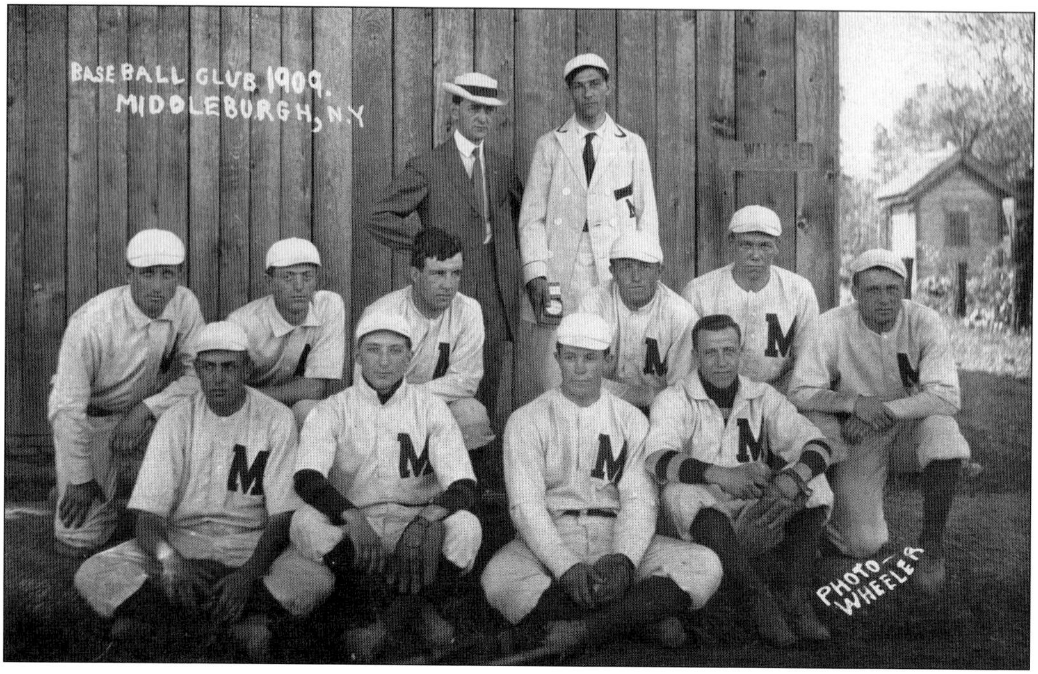

The Schoharie Valley Baseball League. Shown here are the 1909 Middleburgh team (above) and the 1910 Schoharie team (below). The men may have played against each other. According to the August 18, 1910, edition of the *Middleburgh News*, the other league members were Lakeside and Cobleskill. In 1910, Lakeside was league champion with Schoharie and Middleburgh coming last. (Above, courtesy of MLHR; below, courtesy of author's collection.)

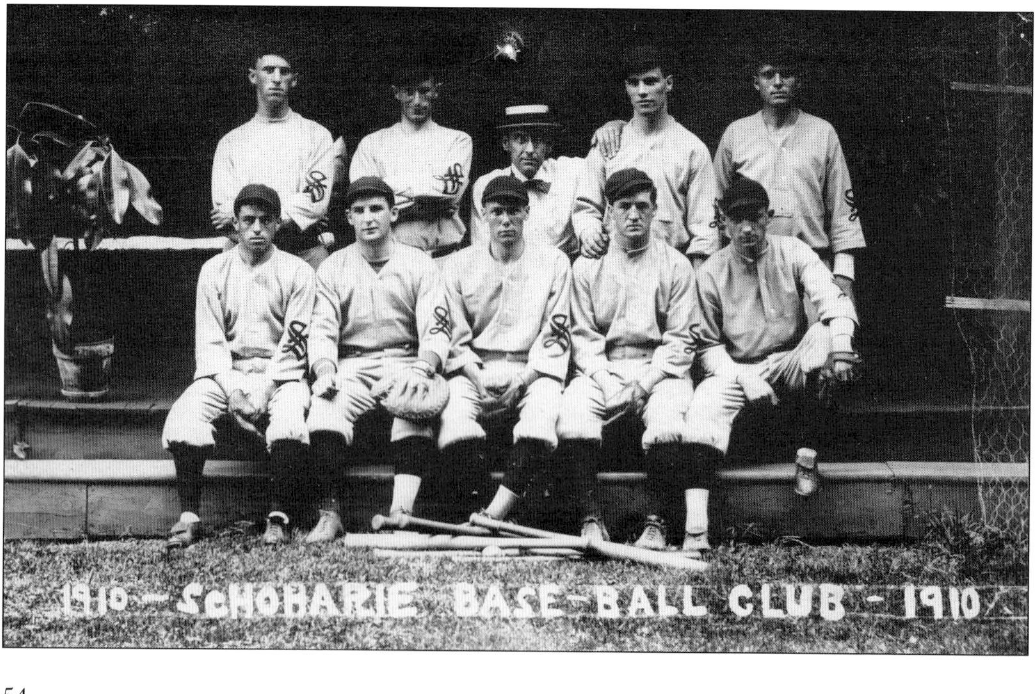

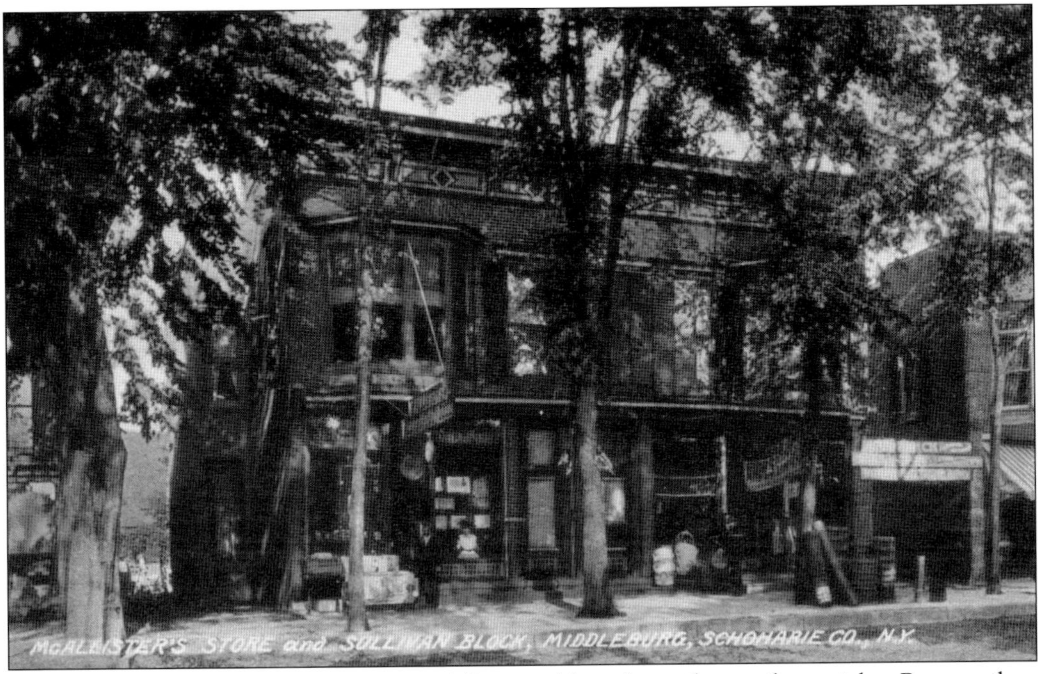

LEWIS MCALLISTER'S STORE, 1909. McAllister sold sterling silver toilet articles, Rogers silver plate, fine china, jewelry, watches, and novelties. In 1911, he opened the Gem Theater upstairs for his three-hour shows. He installed electric fans and called the theater "the coolest and best ventilated place in town." Today, it is the site of Middleburgh Hardware and Mrs. K's Restaurant. (Courtesy of author's collection.)

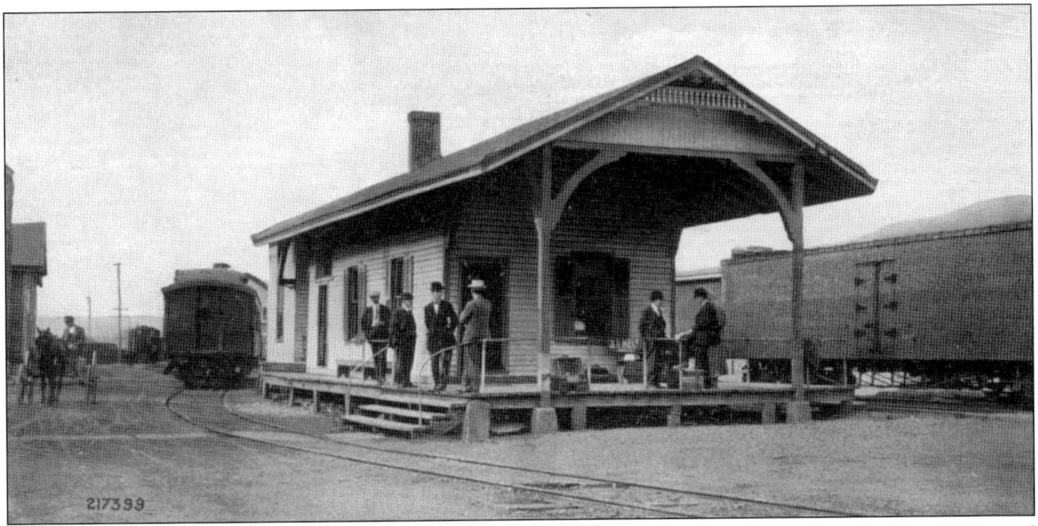

THE MIDDLEBURGH DEPOT. The Middleburgh & Schoharie Railroad was founded in 1867, and the tracks were laid as far as Schoharie where they met the Schoharie Valley Railroad's tracks. Here, men await the train at the station around 1910. (Courtesy of MLHR.)

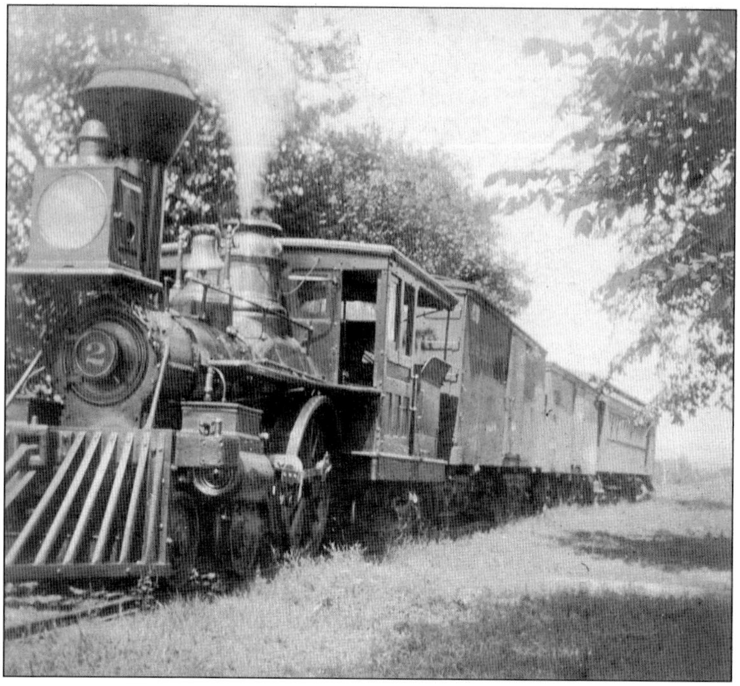

The Pony, 1868–1895. The Pony was the first locomotive purchased in 1868 by the Middleburgh & Schoharie Railroad. It was built in 1855 by the Danforth Locomotive and Machine Works. The locomotive had only one set of drive wheels. Here, it pulls a passenger car and several freight cars. (Courtesy of MLHR.)

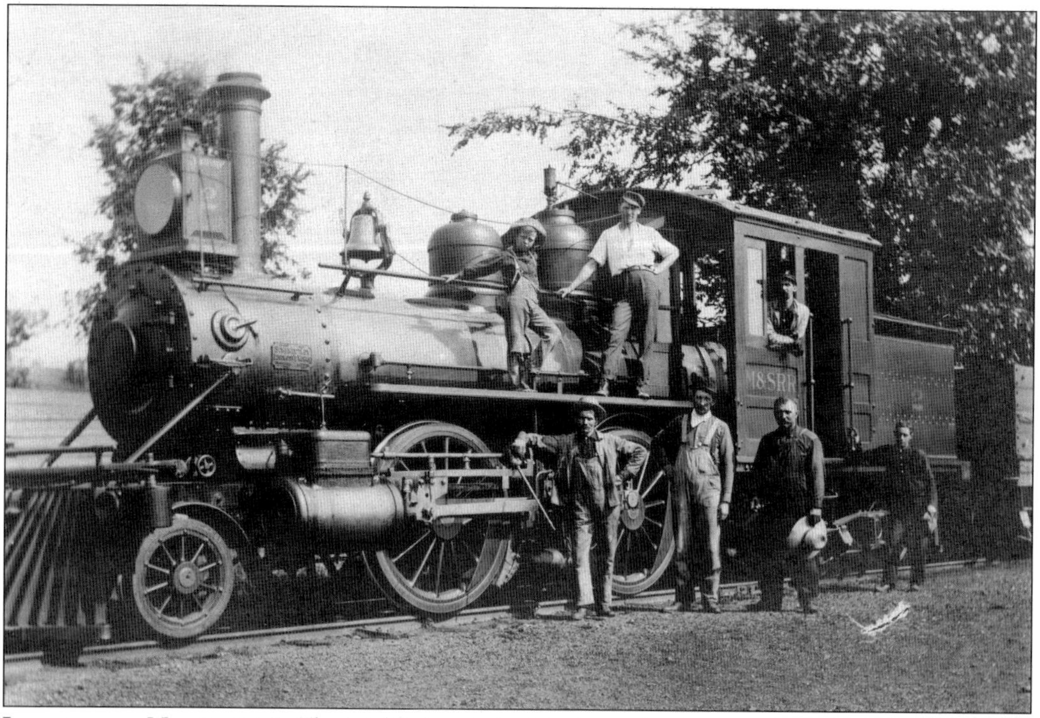

Locomotive No. 2, 1895. The Middleburgh & Schoharie Railroad replaced the Pony with this engine in 1895. This photograph was taken at Schoharie Junction, where the valley railroads met the Delaware & Hudson Railroad. The engineer is John Reynolds. The boy on the engine is Andrew Cartwright. W. Warner (left) and Chauncey Winegar (center) stand by the wheels. (Courtesy of MLHR.)

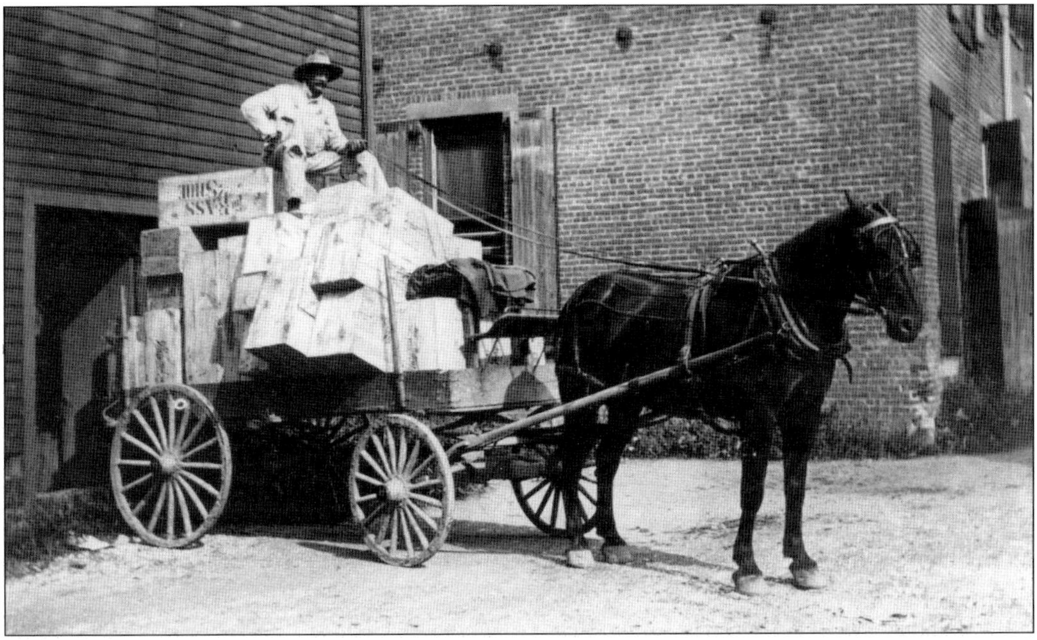

DELIVERIES AT MIDDLEBURGH. Merchandise was brought to Middleburgh by rail and off-loaded, then delivered by wagon. George Rivenburg sits atop a pile of boxes that are haberdashery items on their way to the Bulson Brothers Department Store. The top box says, "The Bass Shoe." (Courtesy of MLHR.)

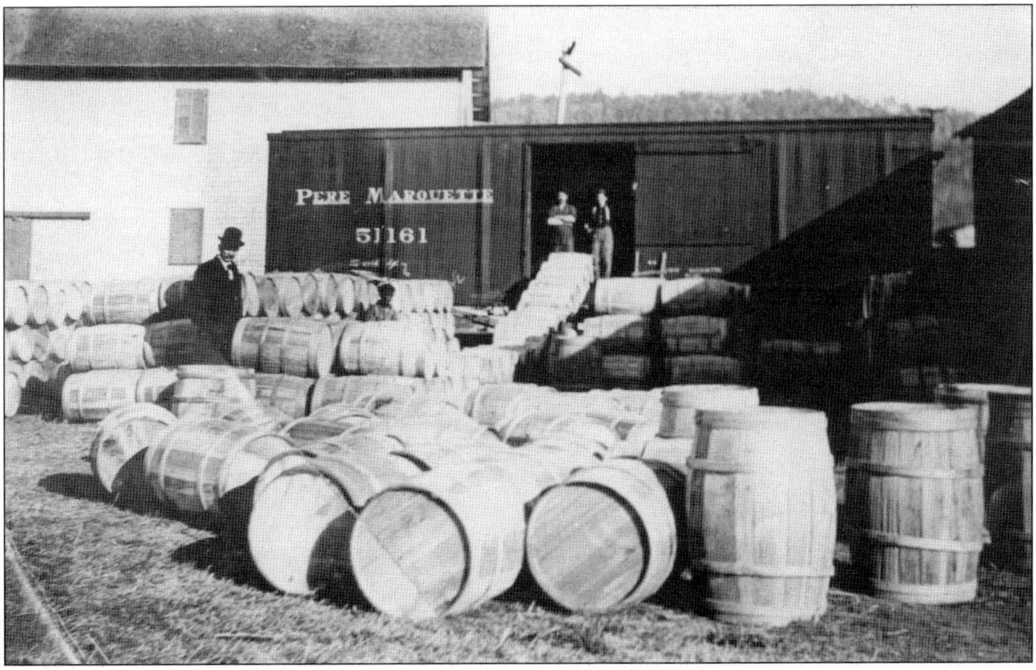

A FREIGHT CAR OF BARRELS. Over 100 wooden barrels of flour are delivered to Middleburgh by freight service. The Middleburgh & Schoharie Railroad was central to the prosperity of the region because it connected the village to the outside world. (Courtesy of MLHR.)

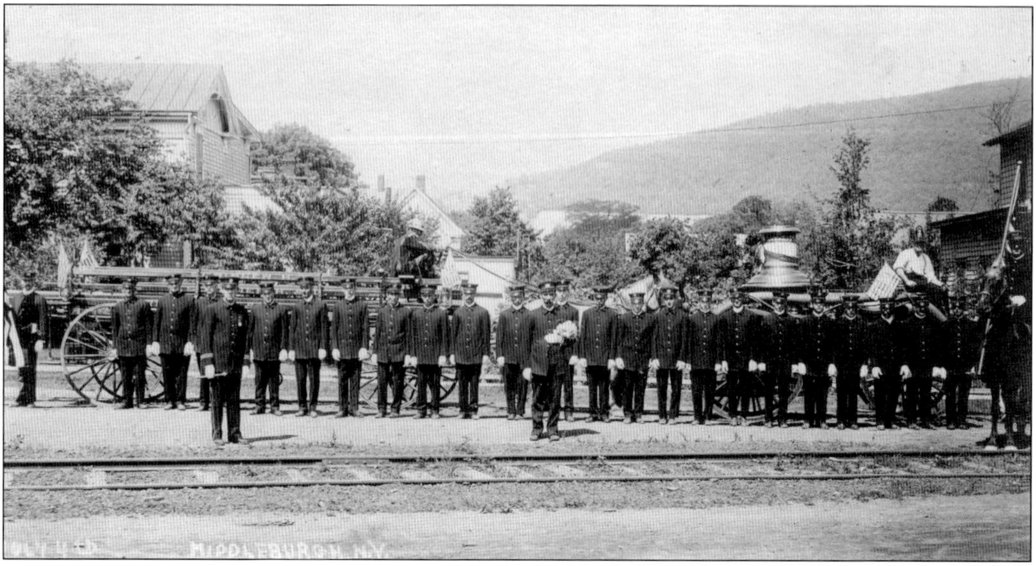

The Middleburgh Fire Company. The company stands at attention at the depot during the Fourth of July celebrations around 1900. Horses were used to pull the hose and ladders. Norman Vroman and John Reynolds stand in front. The group contains Charley Zeh, Eugene Sprague, Lawyer King, Robert Whittaker, Charles Henry Warner, Miles Hazelton, and Roswell Spoore. (Courtesy of MLHR.)

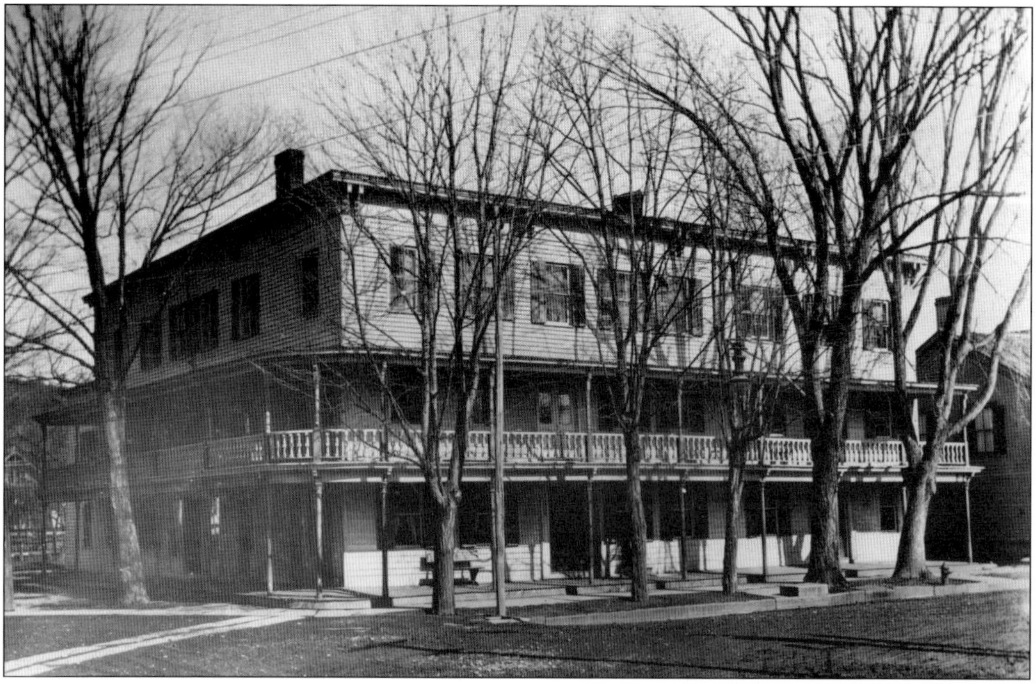

The Traver Hotel. The hotel stood at the corner of Main and River Streets where a convenience store now stands. Built around 1830, it was successively owned by E.P. Atchinson, William Sidney White, and David Traver. It was one of the many hotels in the village that hosted visitors and traveling salesmen. The building was removed in 1921 to make way for a gasoline station. (Courtesy of MLHR.)

The Kelsey and Vroman Store. The building still stands next door to St. Mark's Evangelical Lutheran Church. It is beautifully decorated in the Victorian manner with cornices and decorative fringe at the roofline. Joshua T. Kelsey was the owner and sold haberdashery, notions, and, judging by the shop window, a wide variety of decorative umbrellas. (Courtesy of Skip Edmonds.)

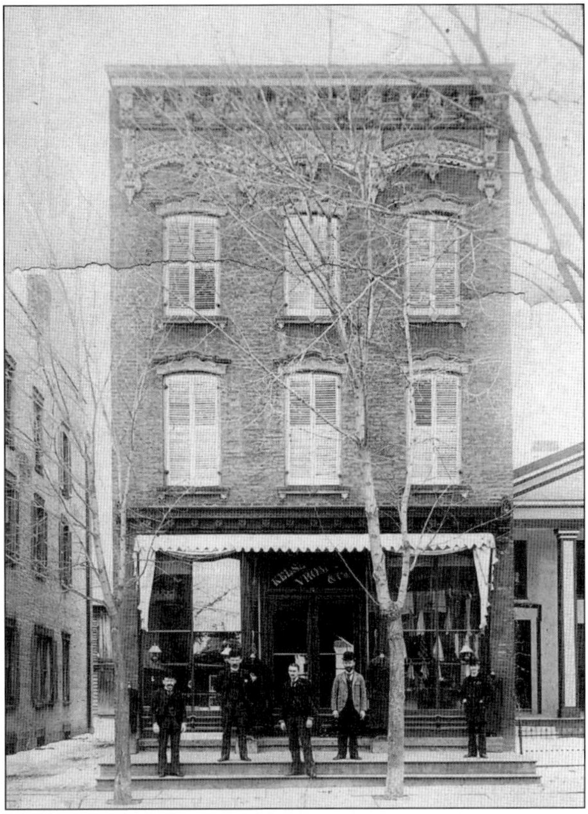

A Middleburgh Birthday Party. Birthdays were important then as now. Here, Marion Kelsey (Guernsey) stands at the center of her friends to celebrate her 10th birthday in 1910. Her mother, Jennie Sheldon Kelsey, is at the back left. They resided on Grove Street, where this photograph was taken. The home now belongs to Tom and Jo-Anne Gruning. (Courtesy of Skip Edmonds.)

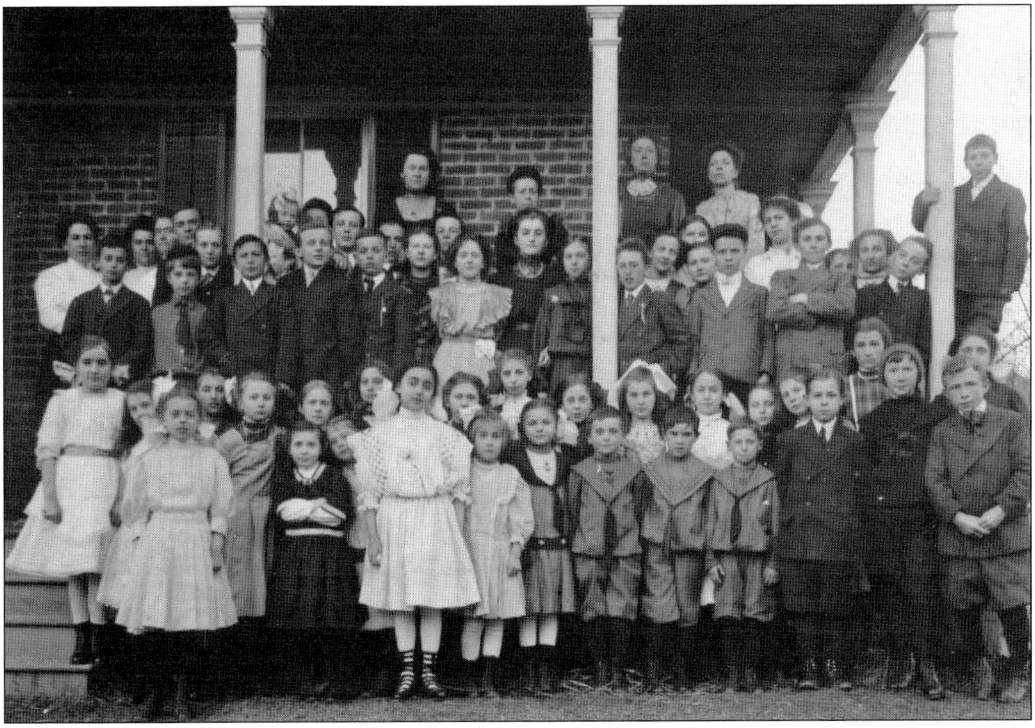

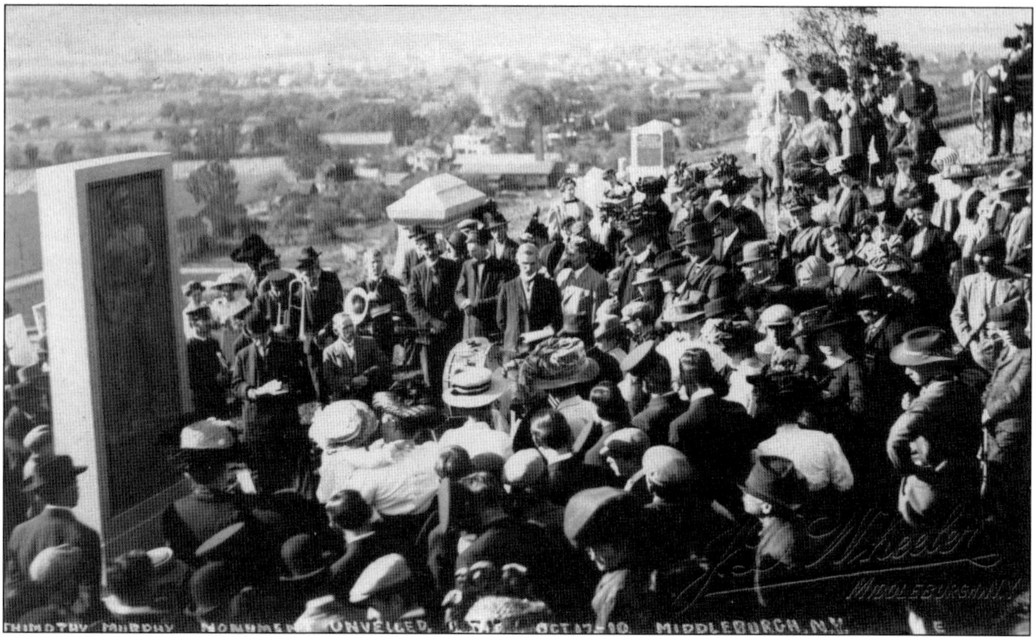

TIMOTHY MURPHY DEDICATION. Local hero Timothy Murphy, a sharpshooter, is reputed to have fired the shot that mortally wounded the British general Simon Fraser at the battle of Saratoga in 1777, turning the tide of the American Revolution. He and his wife, Peggy Feeck, were buried near his home in Fultonham. His remains were moved to Middleburgh where this monument was dedicated in the Middleburgh Cemetery in 1910. (Courtesy of OSFM, Chester Zimmer collection.)

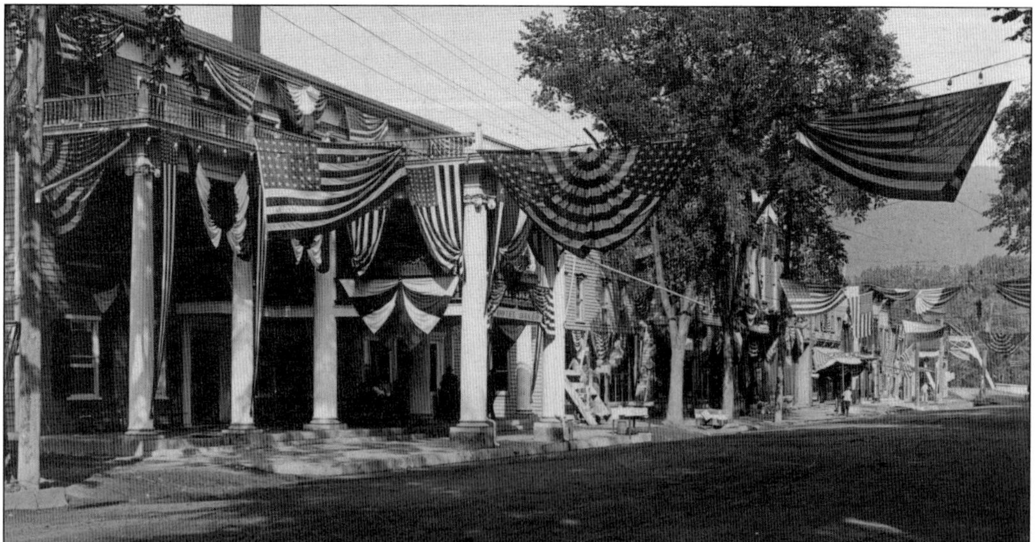

OLD HOME WEEK, MIDDLEBURGH. The year 1912 marked the 200th anniversary of the settlement of the Middleburgh area. The bicentennial was celebrated by a weeklong Old Home Week on August 11–16. Banners, flags, and bunting decorated the streets, and parades, games, plays, and competitions were held. (Courtesy of author's collection.)

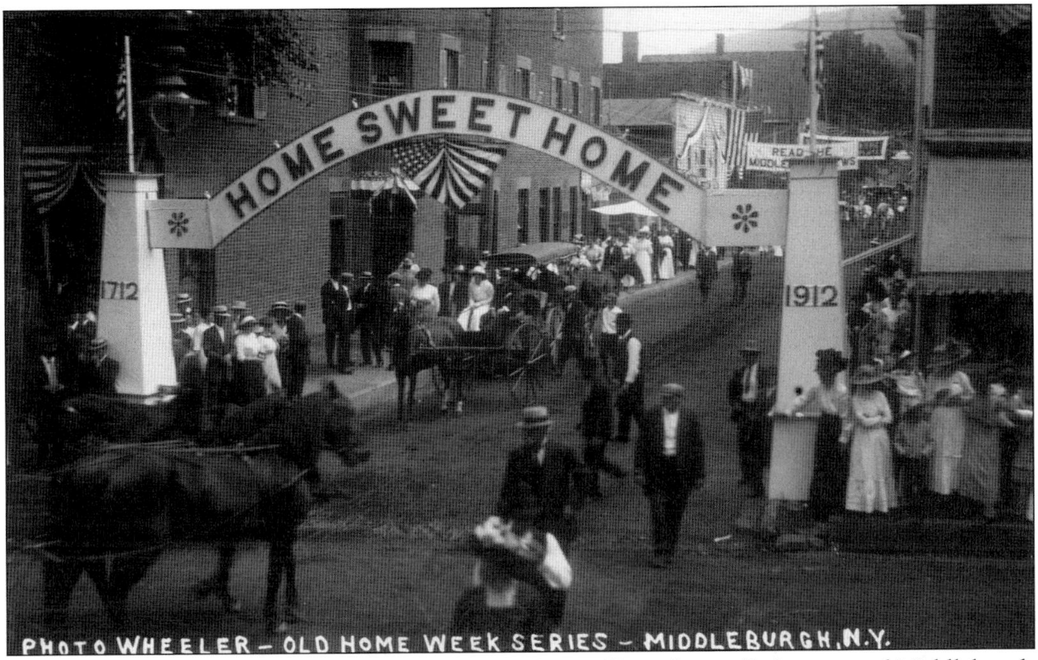

"Home Sweet Home," Middleburgh. "Home Sweet Home" is still the view of Middleburgh residents. The arch straddled Railroad Avenue. Of note are the horse and carriage and the well-dressed men and women attending Old Home Week celebrations. In the background, a sign across the road proclaims, "Read the Middleburgh News." (Courtesy of author's collection.)

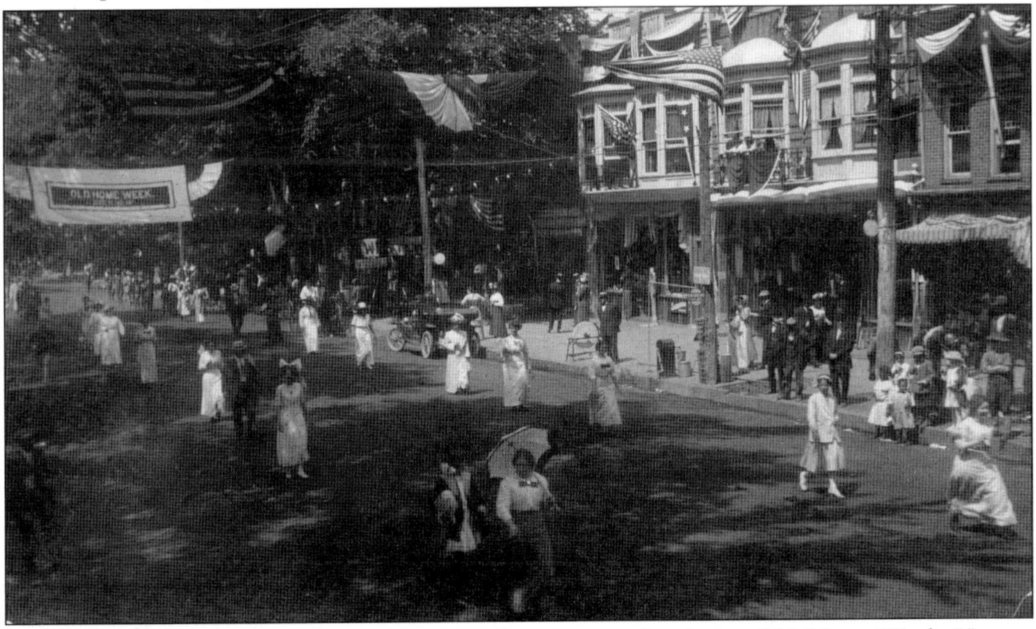

Old Home Week Parade. Many participated in the parades during Old Home Week. Here, a group of women march down Main Street. Though not visible except under magnification, there is a sign near the automobile parked along the road that says, "Motor Gas & Oil." In 1912, one could buy gasoline at stores. The bay windows (above right) indicate the scene is across from the Bauer Block. (Courtesy of author's collection.)

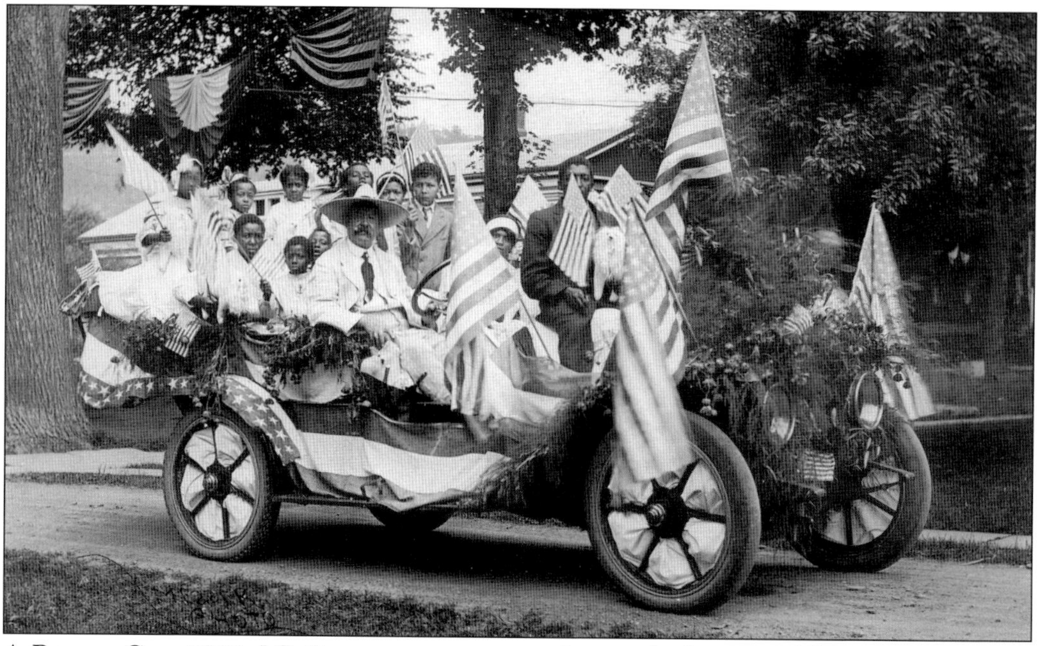

A Parade Car, 1912. J.C. Borst prepares to join the parade during Middleburgh's Old Home Week. His car is decorated with flowers, greenery, bunting, and flags. His passengers are African American youngsters from the neighborhood. (Courtesy of MLHR.)

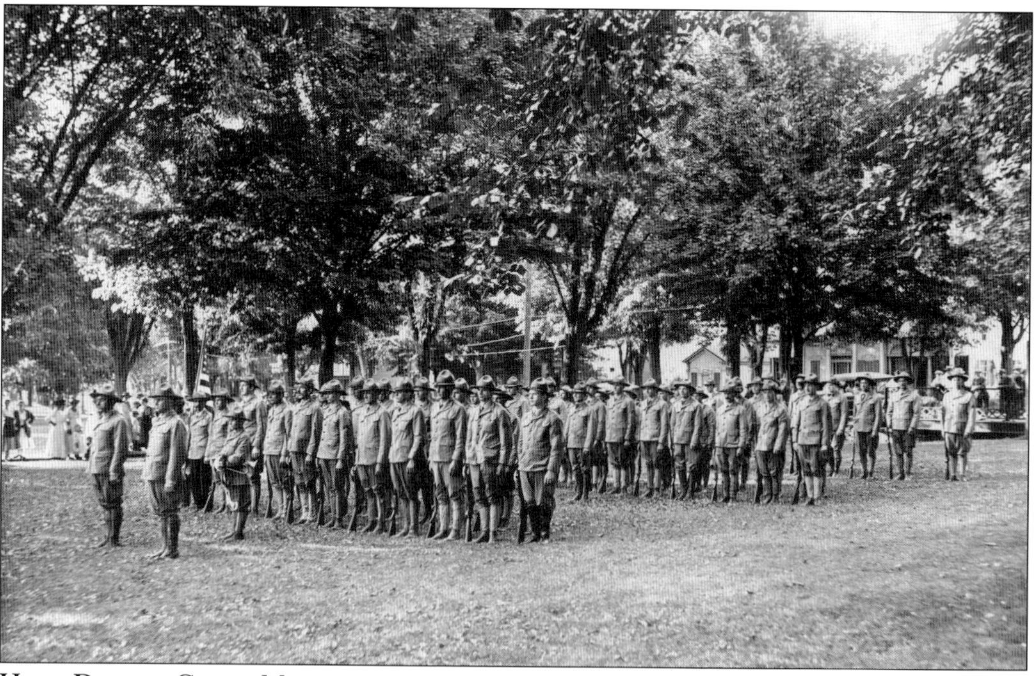

Home Defense Corps, Middleburgh, 1917. During World War I, the Home Defense Corps was composed of men who were not in the military. The purpose was for readiness, to stimulate recruiting, and for general police duties as required. Here, in 1917, the Middleburgh corps holds a drill. The captain was Paul Mattice. Sidney Daniels and W.W. King were lieutenants. (Courtesy of OSFM.)

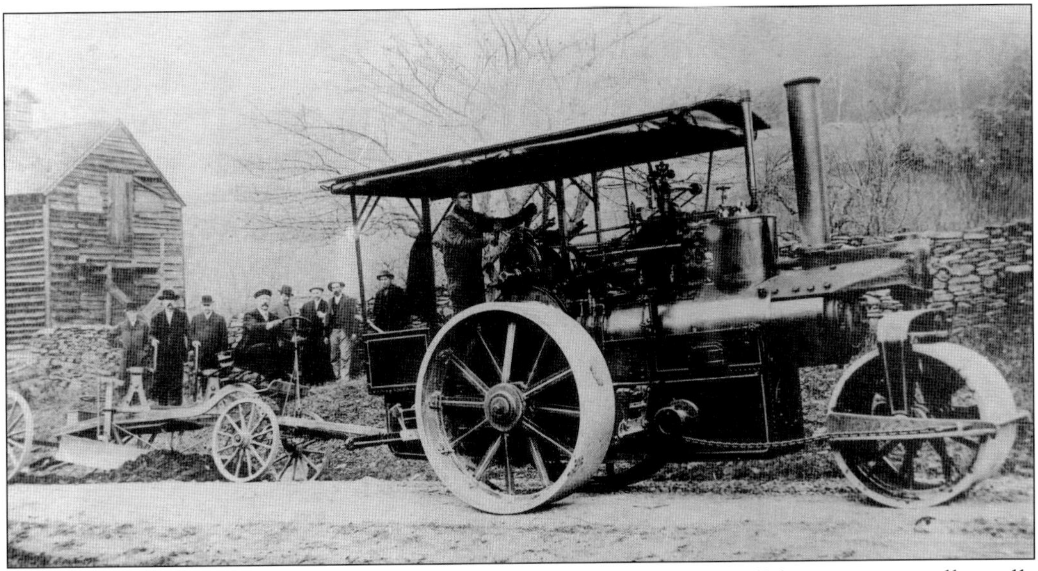

ROADWORK DEMONSTRATION, MIDDLEBURGH, NOVEMBER 1911. A Buffalo-Pitts steamroller pulls a Climax road machine as the town fathers look on. The road machine appears to be a scraper. Mounted on it are two men—one steers while one controls the scraper tilt. (Courtesy of OSFM, Chester Zimmer collection.)

COVERED BRIDGE, MIDDLEBURGH, 1900. There were numerous covered bridges across the Schoharie Creek. This is the old covered bridge in Middleburgh, and the third covered bridge to be built at this crossing. The 300-foot-long bridge was built in 1859 and served until 1905, when it was replaced by an iron bridge, which later was replaced by the current bridge. (Courtesy of Edwin Truax.)

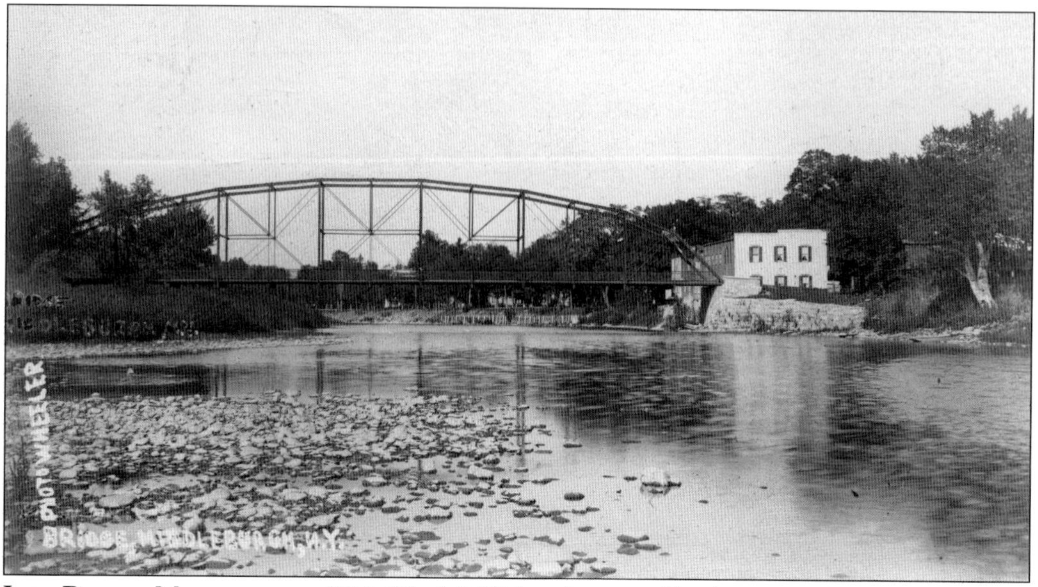

IRON BRIDGE, MIDDLEBURGH, 1910. The Middleburgh covered bridge was replaced in 1905 by an iron bridge, shown in this c. 1910 photograph. This bridge was in turn replaced by the current bridge in 1958. It was left in place for traffic until the new one was built. The building on the right, a gasoline station, was removed at that time. (Courtesy of OSFM, Robert Mahar collection.)

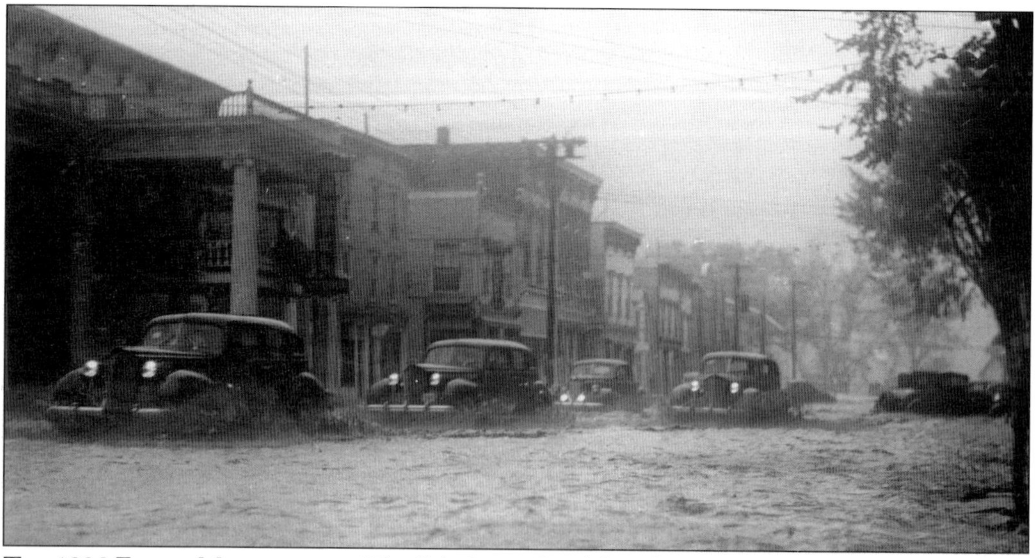

THE 1938 FLOOD, MIDDLEBURGH. The Schoharie Creek has flooded periodically. The waters rise to cover the nearby fields for many miles, and village homes and businesses suffer with damaged basements. Sometimes, the first floors of buildings are also inundated. Here, motorists push through the rising waters on Main Street in Middleburgh during the flood of 1938. Hotel Baker is on the left. (Courtesy of MLHR.)

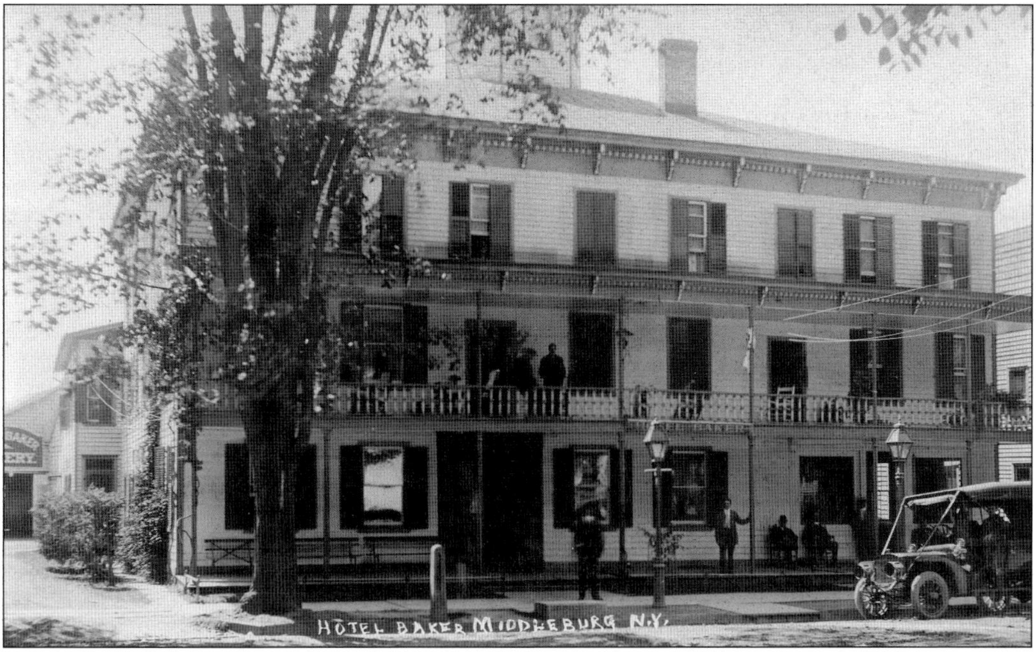

HOTEL BAKER, MIDDLEBURGH, 1910. This early view of Hotel Baker shows the 1824 building as it was around 1910. Menzo Baker purchased the hotel in 1896. Later, his son James took over the establishment. The hotel had 50 rooms as well as stables. Uniformed drivers would meet the trains at the Middleburgh depot using the 1906 Wayne touring car shown at right. (Courtesy of OSFM.)

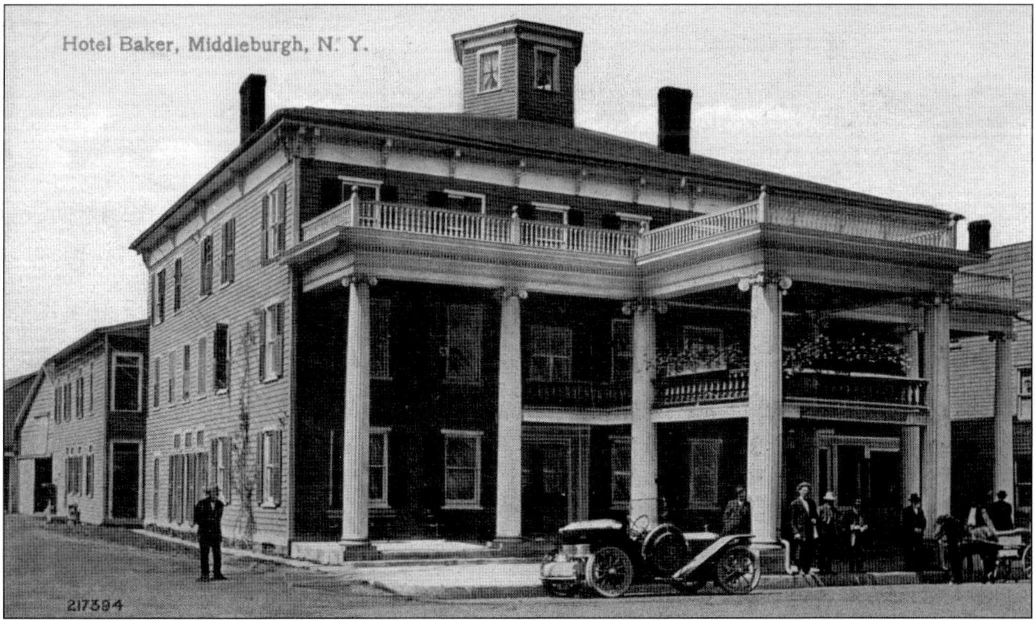

HOTEL BAKER, MIDDLEBURGH, 1915. James Baker, the hotel owner, made many improvements, as this view shows. He added the porch and colonnade as well as an upstairs ballroom. The hotel hosted society balls, political rallies, and music recitals. Weekly band concerts were held in the summer under the front portico. (Courtesy of author's collection.)

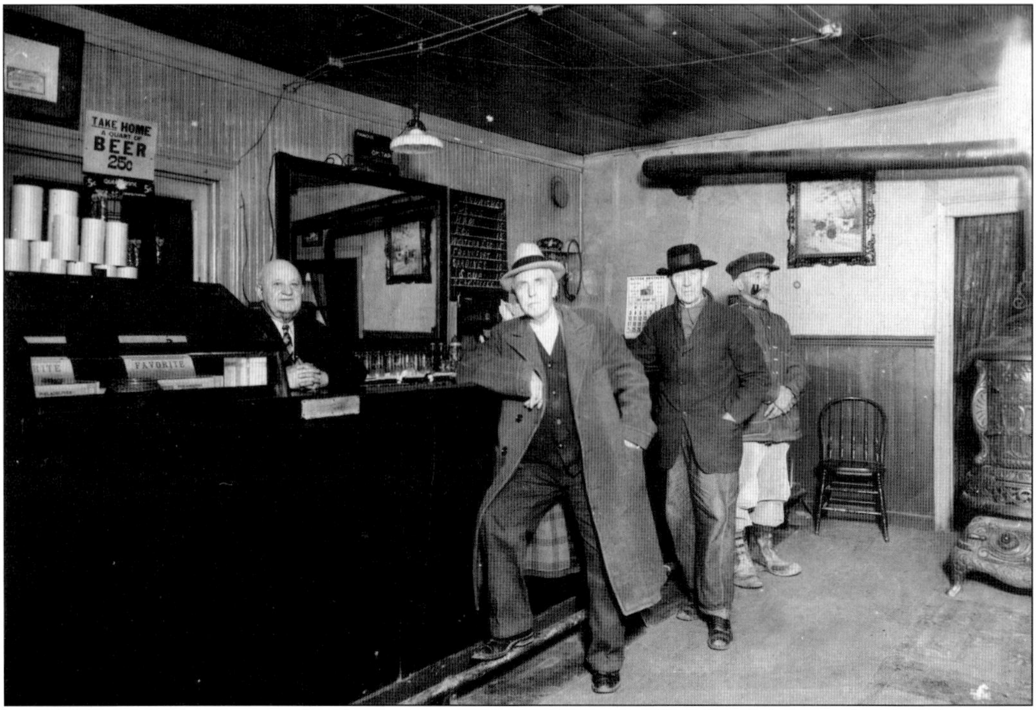

THE HOTEL BAKER BAR, 1937. According to the calendar on the wall of the Hotel Baker bar, it is January 1937, four years after the repeal of Prohibition. Here, three men are at the bar. The menu has sandwiches for 10¢–15¢ each, and patrons could take home a quart of beer for 25¢. Of note is the woodstove to the right with the stovepipe leading to the chimney. (Courtesy of MLHR.)

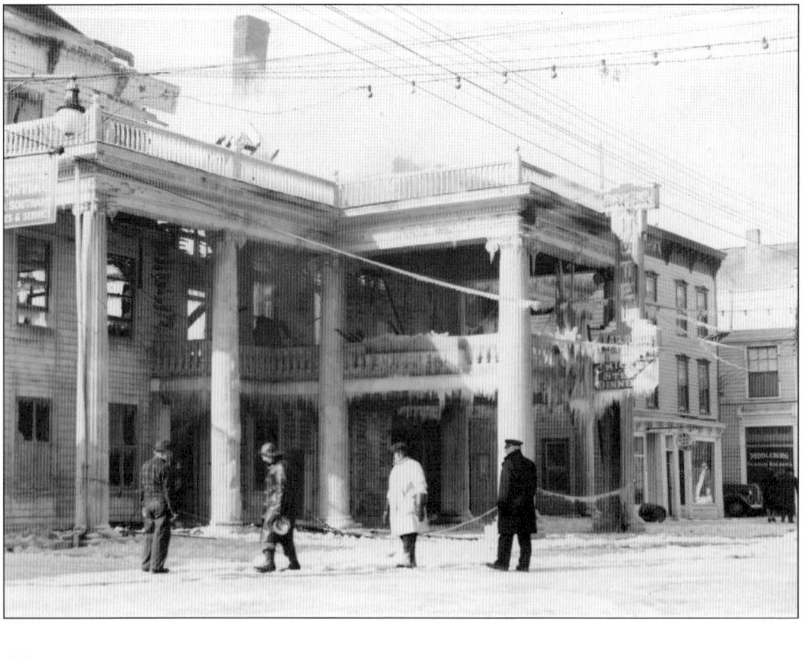

HOTEL BAKER AFTER THE FIRE, 1942. Hotel Baker burned on the night of February 13, 1942. Freezing weather prevented any saving of the structure. The Middleburgh Library, completed in 2004, now occupies the site of the old hotel. (Courtesy of OSFM.)

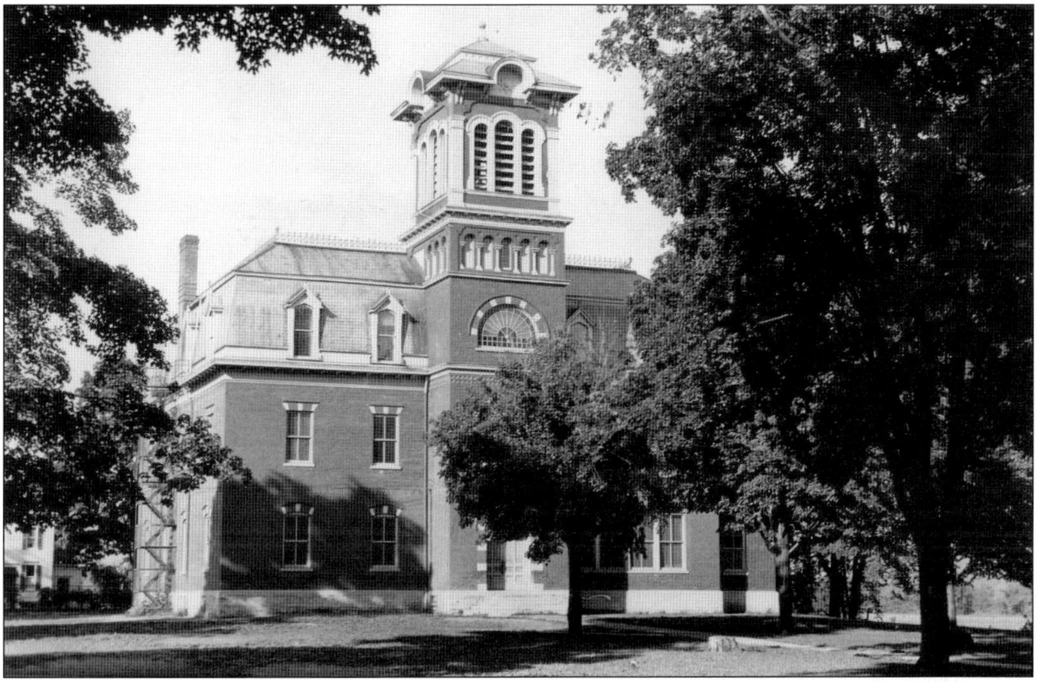

The Union Free School, Middleburgh. The school was built in 1883 to consolidate several local school districts. It was to be the center of many community activities in the following years. The structure was replaced in 1933 by the current school building. (Courtesy of OSFM.)

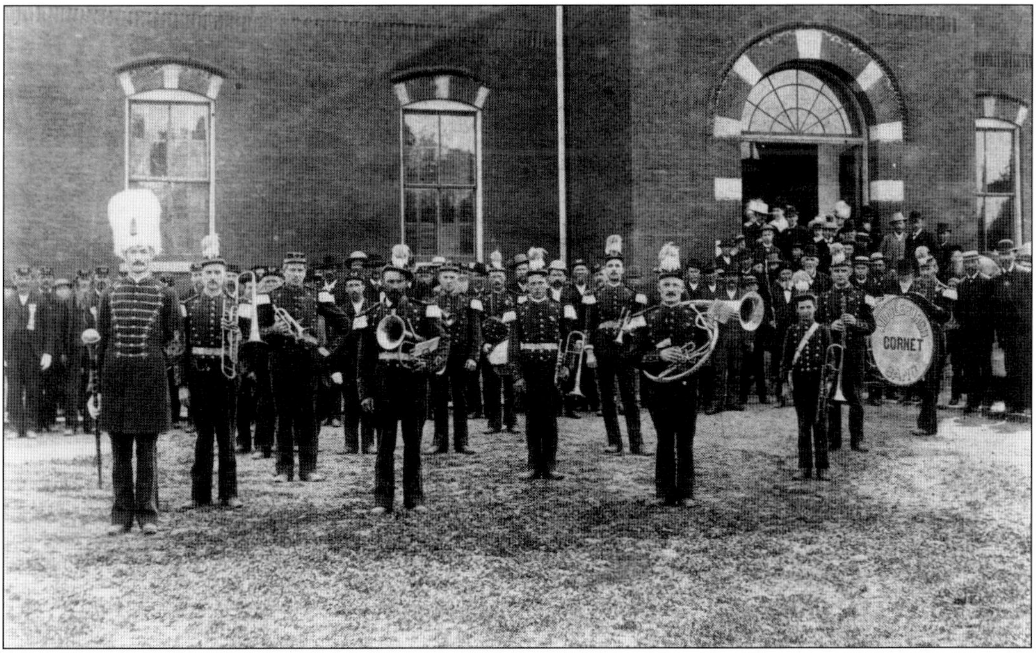

The Middleburgh Cornet Band, 1886. The cornet band played on Memorial Day, May 30, 1886. This photograph was taken in front of the old Middleburgh High School. Some of the people in the picture are Miles Hazelton (drum major, left), Henry B. Snyder (tuba, center right), and Henry Tibbetts (bass drum, right). (Courtesy of OSFM.)

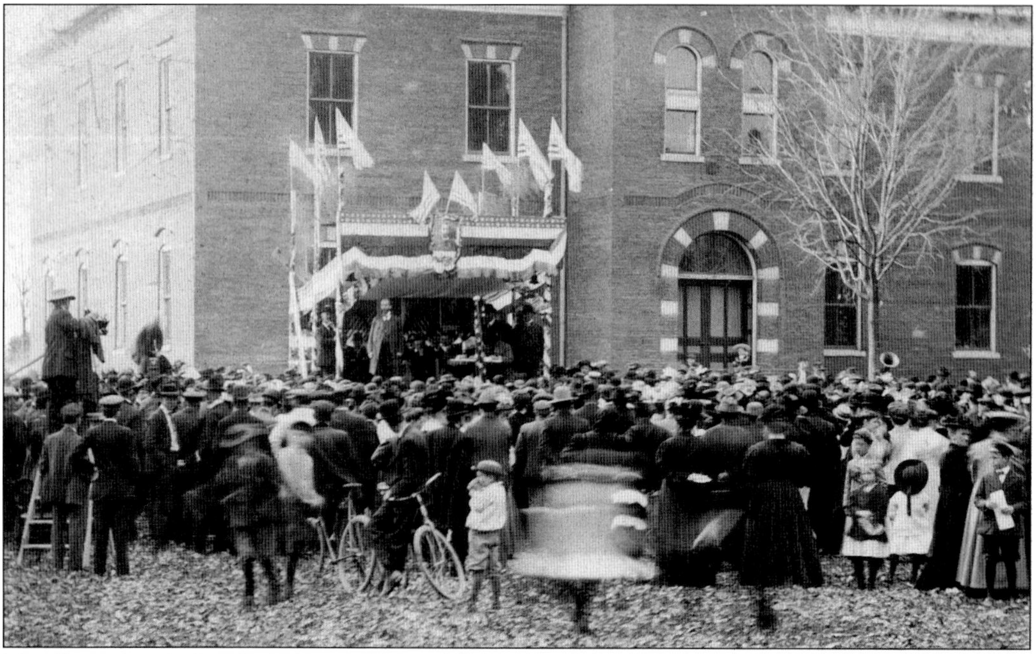

THE GOVERNOR'S STUMP SPEECH. New York's governor Charles Evan Hughes Sr. visits Middleburgh around 1910. He speaks in front of the high school on a raised platform complete with a panoply emblazoned with his image. A band is in attendance, and photographers record the event. Hughes was the Republican presidential candidate defeated by Woodrow Wilson in 1916 and was later chief justice of the US Supreme Court. (Courtesy of MLHR.)

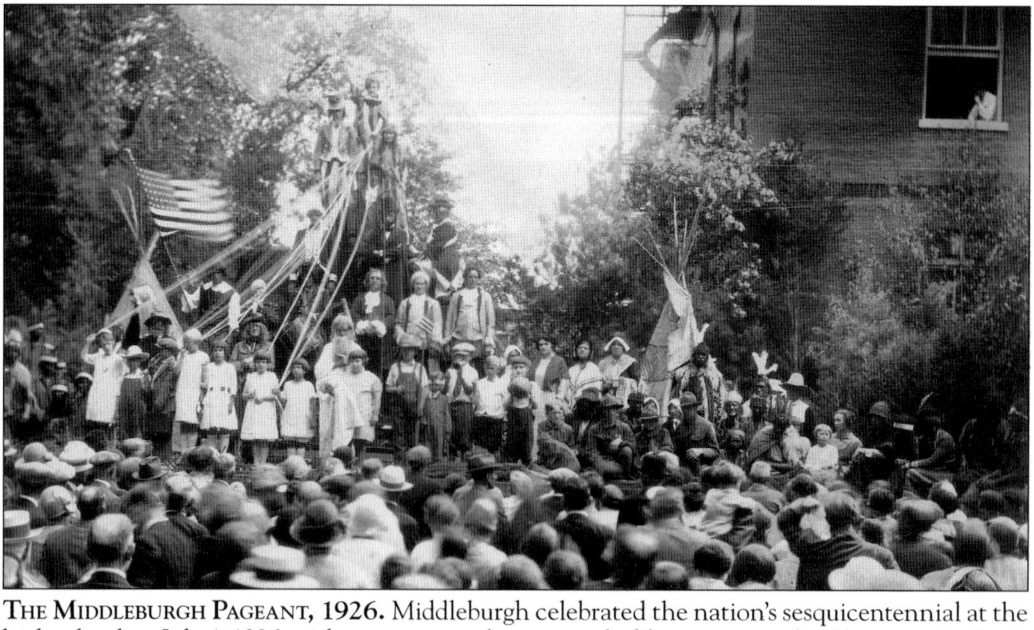

THE MIDDLEBURGH PAGEANT, 1926. Middleburgh celebrated the nation's sesquicentennial at the high school on July 4, 1926, with a pageant with a series of tableaux written by Chauncey Rickard. Here, Florence Vroman is Miss Liberty, Charis Sunderland is Columbia, and Hollis Harrington is Uncle Sam. The rest of the cast, including George Washington and Abraham Lincoln, are also present. Some 5,000 people attended the festivities. (Courtesy of MLHR.)

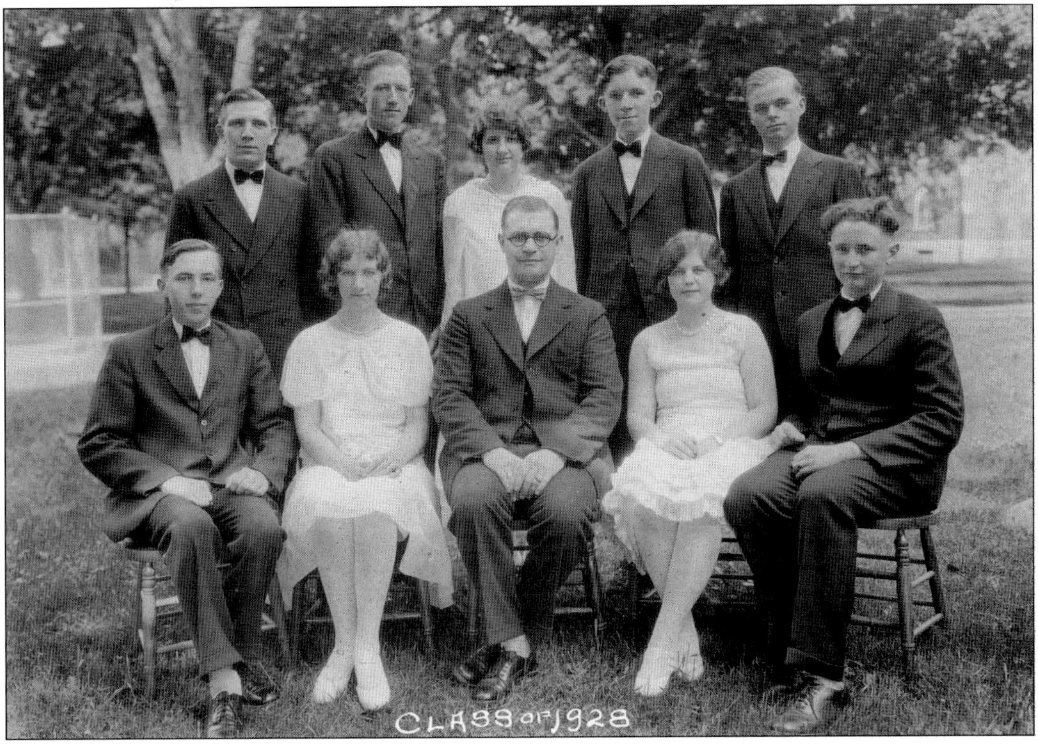

MIDDLEBURGH HIGH SCHOOL CLASS OF 1928. The class was very small compared to the present-day classes. From left to right are (first row) Howard Mann, Esther Braymen, Professor Morrison, Edith Losee Young, and John Spickerman; (second row) Russell Bergh, Kenneth Nelson, Wilhelmina Keyser, Kenneth Bouck, and Omer Youmans. (Courtesy of MLHR.)

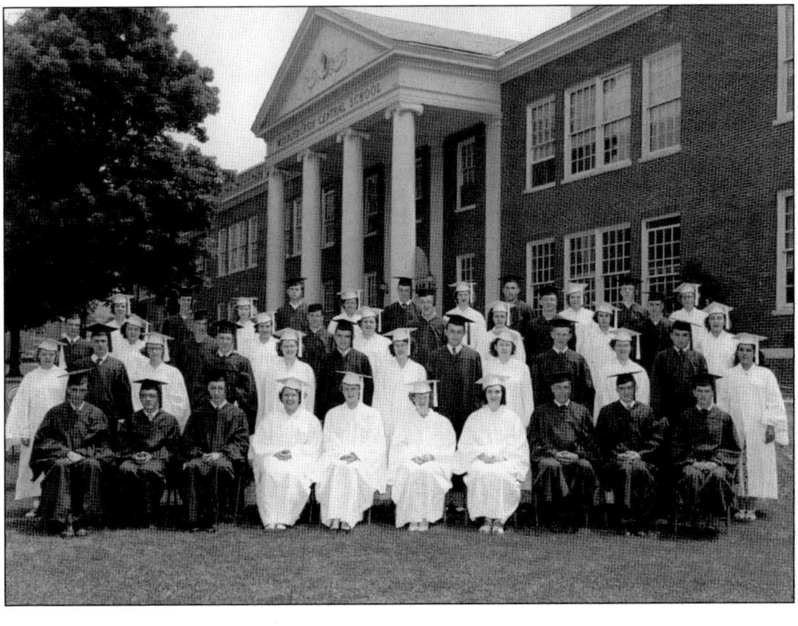

THE MIDDLEBURGH HIGH SCHOOL CLASS OF 1951. The 1951 graduating class of Middleburgh High School is shown in front of the current high school building. Many community events are held on this lawn in front of the colonnaded portico. (Courtesy of MLHR.)

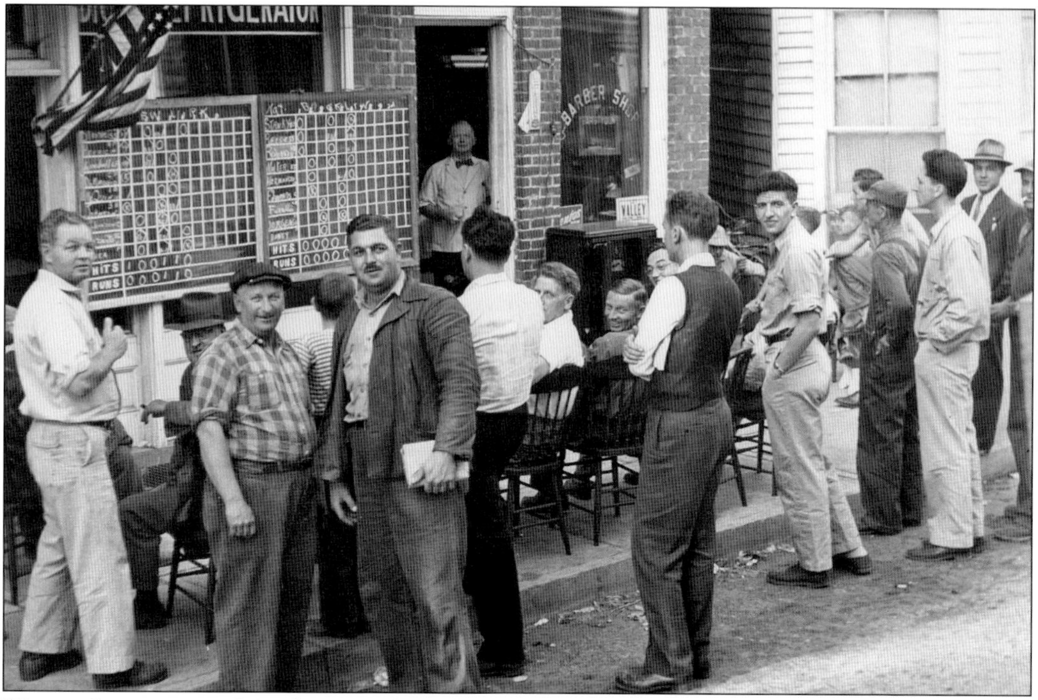

World Series, 1947. Men listen to the radio outside G.J. "Barb" Young's barbershop on Railroad Avenue in Middleburgh. The scoreboards indicate that it is the sixth inning of Game 5 of the 1947 World Series—the New York Yankees vs. the Brooklyn Dodgers. Joe DiMaggio has just hit a home run in the fifth inning. Playing for the Dodgers, Jackie Robinson was the first African American ball player in the major leagues that year. (Courtesy of OSFM.)

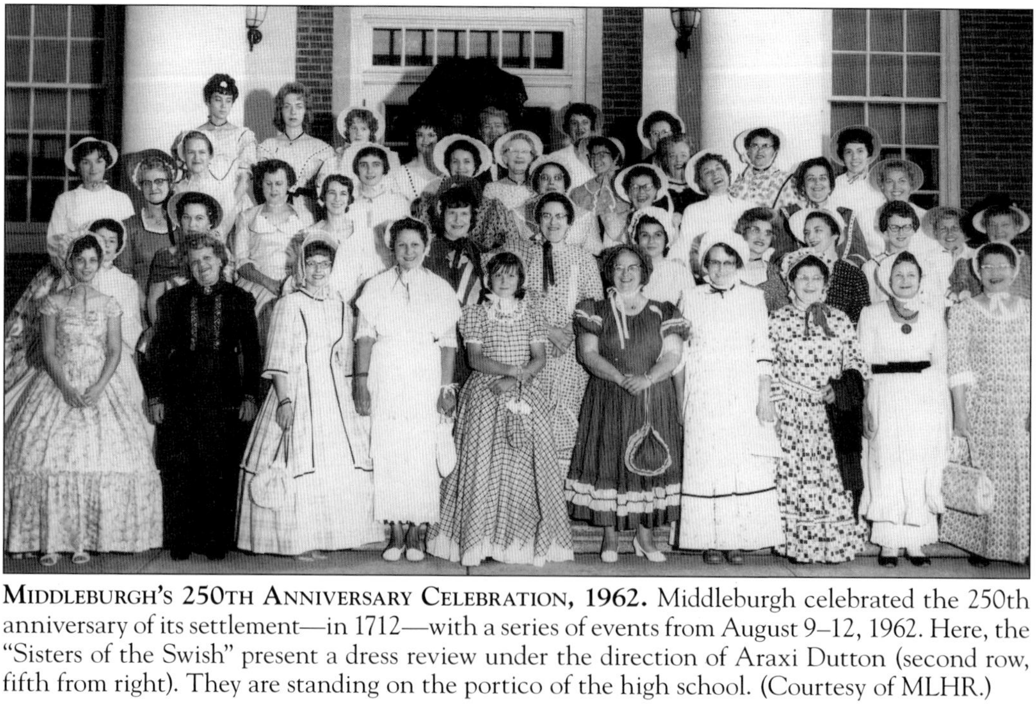

Middleburgh's 250th Anniversary Celebration, 1962. Middleburgh celebrated the 250th anniversary of its settlement—in 1712—with a series of events from August 9–12, 1962. Here, the "Sisters of the Swish" present a dress review under the direction of Araxi Dutton (second row, fifth from right). They are standing on the portico of the high school. (Courtesy of MLHR.)

Five

SCHOHARIE

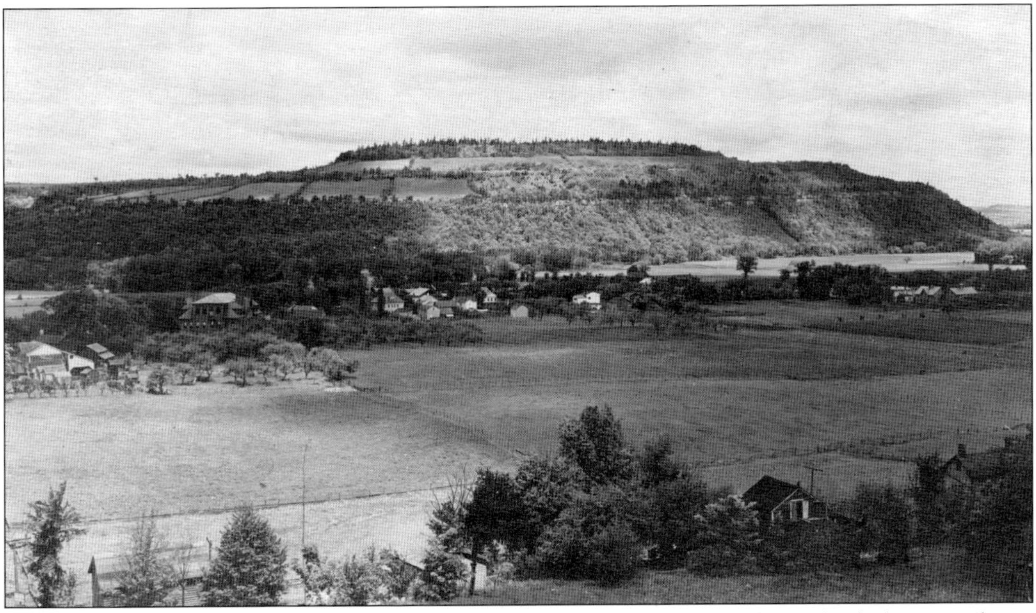

TERRACE MOUNTAIN, SCHOHARIE. Terrace Mountain looks over the village of Schoharie in this c. 1920 view. Unlike today's view, fields are visible on the top of the mountain. The large structure at the left is the old Schoharie High School building, which burned in 1926. The fields in the right foreground belong to the John Borst farm. (Courtesy of author's collection.)

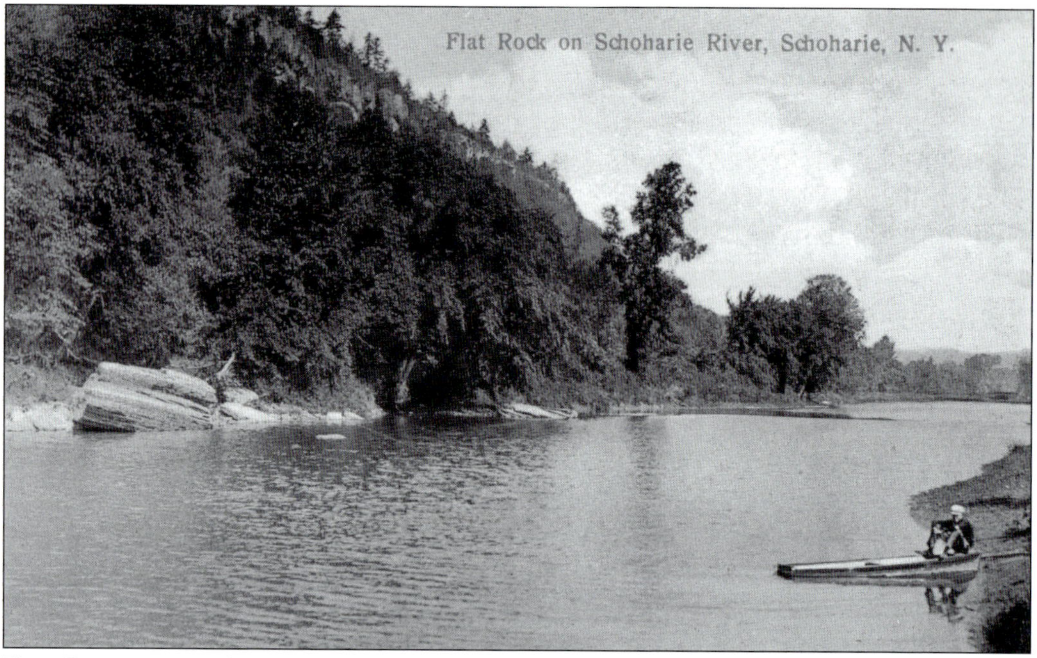

FLAT ROCK ON THE SCHOHARIE CREEK. The Schoharie Creek flows past Terrace Mountain in this pastoral 1910 view. The flat rock on the left has been used by generations of residents as a picnic spot on the river. (Courtesy of author's collection.)

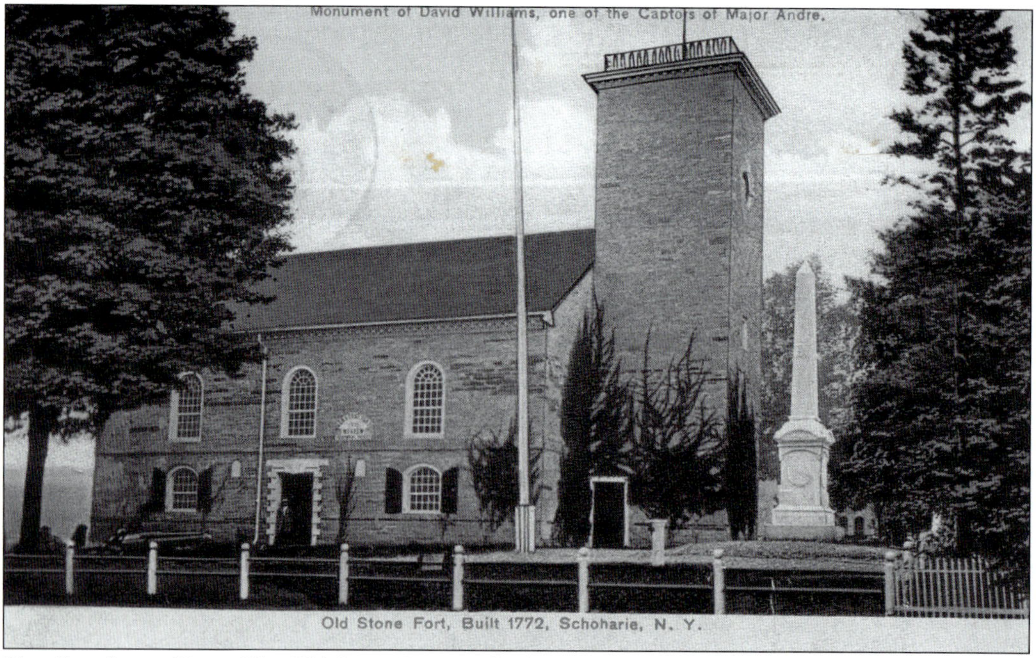

THE OLD STONE FORT. The Old Stone Fort was built in 1772 as a Reformed church. It was stockaded in 1777 and proved its worth in 1780 when the British attacked the Schoharie Valley. Names of the original builders are carved into its walls. After the Reformed Church congregation moved to the village in 1844, the building became an armory. In 1894, Schoharie County acquired the building, which is now a museum. (Courtesy of author's collection.)

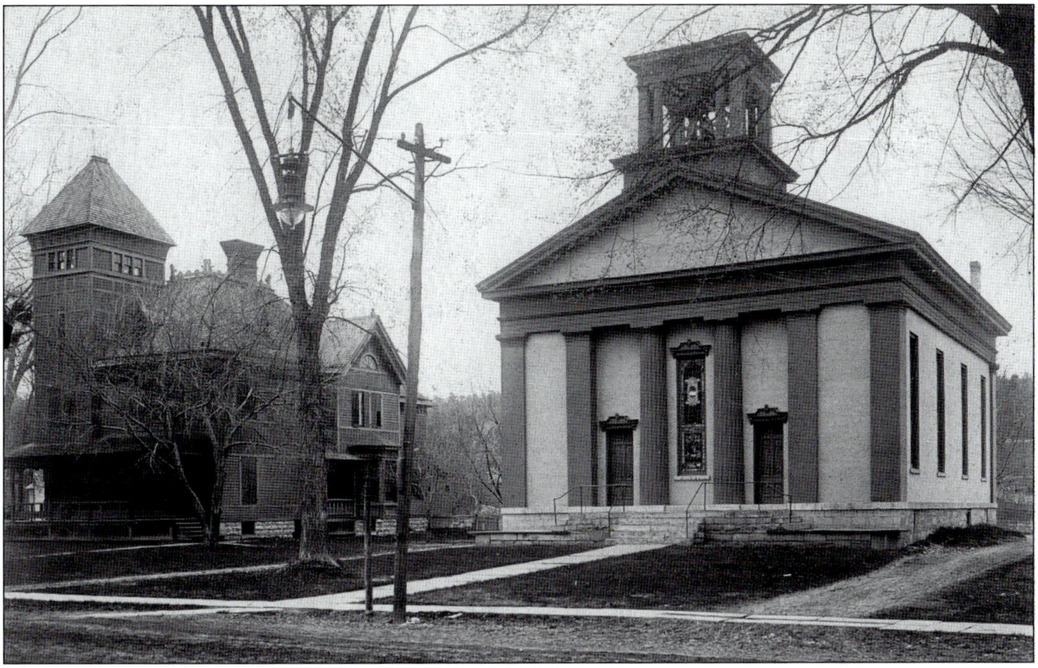

THE SCHOHARIE REFORMED CHURCH, 1904. The building was erected in 1844 when the congregation moved from the stone church now known as the Old Stone Fort. The contract to build the church was awarded to William Babcock for $3,370. Next door, the parsonage (now known as the Heritage House) was built in high Victorian style in 1886 and housed ministers until 1960. Of note is the electric street lamp in this photograph. (Courtesy of OSFM.)

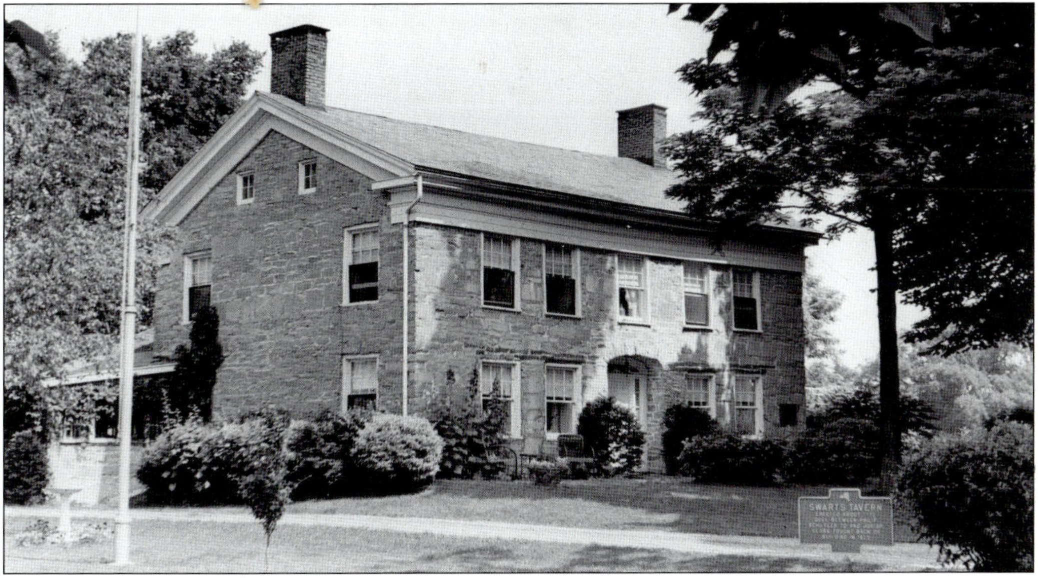

SWART'S TAVERN, AROUND 1950. The tavern was built by Teunis Swart around 1772. Its local limestone construction is similar to that of the Old Stone Fort. During the Revolutionary War, it was one of the few buildings left standing after the British raid of 1780. In 1820, Josias Clark and Philip Schuyler (nephew of Alexander Hamilton) dueled here with pistols. Today, the house is owned by the John Poorman family. (Courtesy of MLHR.)

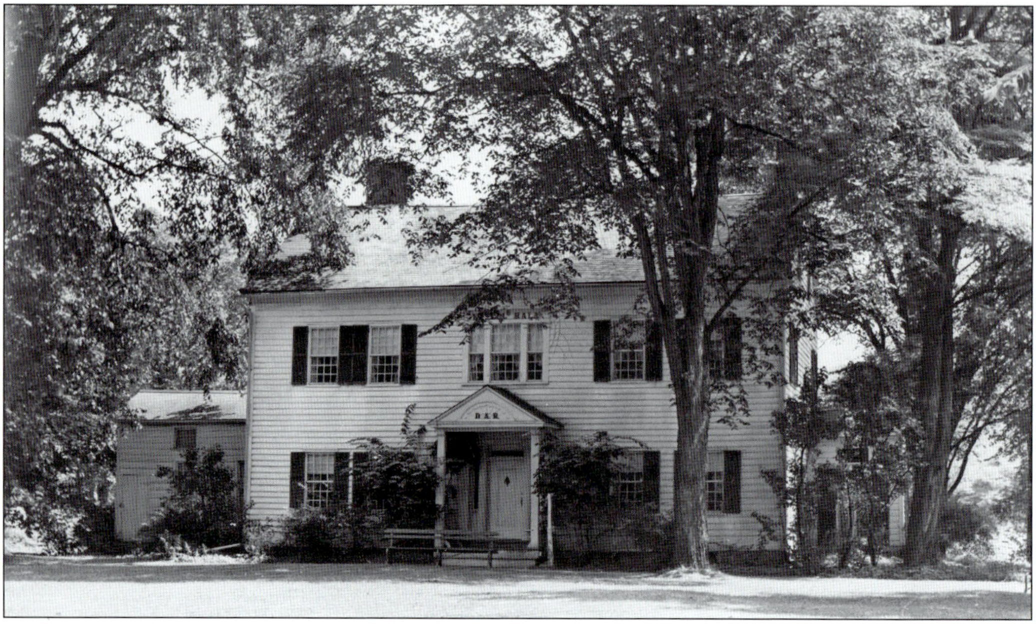

Lasell Hall, Schoharie. Johannes J. Lawyer erected this building as a tavern in 1795. There were several proprietors before it came into possession of the Lasell family. On September 29, 1913, the heirs of Josiah Lasell deeded the old tavern property, then vacant, to the Schoharie Chapter, National Society Daughters of the American Revolution (NSDAR). This view dates from around 1950. (Courtesy of MLHR.)

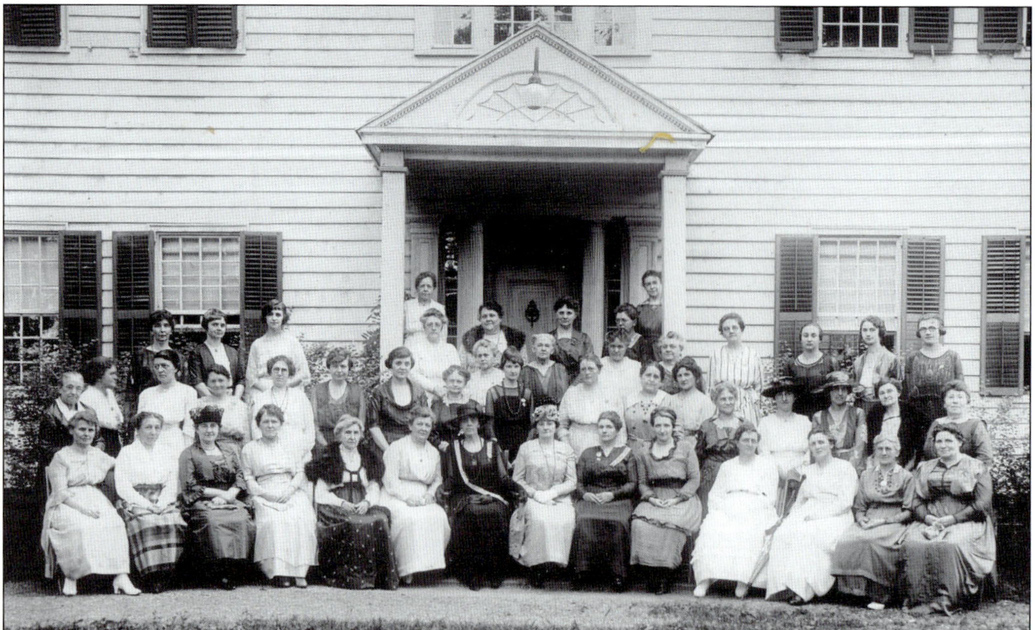

Chapter House Dedication, Schoharie DAR, 1914. The Schoharie Chapter, NSDAR held its first meeting in the newly refurbished Lasell Hall on October 18, 1914. The chapter was founded in 1910 by 30 Schoharie women. They are joined here by members from other chapters. (Courtesy of the Schoharie Chapter, NSDAR.)

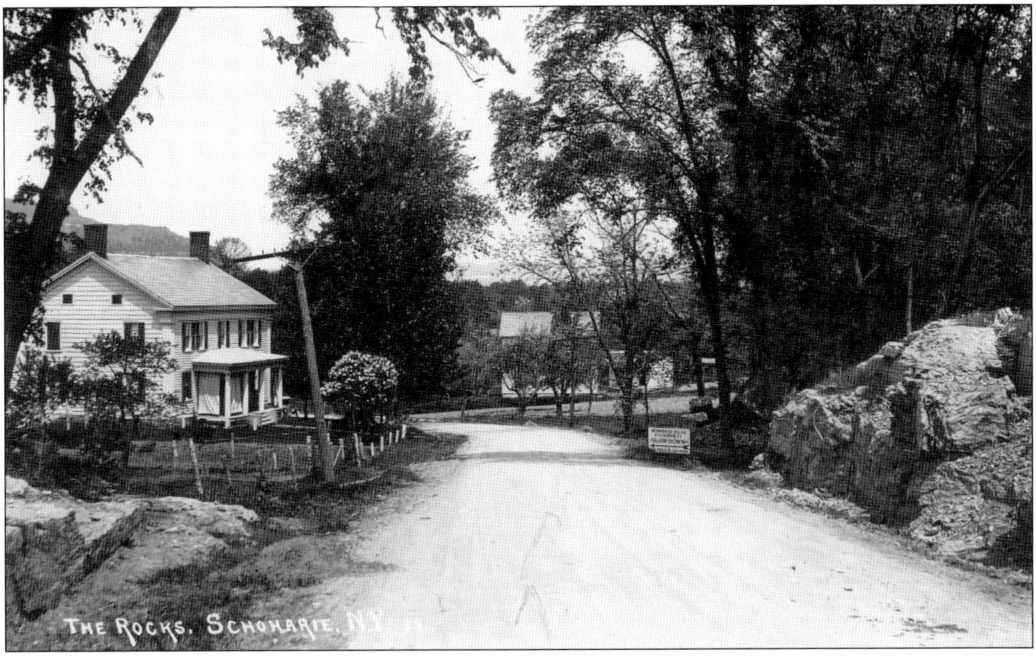

The Rocks. This was the home of Hendrick Schaeffer (1698–1776), one of the early settlers of Schoharie. Some portions of the house date to around 1745. The home sits at the picturesque southern entrance of Schoharie near a rock ledge that gives the house its name. Today, it is home to Mary Arnold and Joseph Gluck. (Courtesy of Edwin Truax.)

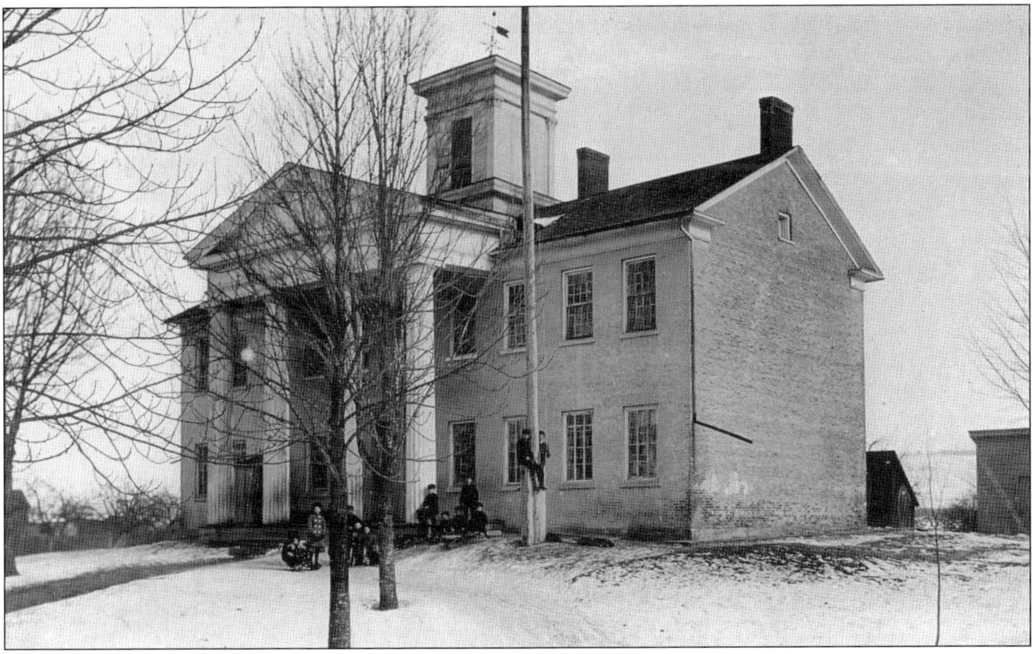

Schoharie Academy. The Schoharie Academy was constructed in 1835 and was torn down in 1904 to make way for a new, larger brick school building. This winter scene shows a group of children waiting to sled down the hill, and two boys perched on the flagpole supports. (Courtesy of OSFM.)

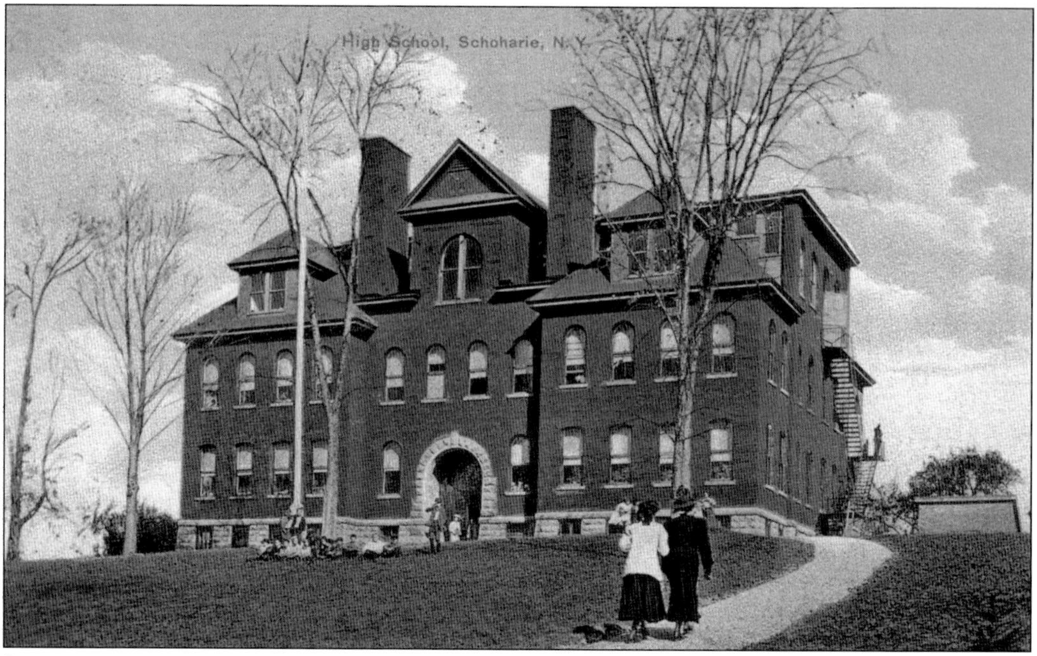

SCHOHARIE HIGH SCHOOL, 1910. Schoharie's new redbrick school was built a short time after 1904. It was a magnificent three-story building with arched windows and tall chimneys. It even boasted iron fire escapes. This c. 1910 view shows two well-dressed women (perhaps teachers) walking up the path to school while a small group of students is seated around the flagpole. (Courtesy of Edwin Truax.)

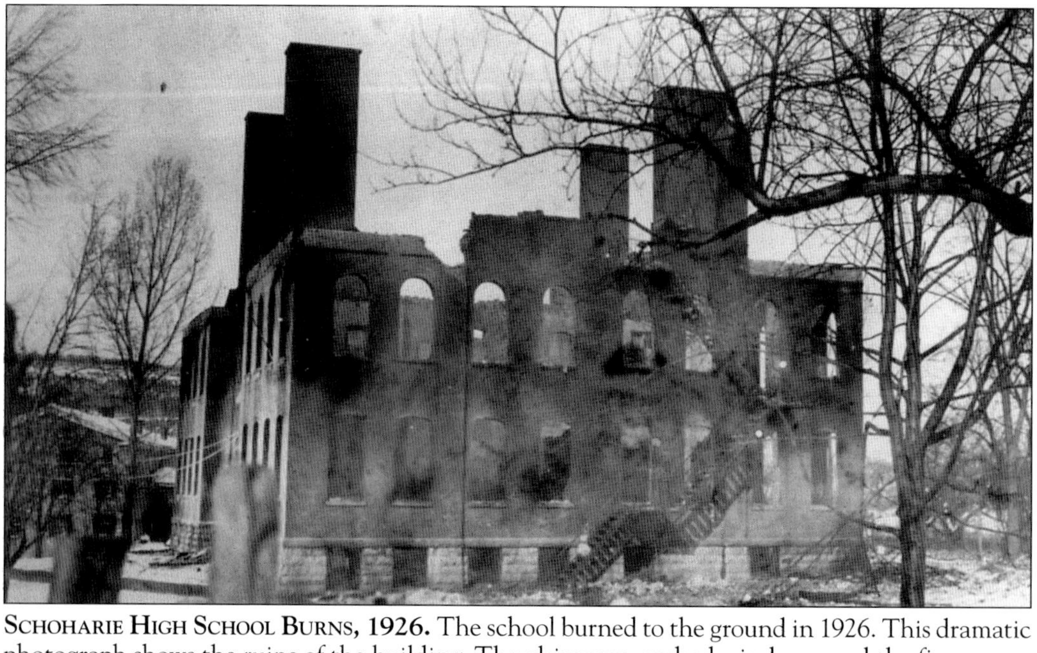

SCHOHARIE HIGH SCHOOL BURNS, 1926. The school burned to the ground in 1926. This dramatic photograph shows the ruins of the building. The chimneys, arched windows, and the fire escape still stood, but all else was lost. (Courtesy of Skip Edmonds.)

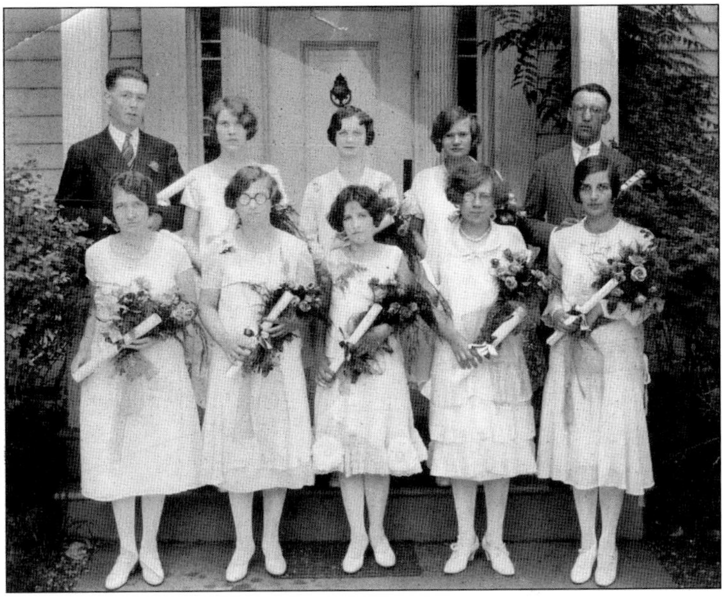

Schoharie High School Class of 1926. Because the high school had burned, the class of 1926 had their graduation at Lasell Hall. Here, the 10 graduates pose on the Lasell Hall steps with their flowers and certificates. From left to right are (first row) two unidentified, Elizabeth Becker (Warner), and two unidentified; (second row) ? Schemerhorn, Janet Bergh Webb (Colyer), unidentified, Elizabeth Von Linden, and Edward Scribner. (Courtesy of Betsy Colyer Guernsey.)

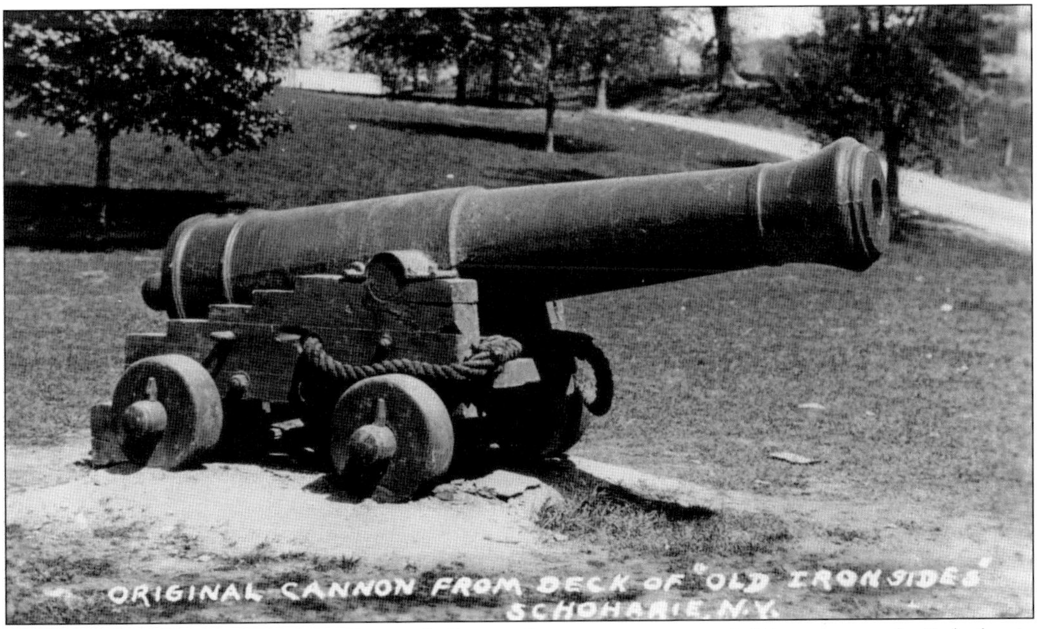

The School Cannon. In 1928, Gertrude Spawn Leininger presented this canon to the Schoharie School Board. The canon has stood on the school lawn since then. It was said to be from the USS *Constitution*. Built in 1797 and known as "Old Ironsides," the ship was made famous during the War of 1812. The ship is now in Boston Harbor. Research by Louis Tremante showed that this canon is a replica cast at the Boston shipyards in 1906 to raise funds to restore "Old Ironsides." (Courtesy of author's collection.)

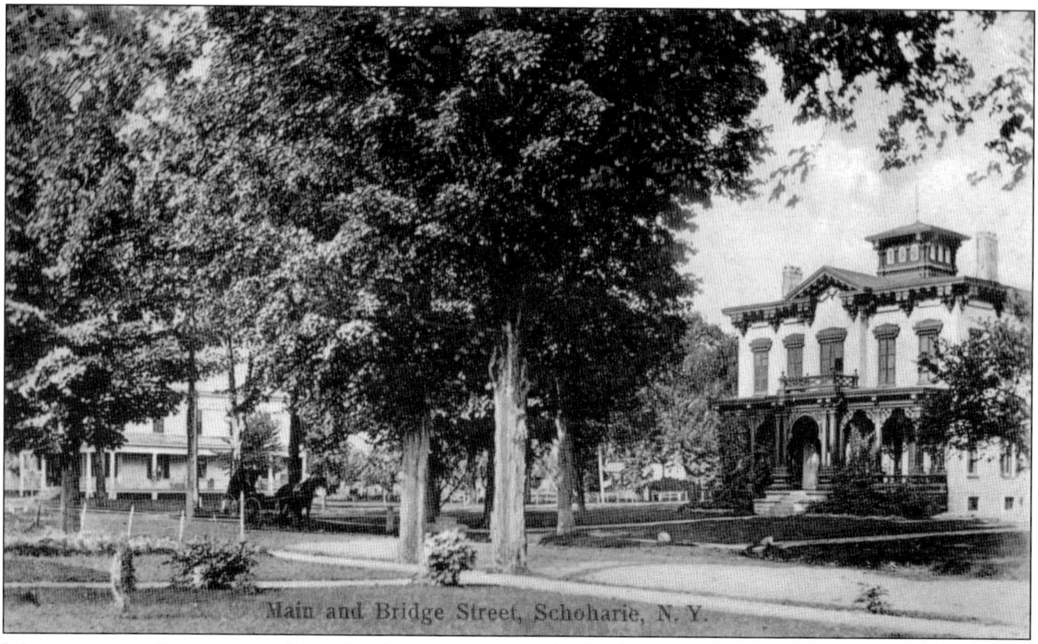

MAINBRIDGE, SCHOHARIE. Mainbridge is a spectacular Italianate Victorian home situated on the corner of Main and Bridge Streets. The house was built around 1883, probably for James O. Williams, a Schoharie banker, who at one time was the county treasurer. (Courtesy of author's collection.)

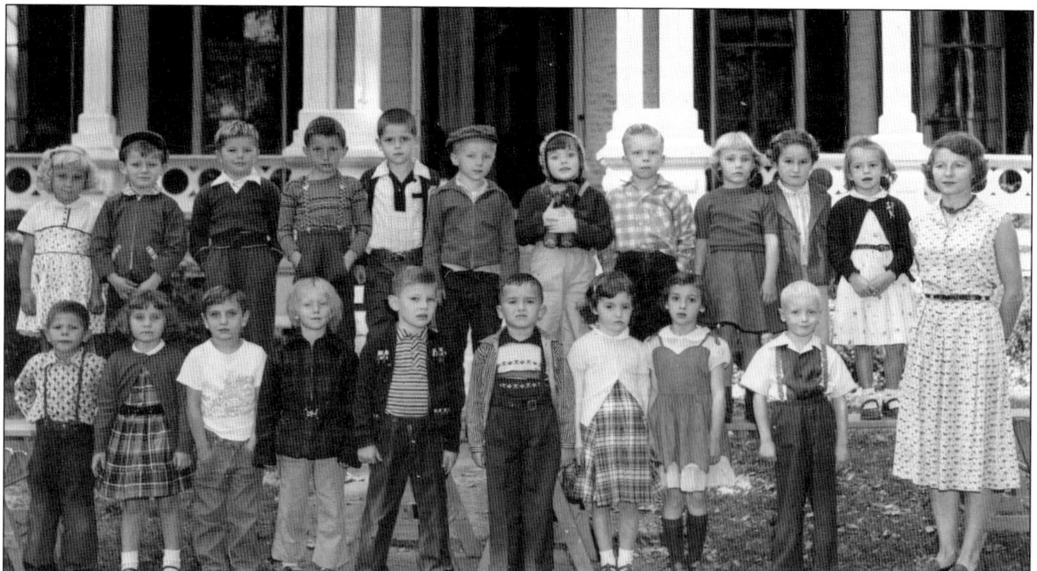

KINDERGARTEN CLASS AT MAINBRIDGE, 1958. During the building of the elementary school, some classes were held at Mainbridge. Here, the kindergarten class of 1958 poses in front of the porch of Mainbridge with their teacher Martha Gallup. Edwin Truax is in the second row, center, wearing the hat. Gallup's mother would knit a pair of mittens for each child in the class. (Courtesy of Edwin Truax.)

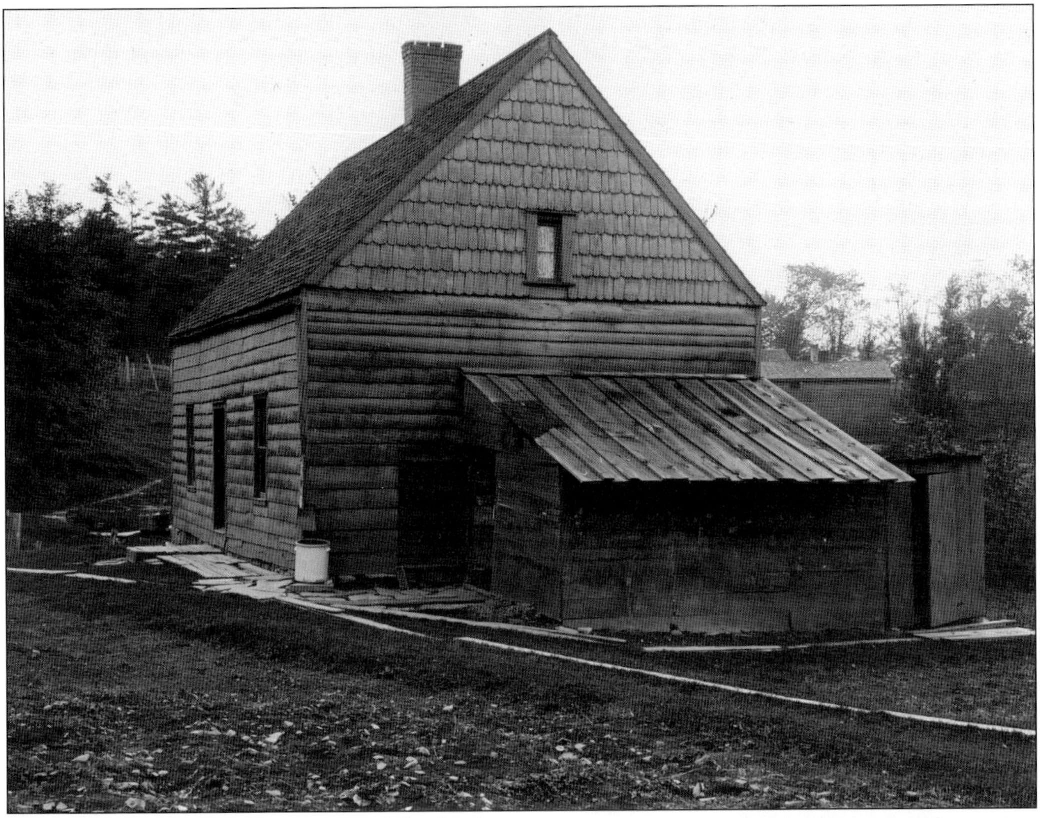

THE 1743 LUTHERAN PARSONAGE. The Lutheran congregation in Schoharie was organized before 1734. The Reverend Peter Nicolas Sommer was called in 1742, and this parsonage was built for him in 1743. He was minister until his death in 1786. The parsonage was restored in 1972 and is listed in the National Register of Historic Places. In 1751, a stone church was built nearby. Names of the builders were carved on its foundation stones. (Courtesy of New York State Archives.)

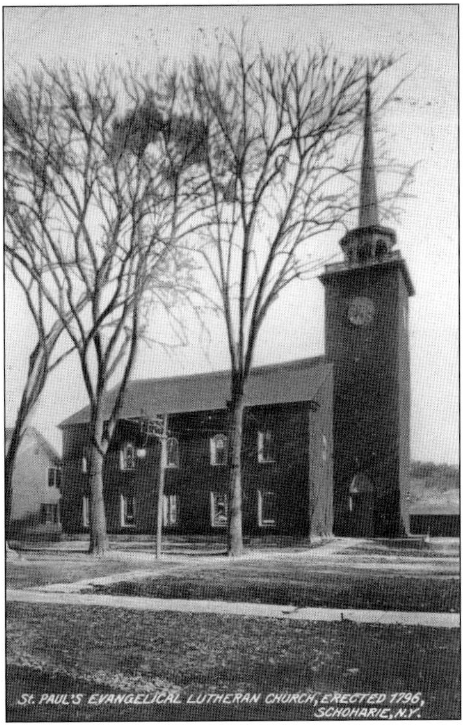

THE 1796 LUTHERAN CHURCH. The Lutheran congregation had Benjamin Niles build a new brick church in 1796. The foundation used the stones of the 1751 church. The names of those associated with the 1751 church are still visible along the base of the foundation facing Main Street. At this time, English (instead of German) began to be used in church services. The building now houses the United Presbyterian Church. (Courtesy of Edwin Truax.)

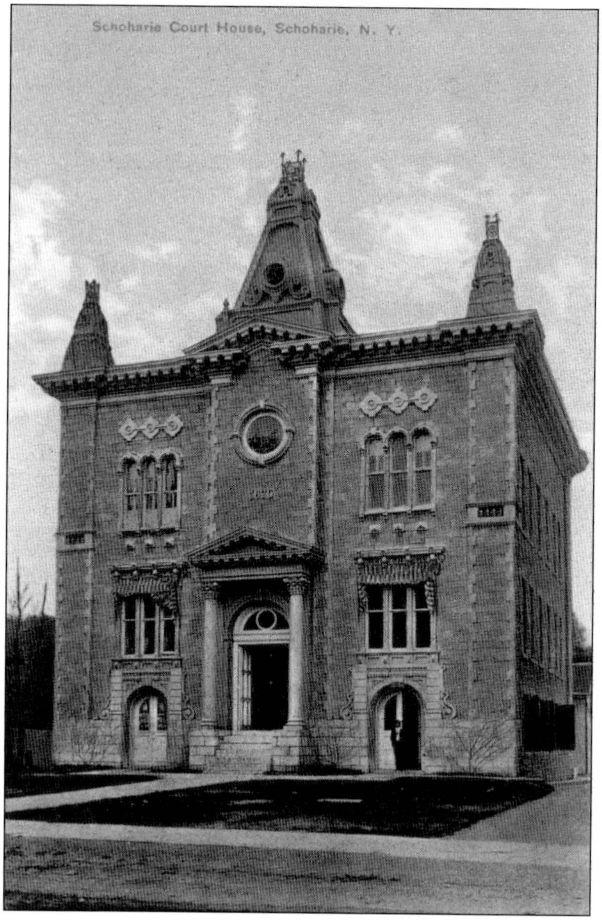

THE 1870 SCHOHARIE COUNTY COURTHOUSE. The courthouse was built in 1870 after a fire that destroyed its predecessor. It is built in the Victorian style of local limestone blocks. Though it originally stood alone in this photograph, the county building office has been erected at the right. (Courtesy of author's collection.)

SCHOHARIE COUNTY COURTHOUSE INTERIOR. The present interior is almost exactly the same as seen in this 1910 view. During a recent redecoration, this view was used to retain the look of the older decor. Of note are the benches for spectators and jury selection, the wainscoting on the walls and ceiling, and the portraits in oil of former judges. (Courtesy of author's collection.)

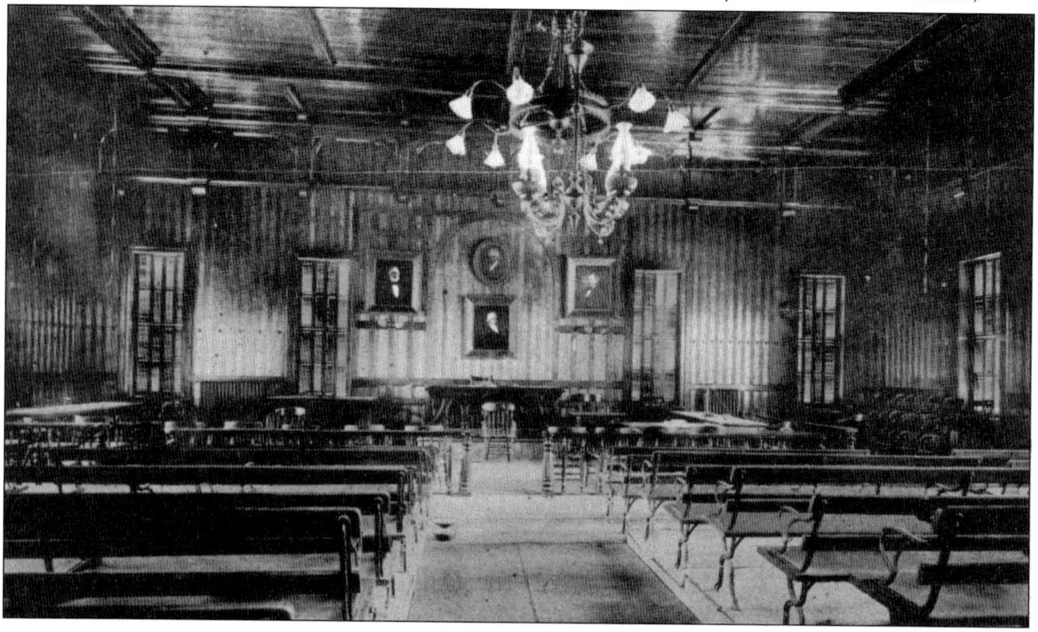

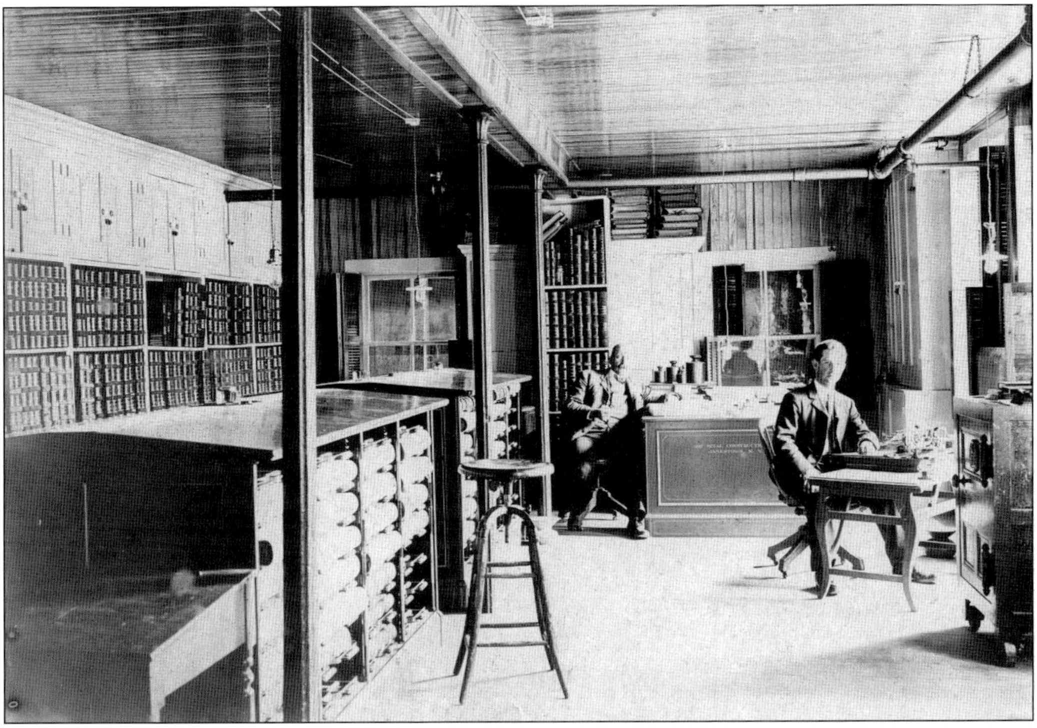

The County Clerk's Office, 1905. County clerk Clarke Shaul and his deputy Herbert A. Shaul are in their office in the old county building. Books of deed and mortgage records line the walls and are stacked under the desk at left. The books are still available today, though many records are now digitized. The clerk's desk (middle) has a set of weights to check merchant scales. At the feet of the deputy (right) is a spittoon. (Courtesy of OSFM.)

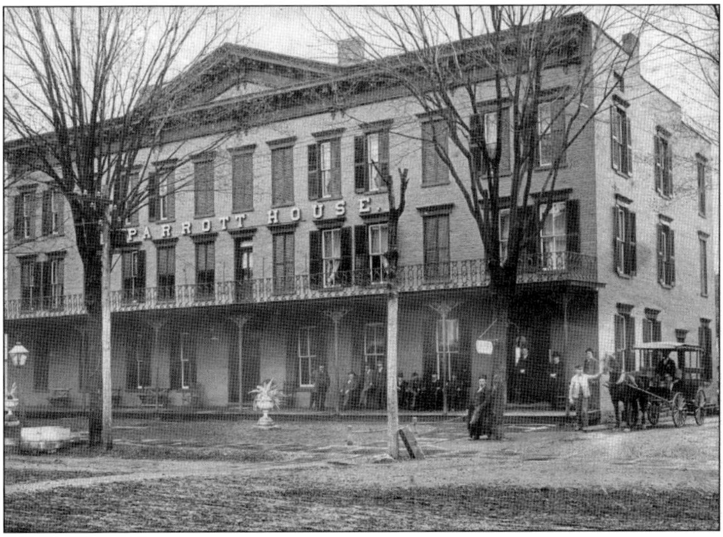

The Parrott House. Built over the ruins of the Eagle Hotel after the disastrous fire of 1870, the Parrott House has served as a place to meet in Schoharie ever since. The carriage on the right was used to bring visitors from the railroad depot. This c. 1910 photograph shows people congregating around the right-hand door, which was then the main entrance, contrary to today's use of the center entrance. (Courtesy of OSFM.)

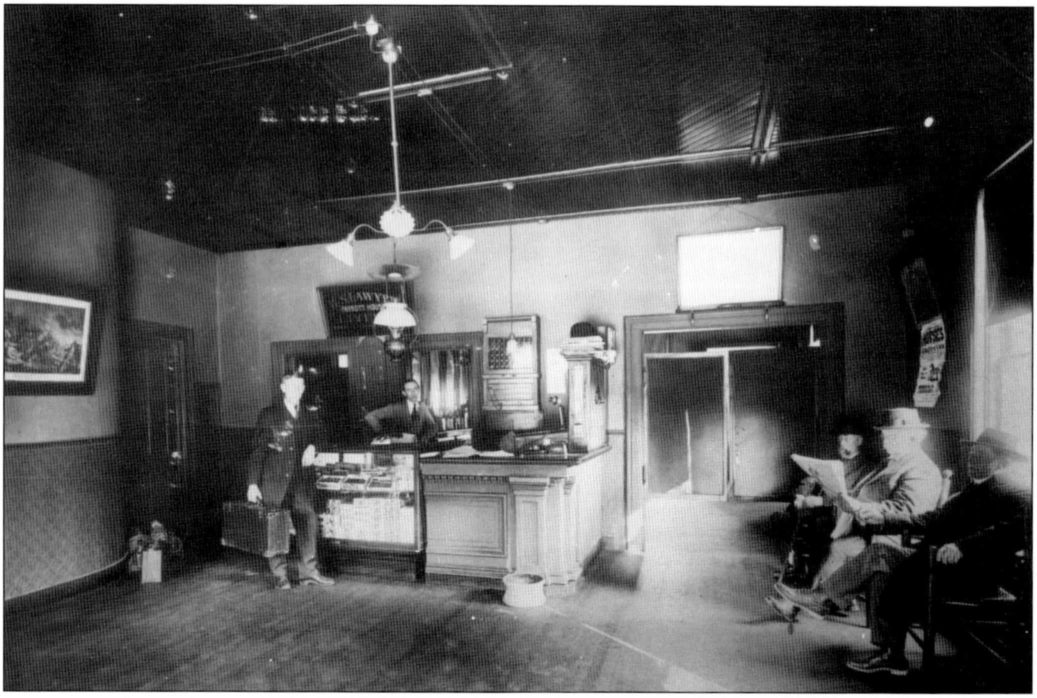

Parrott House Interior, 1910. The reception desk was located toward the right-hand entrance of the Parrott House. Of note are the double electric wires to the lamp (known as knob and tube wiring). The man with the suitcase is Edward Warner; the clerk is Stratton Kilmer. Seated are, from left to right, Seneca Warner, Lyman Holmes, and Lee Auchampaugh. (Courtesy of author's collection.)

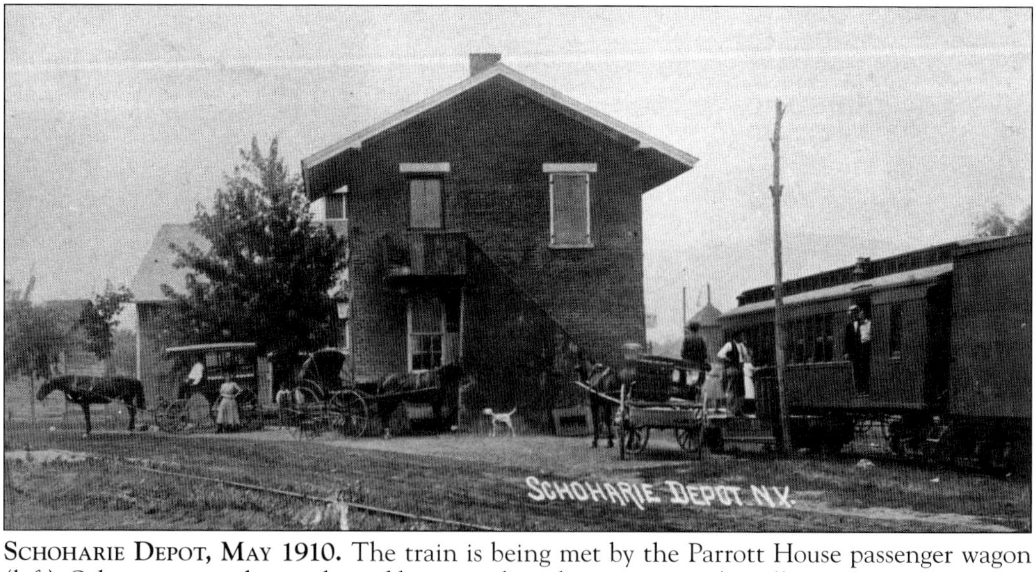

Schoharie Depot, May 1910. The train is being met by the Parrott House passenger wagon (left). Other wagons take trunks and boxes to their destination in the village. The rails ran from Schoharie to Schoharie Junction to connect with the Delaware & Hudson line that ran from Albany to Binghamton. Middleburgh & Schoharie Railroad tracks ran south from Schoharie to Middleburgh. (Courtesy of MLHR.)

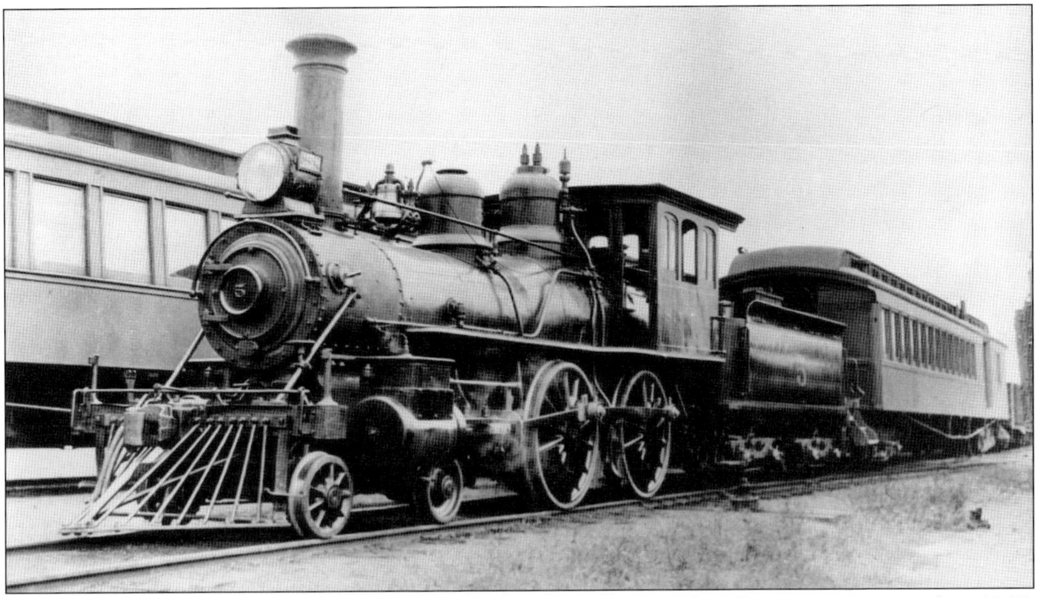

The Schoharie Valley Railroad. The Schoharie Valley Railroad was incorporated in 1865. Engine No. 5 was built in 1874, purchased in 1902, and scrapped in 1925. It is shown here doing passenger service. (Courtesy of MLHR.)

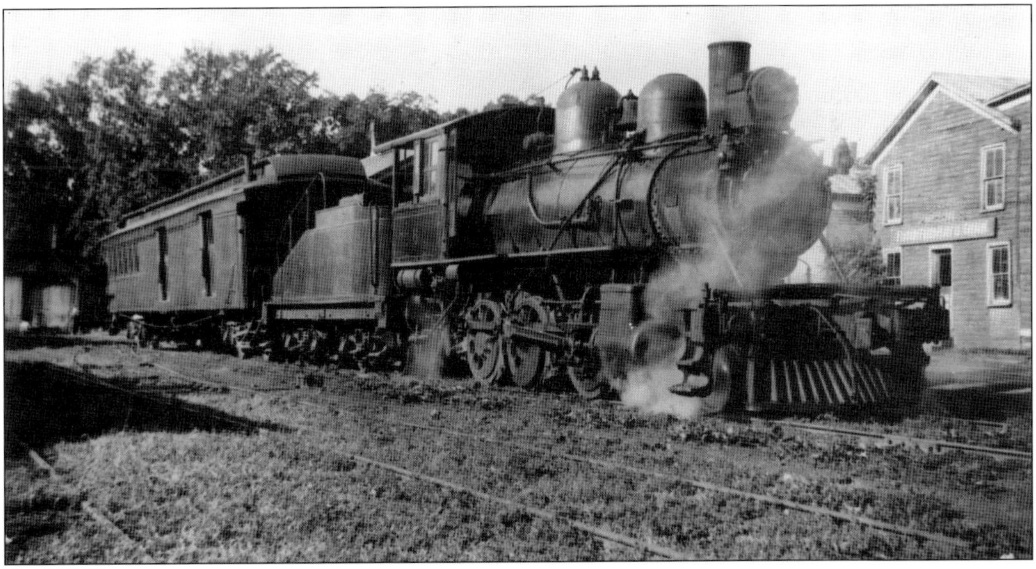

Engine No. 5's Replacement. Engine No. 6 was built in 1913 by the American Locomotive Company. It superseded engine No. 5 in 1925 when it was acquired from the Keeseville, Ausable Chasm & Lake Champlain Railway. It served until 1942 when the railroad assets were sold or scrapped. The engine was sold to the Hoosac Tunnel & Western Railway. Here, the engine is shown in Middleburgh in 1932. (Courtesy of MLHR.)

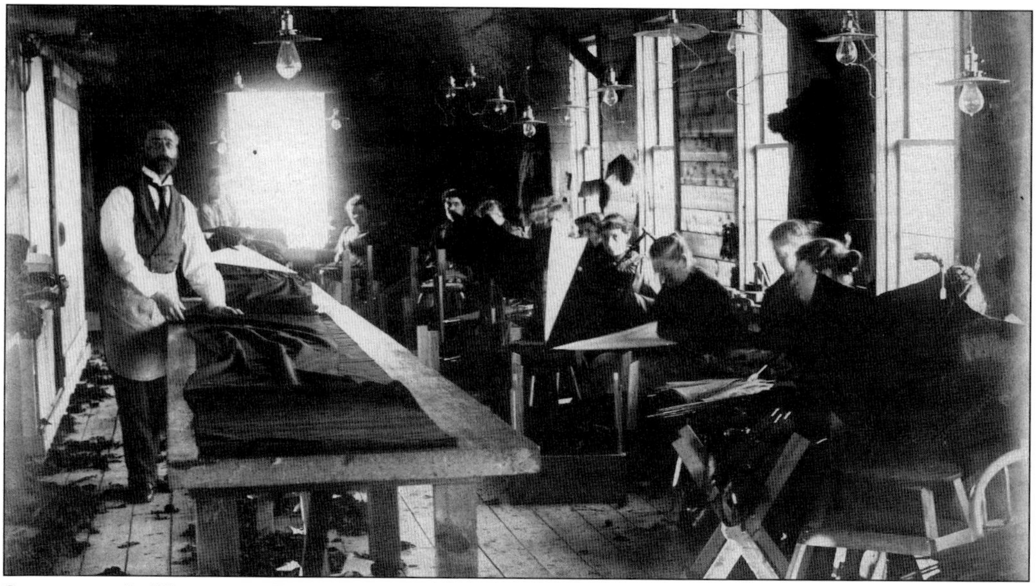

SCHOHARIE'S UMBRELLA FACTORY. At the turn of the 20th century, many business enterprises existed in Schoharie, including a monument maker, a cigar factory, a hat factory, and this umbrella factory situated near the Schoharie depot. Judging from the existing photographs, the umbrella factory employed some 30 men and women. All that remains of this enterprise are a few photographs—nothing is known about the owner. (Courtesy of OSFM.)

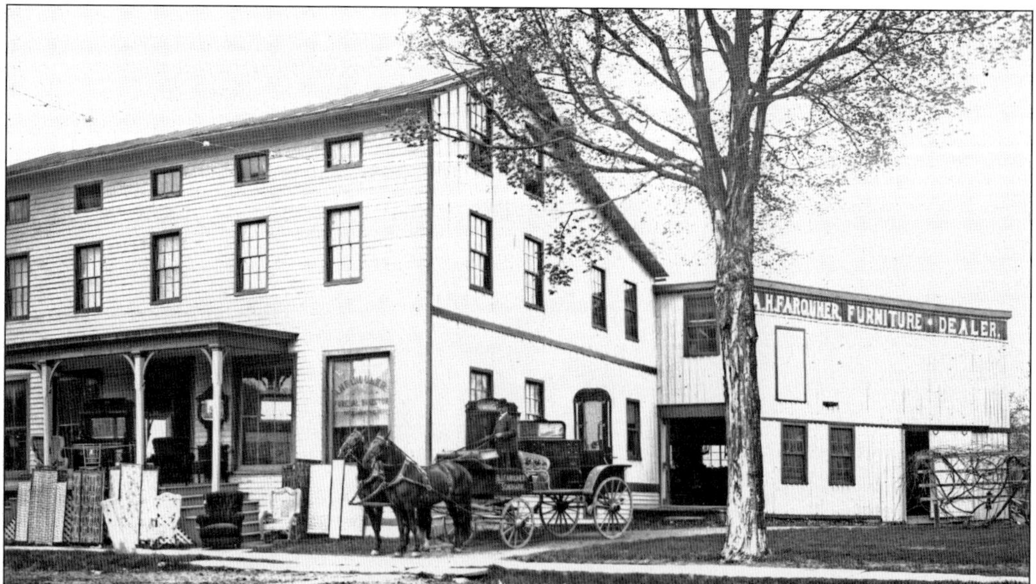

FARQUHER'S FURNITURE AND UNDERTAKING. Benjamin Farquher drives a wagonload of furniture to a customer. In the window, a sign advertises, "A.H. Farquher, Funeral Director, Embalmer." Arthur Farquher was a furniture dealer before his son Benjamin took over the enterprise. The building stood on the corner of Main and Grand Streets. This scene is from a glass plate photograph made by Dr. Samuel A. Scranton around 1900. (Courtesy of Sally Scranton Law.)

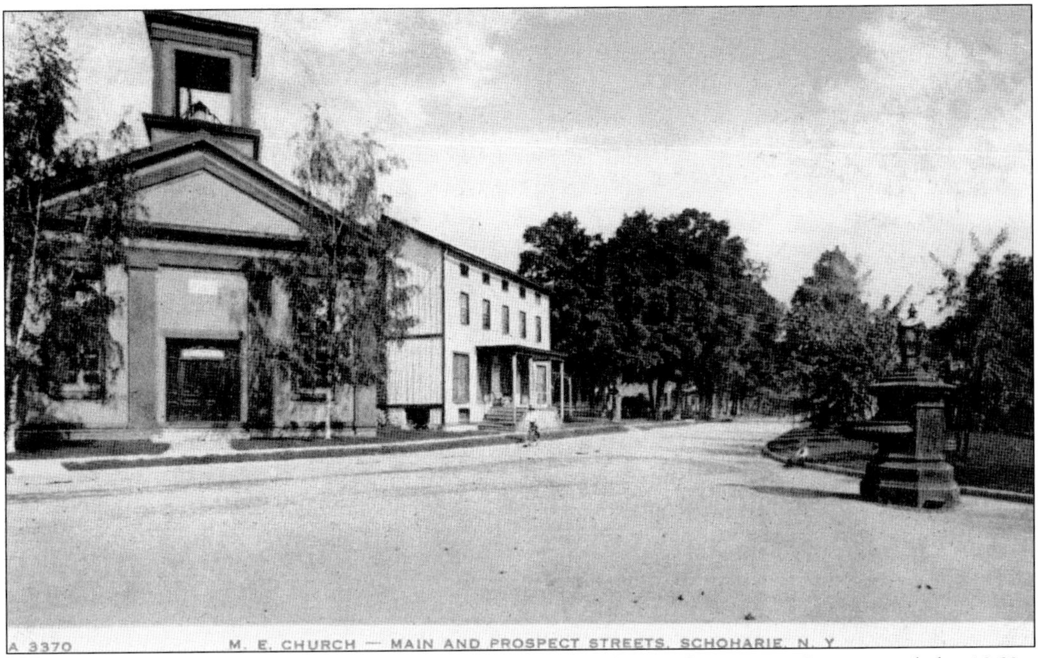

METHODIST EPISCOPAL CHURCH, SCHOHARIE. The church stood on Main Street until the 1960s. The former St. Joseph's Church now occupies the site. The white building was the furniture store of Benjamin J. Farquher. The water fountain (right) now stands near the station house at the Schoharie Valley Railroad complex on Depot Lane. The fountain has three levels of water—one for dogs, one for horses, and one for humans. (Courtesy of Edwin Truax.)

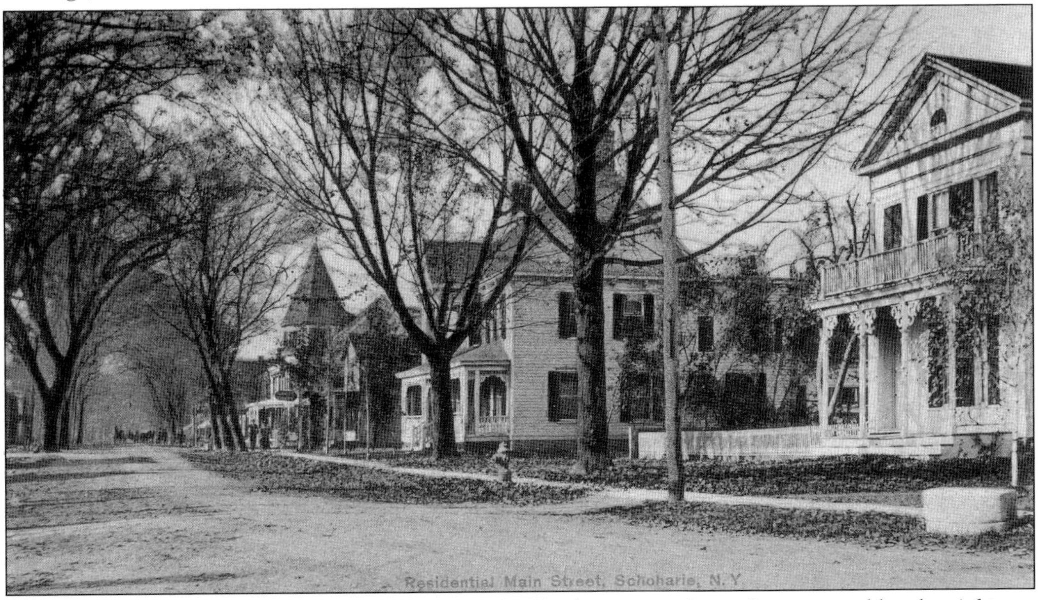

RESIDENTIAL MAIN STREET, SCHOHARIE, 1905. The house on the right was used by the African Methodist Evangelical Zion Church from about 1860 to 1880, when the African American congregation moved to a church on Prospect Street, a half-mile away. The building was situated next to the Methodist Evangelical Church and was later occupied by the Terpenning family. The building at the center is now the Langan funeral home. (Courtesy of Edwin Truax.)

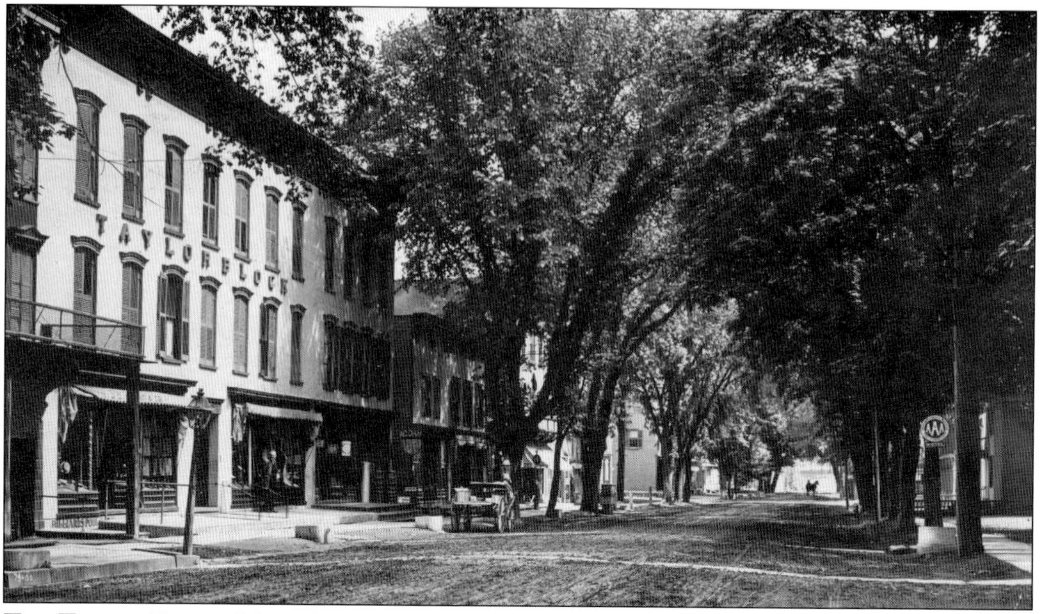

The Taylor Block, Main Street, Schoharie, about 1905. The Taylor Block once housed a hotel with livery stables behind. The AAA sign on the tree (right) indicates that the Parrott House was certified by the organization. The AAA was formed in 1902 to help in improving roads for motorists. Here, Main Street is still a dirt road, though it is quite smooth. (Courtesy of Edwin Truax.)

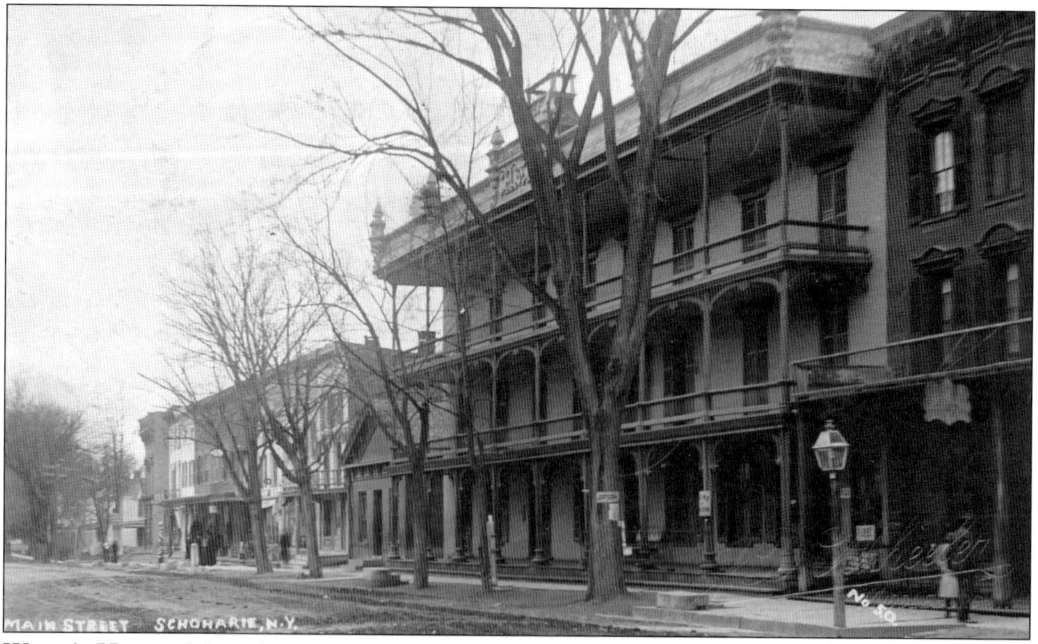

Wood's Hotel, Main Street, Schoharie, 1911. The hotel was situated opposite the Parrott House. It was built around 1860 and run by Francisco Wood until the 1900s. Later, it housed the store of Kilts and Sidney, who tore it down in 1946 to make way for their new store. Of note are the double balconies and the fancy embellishments on the roof. (Courtesy of Edwin Truax.)

Frank Vroman's Grocery Store, Main Street, Schoharie. The store is shown around 1910. Frank used a team of horses and a grocery wagon to haul his goods from the depot, or to make deliveries to customers. Later, this store housed Edward Scribner's appliance and electronics business. It is now the Little Italy pizza restaurant. (Courtesy of Edwin Truax.)

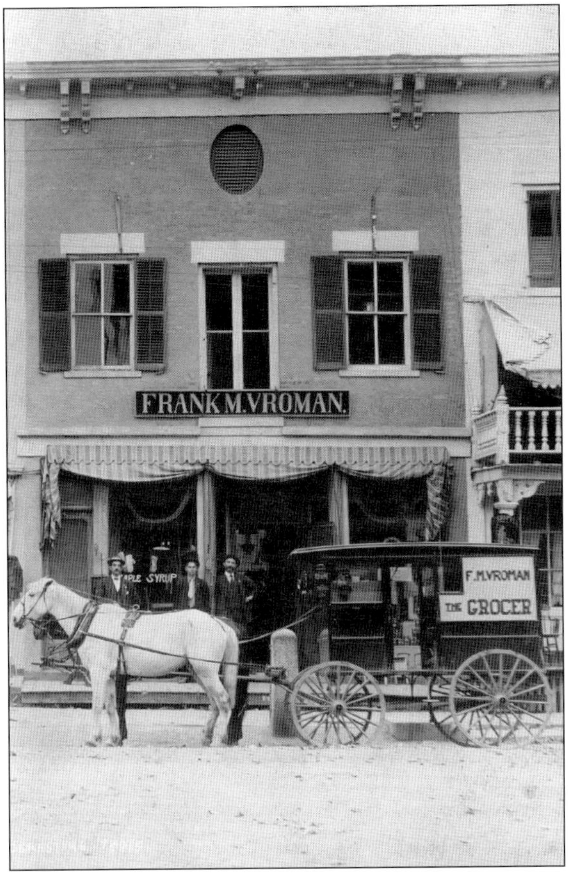

Main Street, Schoharie, Looking North. At the right is the 1877 Union Block containing two stores: the dental office of Dr. Samuel A. Scranton and the office of the *Schoharie Standard* newspaper. Union Block was demolished around 1915 for the county building (now the county health department office). Beyond are three buildings that were removed in 1968 for the present county structure. The courthouse tower is also visible. (Courtesy of Edwin Truax.)

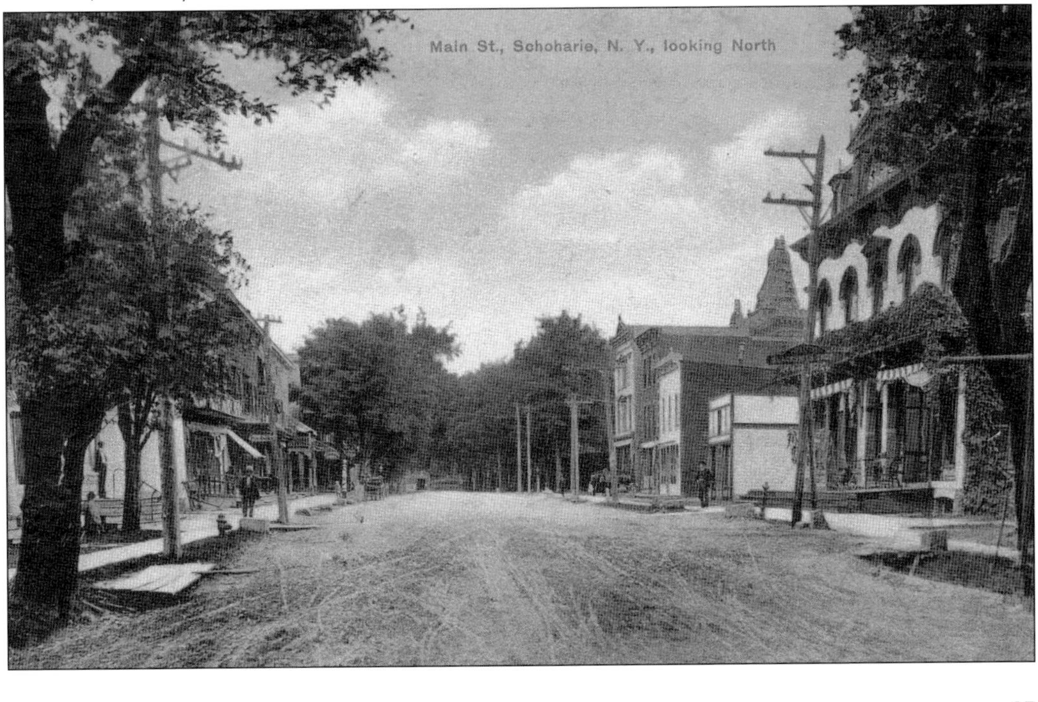

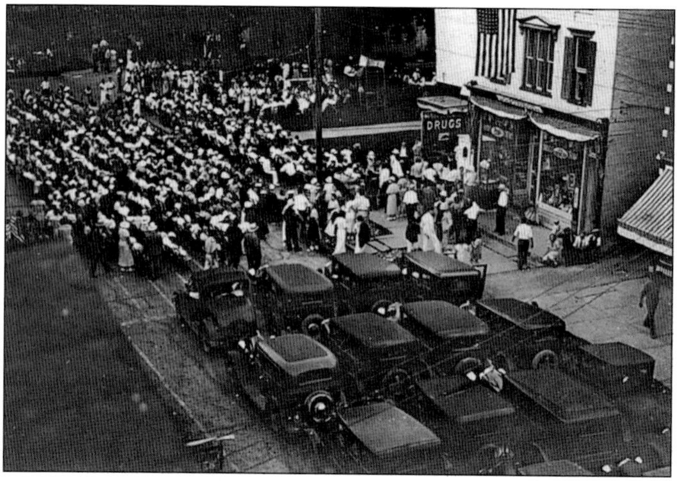

Main Street Movies. From 1917 to 1942, free open-air movies were shown on Schoharie's Main Street on Thursday nights from June to September. The first talking pictures ever shown outdoors anywhere were seen here on July 11, 1931. Edward Scribner, who operated an appliance and electronics store in Schoharie, was the projectionist. The movie screen was hung in front of the courthouse as shown here. (Courtesy of Skip Edmonds.)

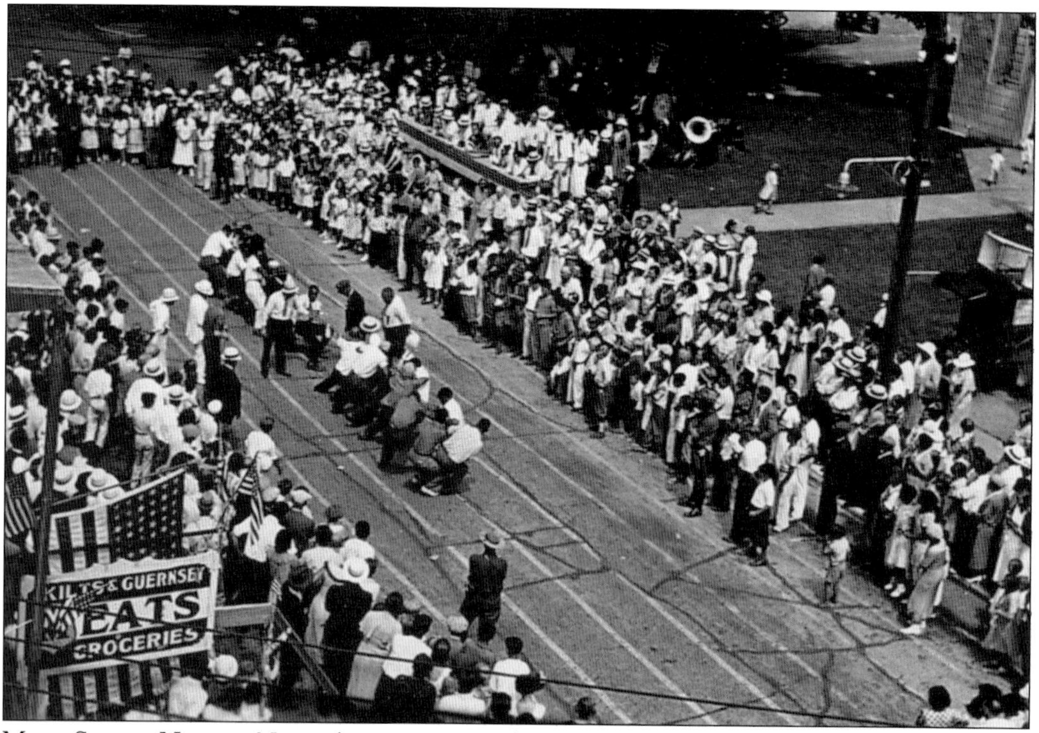

Main Street Nights. Not only were movies shown on Schoharie's Main Street on Thursday nights, but competitions and dances were also held. In this 1930s photograph, a tug-of-war is being held. A panel of judges is seated at a table (upper center). Lines are marked on the street to set up chairs for the free movies that will be shown later. Chairs could be rented for 10¢, though the movies were free. (Courtesy of Skip Edmonds.)

DANCING ON MAIN STREET. After the movies, it was time to dance on Main Street to the music of Ruland's Yo Sko Haro Orchestra. This scene is from the late 1930s or early 1940s. One could also get refreshments at Badgley's ice cream bar or from Boucky's hot dog stand. (Courtesy of Skip Edmonds.)

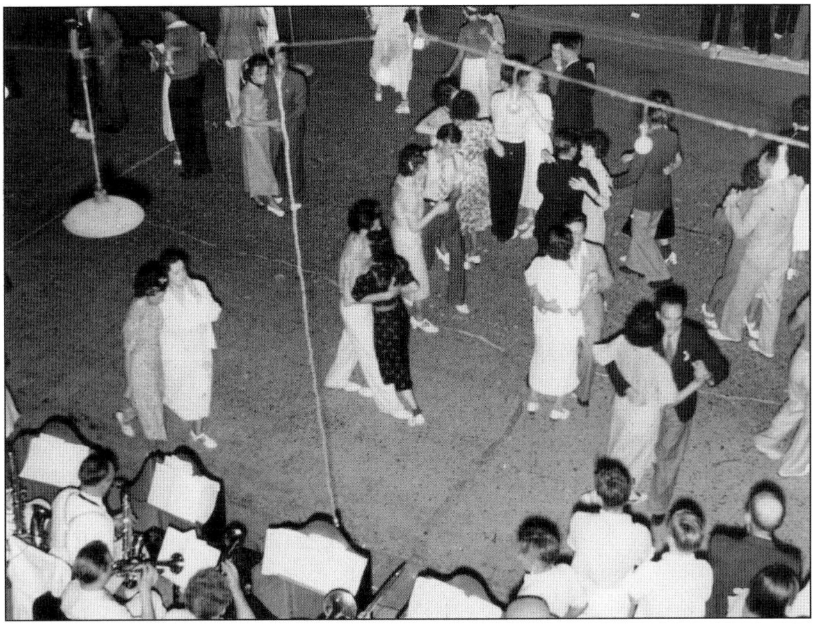

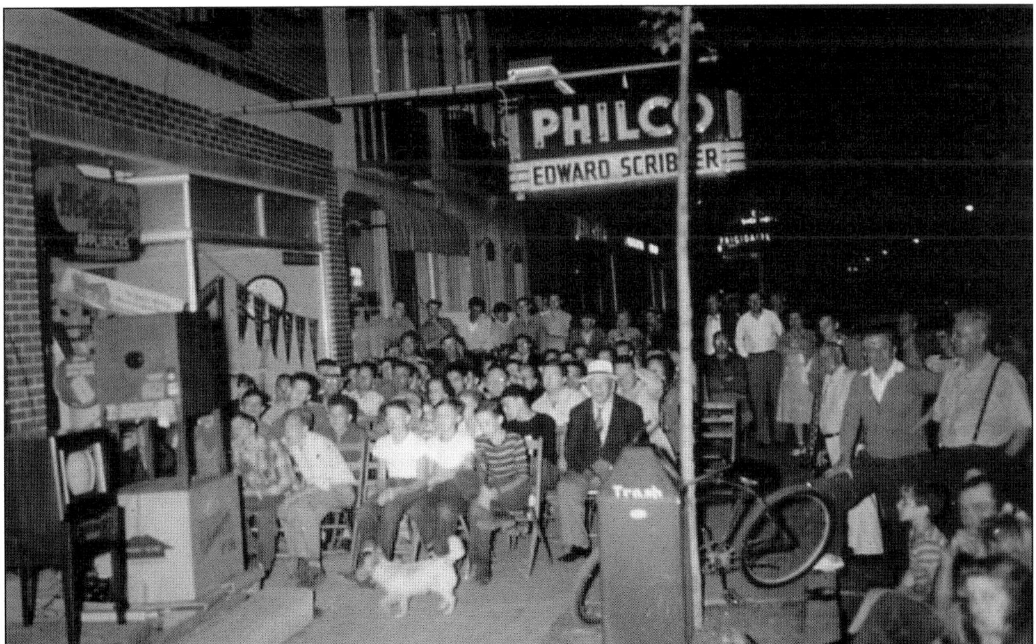

SIDEWALK TELEVISION, MAIN STREET, SCHOHARIE. In the early 1950s, television was quite new and not many families owned one. Edward Scribner ran his appliance store on Main Street. On special nights, he would set up a television on the sidewalk outside his shop. Here, kids are seated near two television sets while adults watch nearby. (Courtesy of Skip Edmonds.)

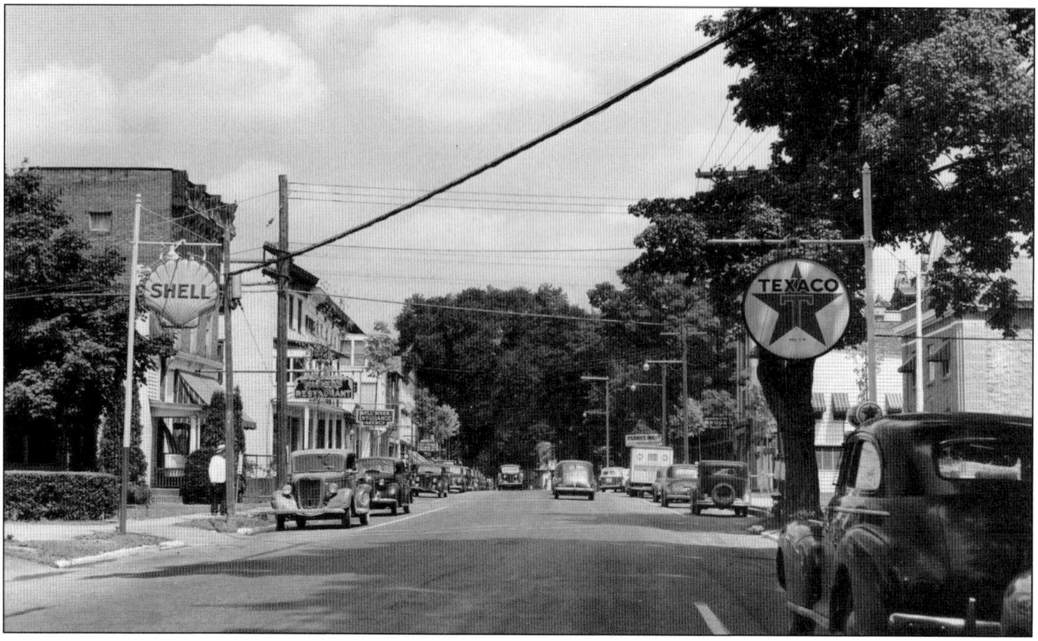

MAIN STREET, SCHOHARIE, AROUND 1950. Shell and Texaco gasoline stations were situated near Spring Street. Wagner's Restaurant (left) later became the American Legion Hall. Bellinger's Insurance Agency and Badgley's Ice Cream Bar were on the left. Harrington's drugstore was next to the courthouse. It was later taken down to make room for the new county office building. (Courtesy of MLHR.)

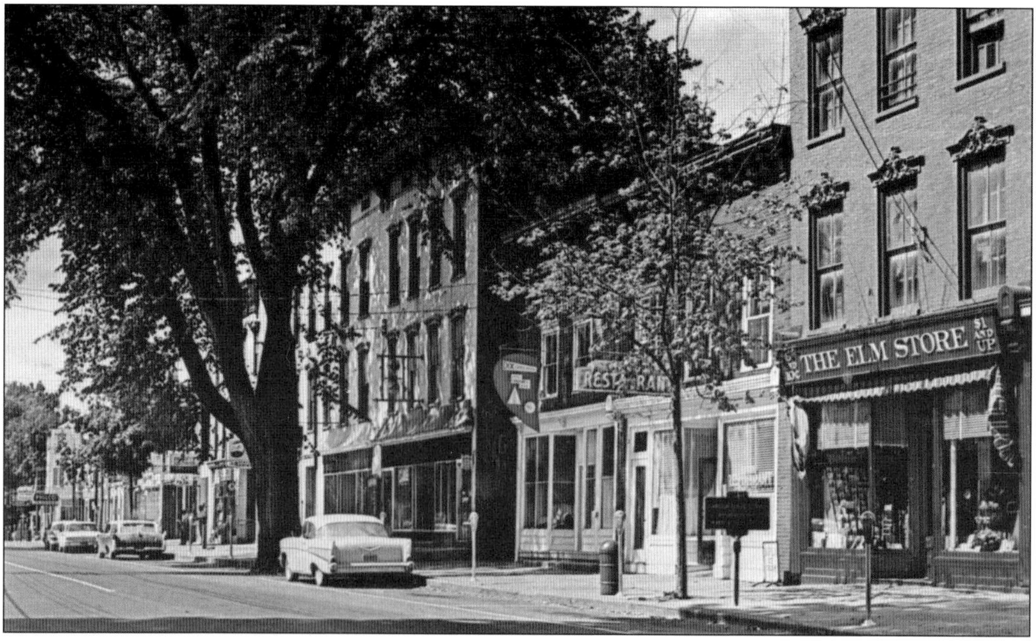

THE ELM STORE. By 1960, Main Street held many small mom-and-pop stores; one was the Elm Store (right). This was a traditional five-and-dime variety store selling everything from sewing notions to candies. It was owned by John and Grace Furman. The historical marker in front shows that the 1877 building once housed the Throop drugstore. (Courtesy of author's collection.)

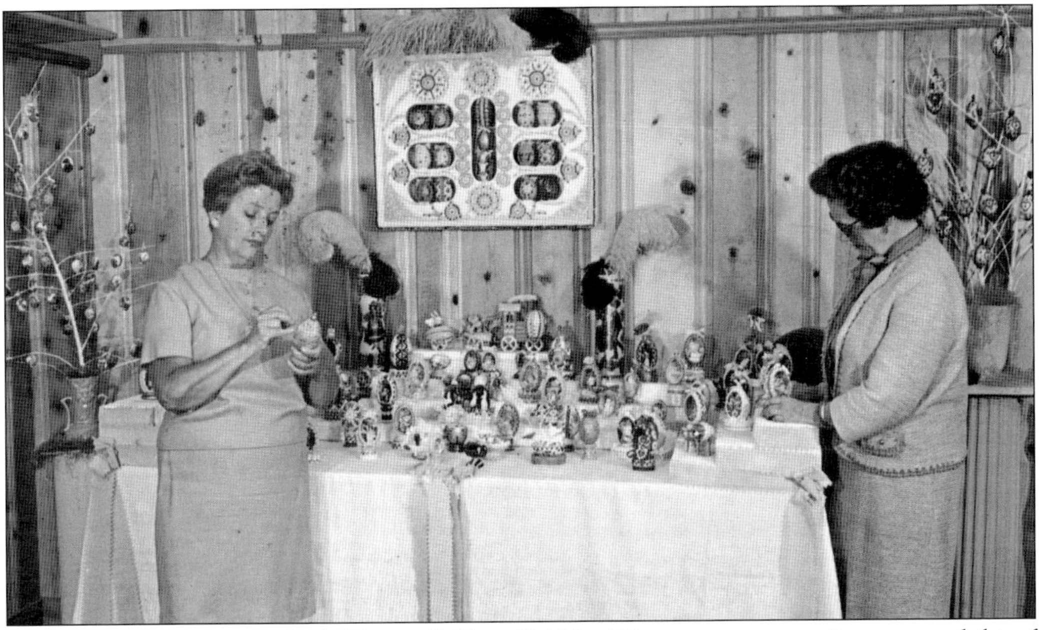

Easter Egg Exhibit. Elizabeth Warner (left) and Mildred Vroman prepare an Easter egg exhibit of their 3,500 hand-painted eggs. According to this 1960s postcard, the idea of an Easter egg exhibit began in 1953 when Easter egg trees were shown at Lasell Hall and in front of the courthouse. Later, the ladies developed the Easter Egg Museum. At its height in 1968, over 14,000 people visited the museum. (Courtesy of Edwin Truax.)

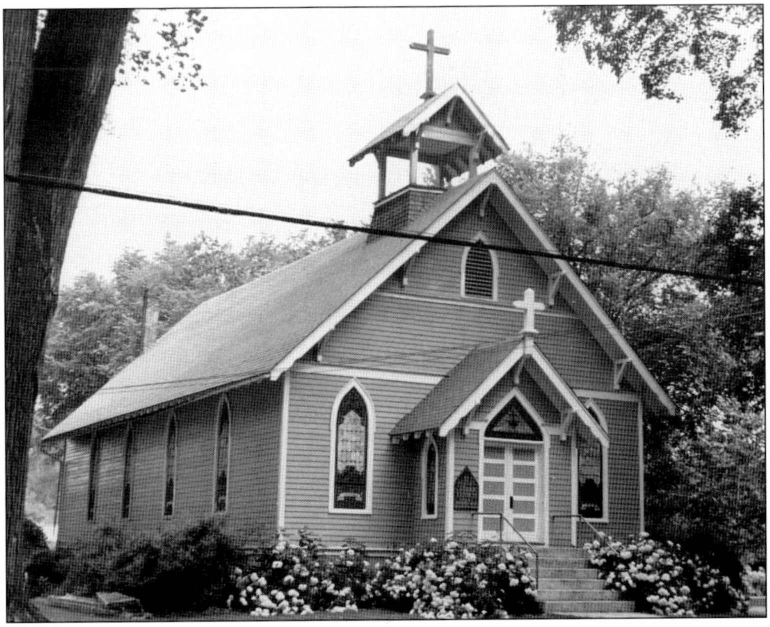

St. Joseph's Catholic Church, Main Street, Schoharie. The church was built in 1918 and used until 1964 when the brick church was erected at the corner of Main and Grand Streets. This building stands next to the village offices and has been since converted into apartments. (Courtesy of MLHR.)

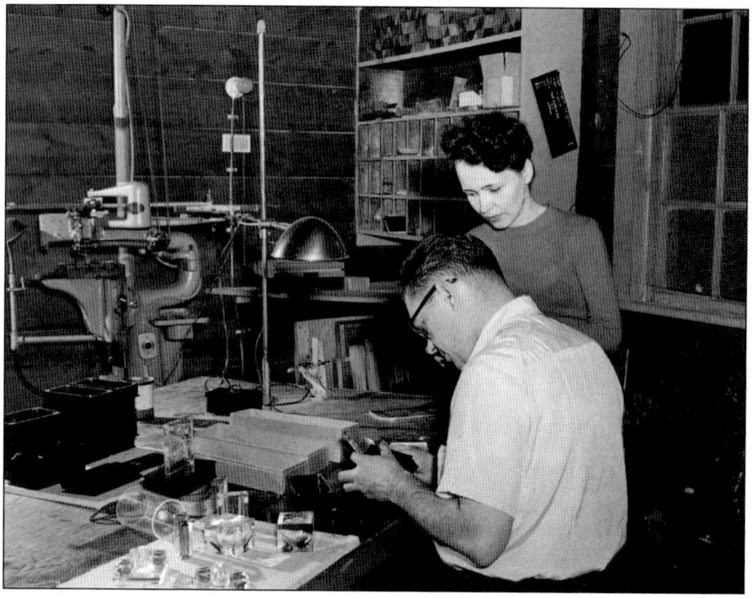

FOUNDERS OF THE HARVA COMPANY, HARRY AND VIRGINIA KINTZ. The Harva Company was founded in the village of Schoharie in 1949. At first, it made costume jewelry but soon expanded its product line into plastics manufacturing. In this c. 1950 view, husband and wife Harry and Virginia are working on jewelry items, including a paperweight and a night light. At left is an engraving machine. (Courtesy of MLHR.)

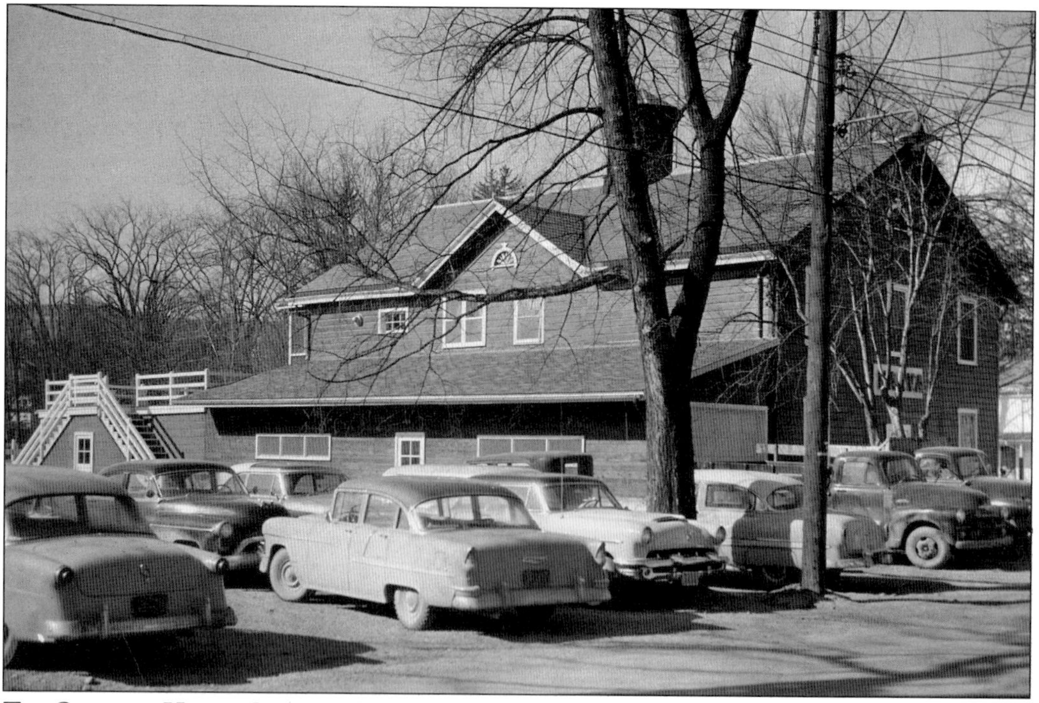

THE ORIGINAL HARVA COMPANY BUILDING, SCHOHARIE. By the early 1950s, the Harva Company was housed in this converted barn, which was soon expanded. Today, the company produces custom engineered parts for several industries, including aerospace, medical, commercial, and food service. The company has won numerous quality awards from customers, including Lockheed Martin, IBM, GE, and General Dynamics, and it continues as a three-generation family business. (Courtesy of Susan Kintz McGiver.)

Six

GALLUPVILLE

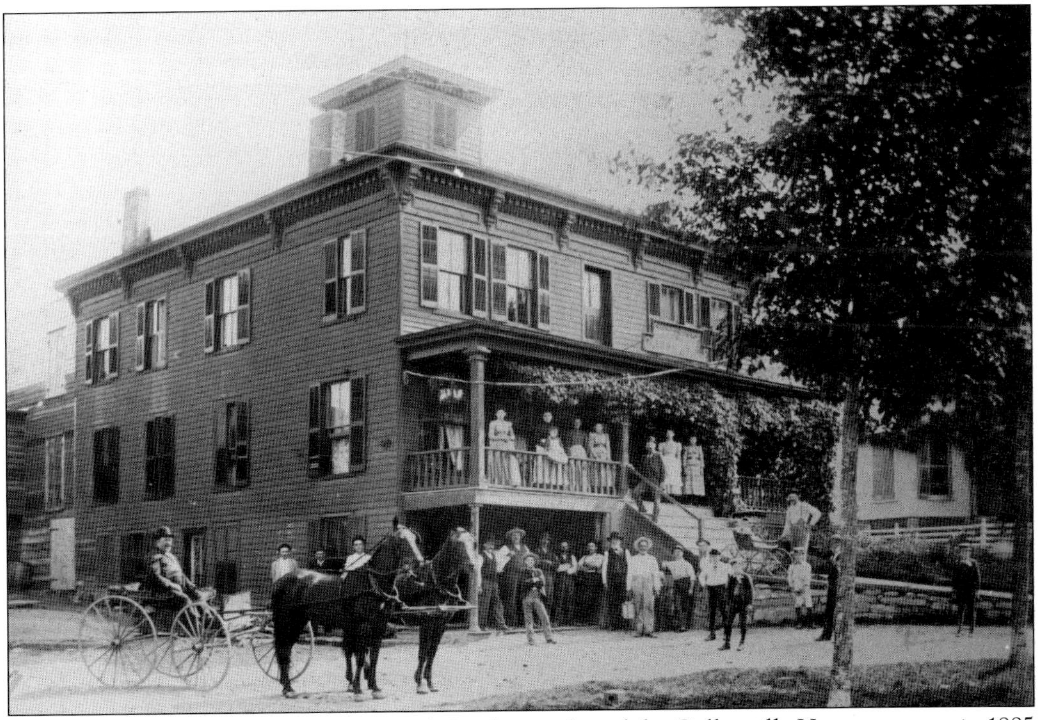

GALLUPVILLE HOUSE, GALLUPVILLE. Jacob Snyder purchased the Gallupville House property in 1885 and ran it as a hotel known as the Snyder House until 1904. He is shown in this 1893 photograph with the horse team and carriage. The Orion Lodge Independent Order of Odd Fellows (IOOF) bought the property in 1920 and rebuilt it for a hall and meeting rooms. Today, the Gallupville House is used as a community meeting place. (Courtesy of OSFM, Chester Zimmer collection.)

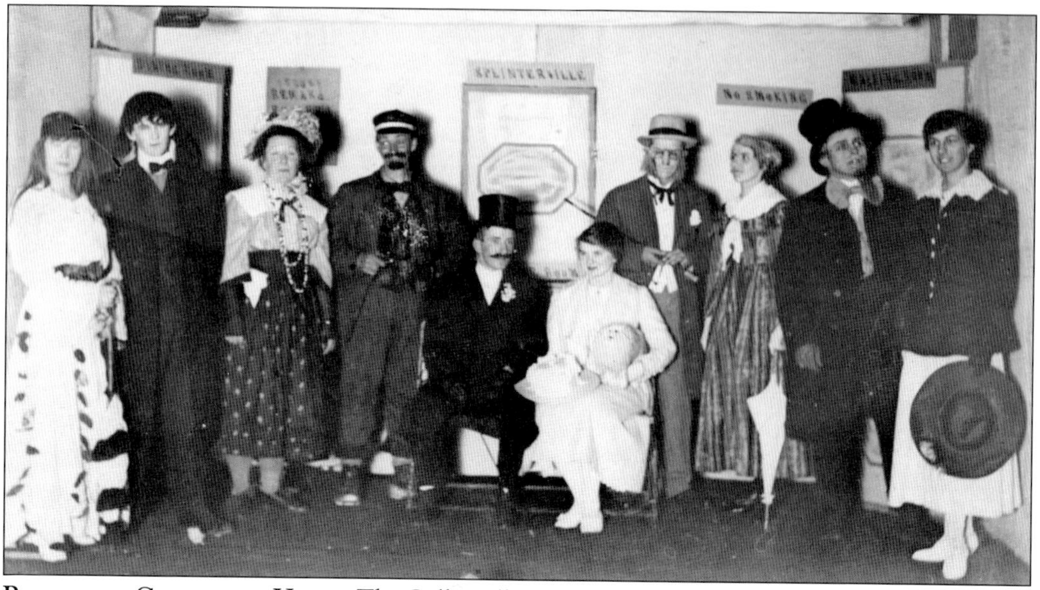

Play at the Gallupville House. The Gallupville House has been used as a community center since the 1930s. Here, the cast of *The Dutch Detective* takes a bow. Josephine and Wallace Stahlman are third and fourth from left. The others are unidentified. (Courtesy of Naomi Zimmer Wikane.)

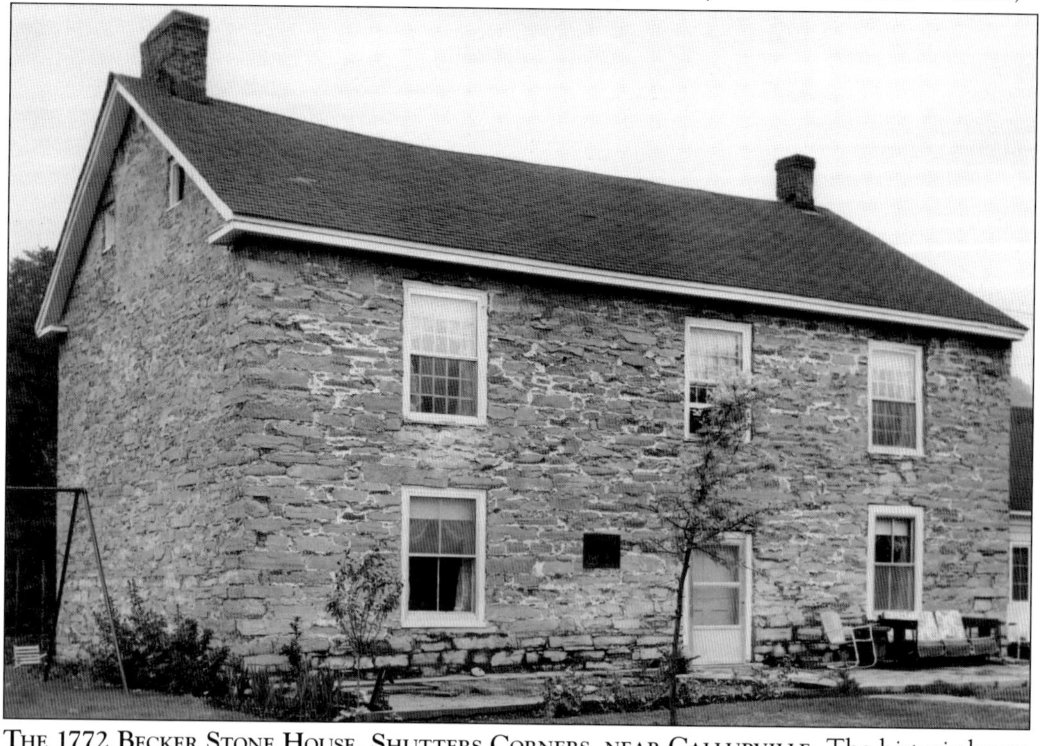

The 1772 Becker Stone House, Shutters Corners, near Gallupville. The historic house was built by Johannes Becker. During the British and Indian raid of 1780, his son Maj. Joseph Becker commanded the patriots at the Old Stone Fort. In 1781, the loyalist Adam Crysler with Indian allies attempted to burn the house but was repulsed. Todd and Sue Rolfe now own the house. (Courtesy of OSFM.)

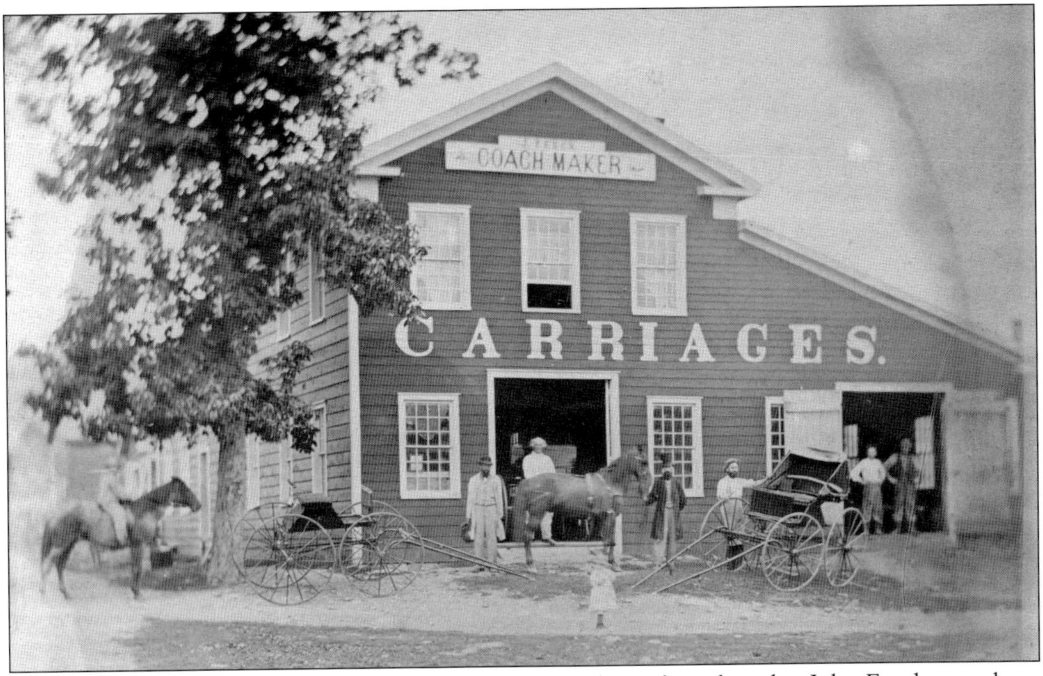

The Carriage Maker, about 1860. The Gallupville shop of coach maker John Feeck was a busy place in 1860. Here, two carriages are ready for sale while son Peter Feeck (second from right) works in the blacksmith shop. The little girl in the foreground may be Sarah Feeck. The building was erected in 1859 and was a carriage factory until 1866. The Orion Lodge IOOF converted it into a hall in 1892. It was situated at the corner of State Routes 443 and 146. (Courtesy of OSFM.)

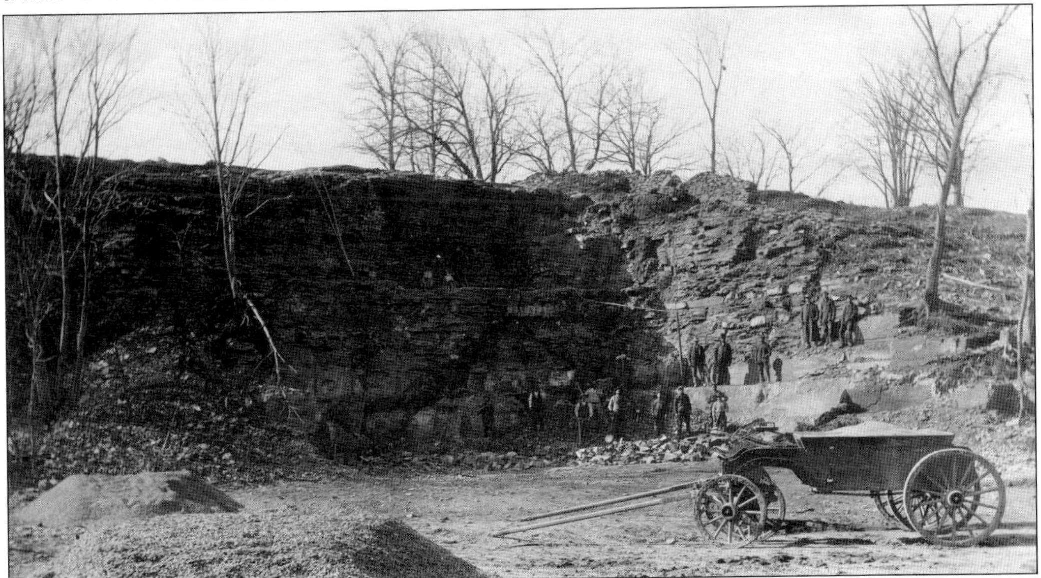

Building the Gallupville to West Berne Road. In the days before steam driven machinery, it took muscle and brawn to built roads. Here, 16 men are working on the Gallupville to West Berne road. They use picks and shovels and horse-drawn wagons to do the work. By 1911, this road was the first macadam road in Schoharie County and was suitable for motorized traffic. (Courtesy of OSFM, Chester Zimmer collection.)

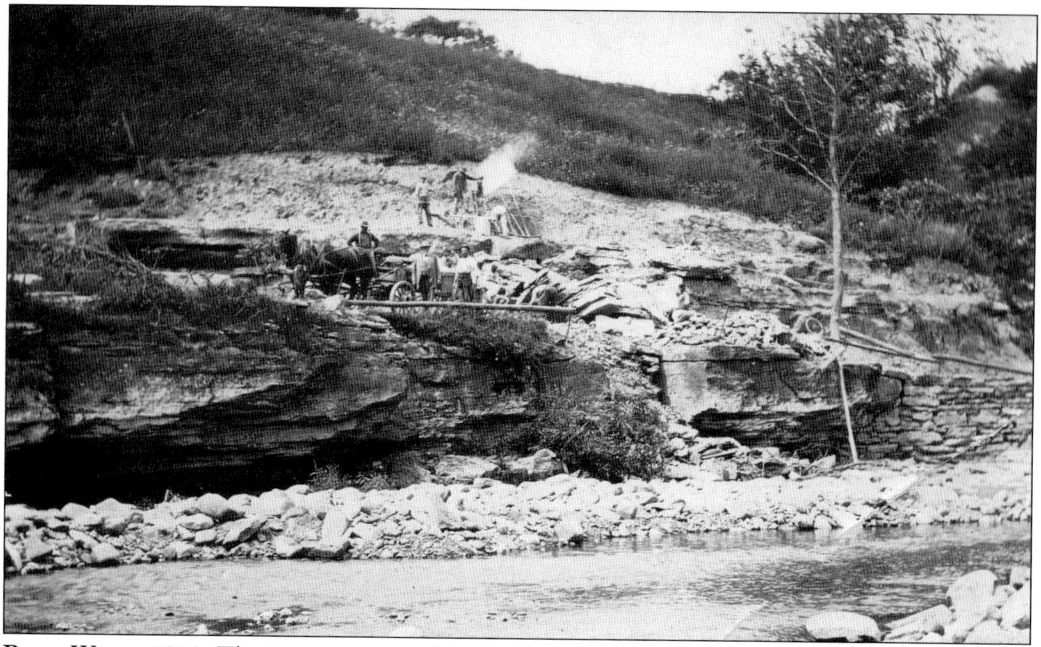

ROAD WORK, 1910. The improvement of the Gallupville to West Berne road was a big enterprise. Though the road had been used for years, the advent of motorcars made upgrades necessary. In this c. 1910 view, a dozen men widen the road by digging into the shale and limestone bank above Fox Creek. The horse-drawn wagon is loaded with rocks for use elsewhere on the road. (Courtesy of OSFM, Chester Zimmer collection.)

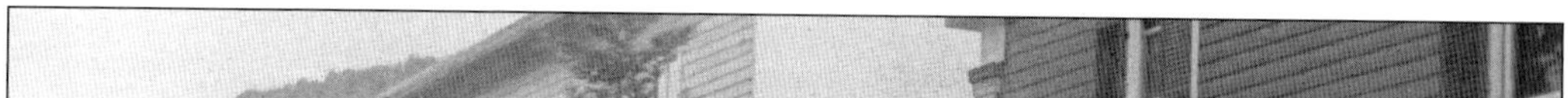

THE GALLUPVILLE TO ALBANY BUS, 1912. The *Schoharie Republican* newspaper of June 6, 1912, wrote: "The Berne bus now leaves Gallupville every day at 6:30 a.m. for Albany and returning leaves Albany at 3:30 p.m. The fare is $1.25. Henry Bliss is manager and Edward Jones chauffeur." (Courtesy of OSFM, Chester Zimmer collection.)

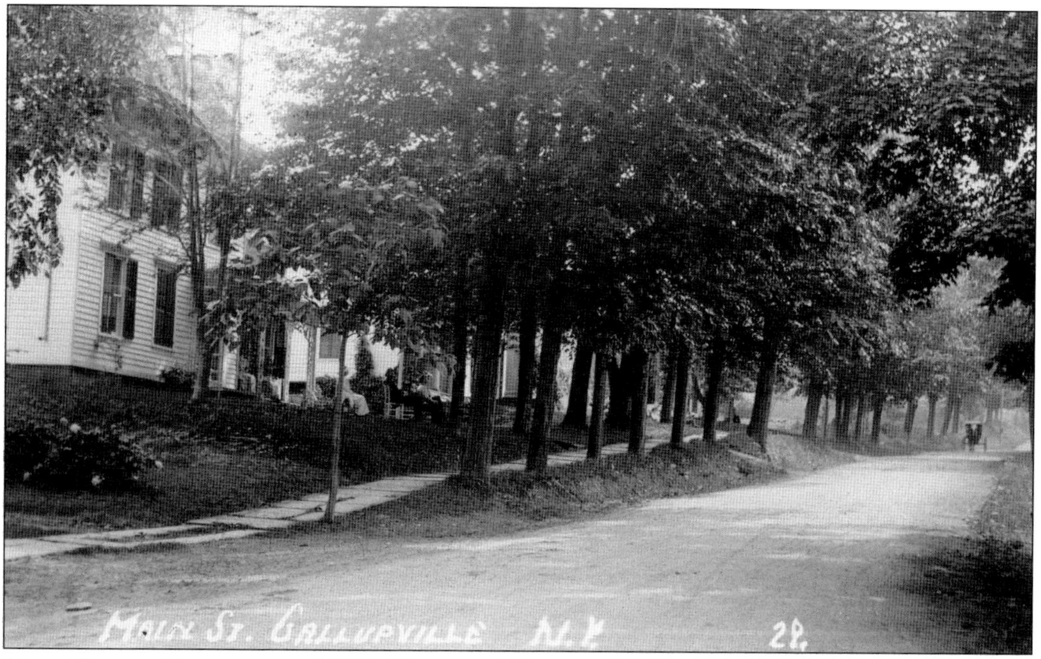

MAIN STREET, GALLUPVILLE, 1900. This peaceful view of Gallupville shows a horse-drawn buggy in the distance. Trees are planted between the sidewalk and the street, making a picturesque scene. Several residents are relaxing on their front porches. (Courtesy of OSFM, Robert Mahar collection.)

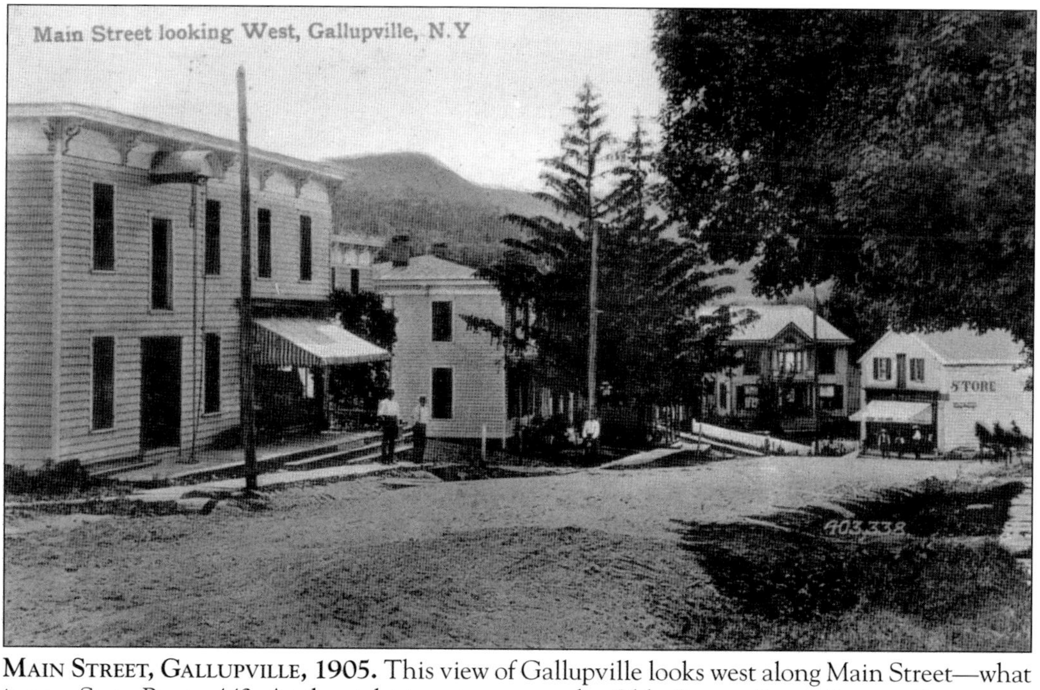

MAIN STREET, GALLUPVILLE, 1905. This view of Gallupville looks west along Main Street—what is now State Route 443. At the right is a store, now the Olde Corner Store. Factory Street goes off to the left at the store. On the left, Alva Becker's grocery and general goods store has a pulley system to haul goods up to the second floor. (Courtesy of author's collection.)

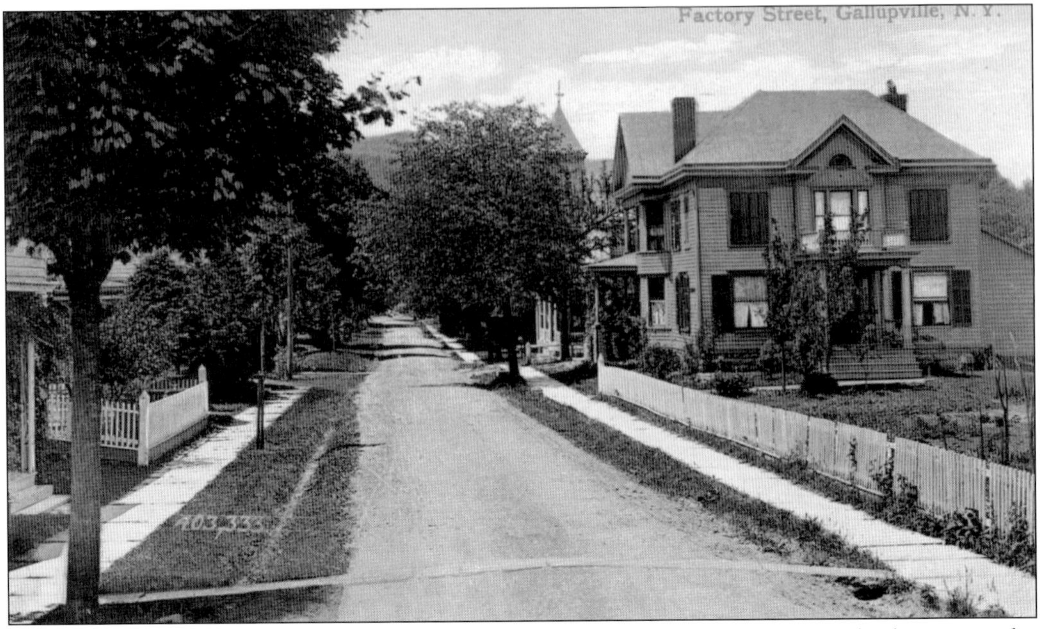

FACTORY STREET, GALLUPVILLE, 1910. The street was named for the tannery, also known as the leather factory, at the end of the road. Picket fences were a common sight along many streets. In the foreground is a stone crossing path on the road, placed there to avoid the mud during rainy days. (Courtesy of author's collection.)

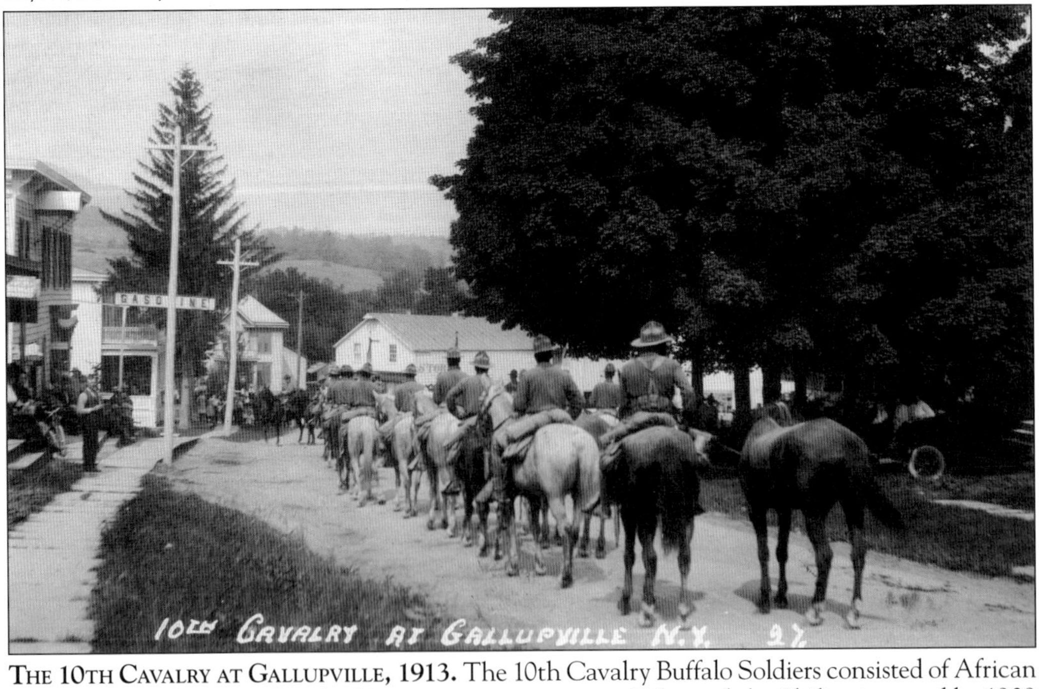

THE 10TH CAVALRY AT GALLUPVILLE, 1913. The 10th Cavalry Buffalo Soldiers consisted of African American cavalrymen. They had been on assignments in Cuba and the Philippines and by 1909 were stationed in Vermont from where they participated in maneuvers, including some in New York State. Here, on June 25, 1913, they are moving into Gallupville on Main Street. Residents are out on the sidewalks to view the troops. (Courtesy of author's collection.)

Seven

Central Bridge

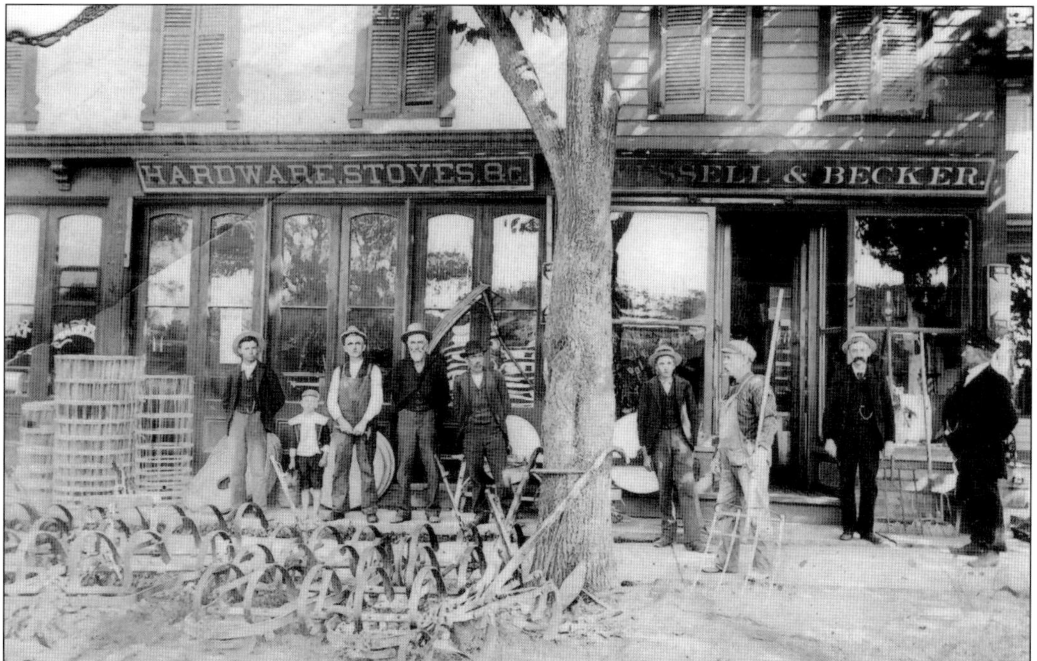

The Wessell & Becker Hardware Store, 1897. The store sold a wide variety of items for the home and farm. On the sidewalk are several types of cultivators, rolls of fence wire, a scythe, and two grinders used to sharpen implements. Standing in front of the store are, from left to right, Jim Storey, unidentified, Julius Carr, Dyke Lansing, Abner Cook, ? Gordon, George Barner (holding a hayfork), store owner Walter Wessell, and Walter Jenkins. (Courtesy of Robert Holt.)

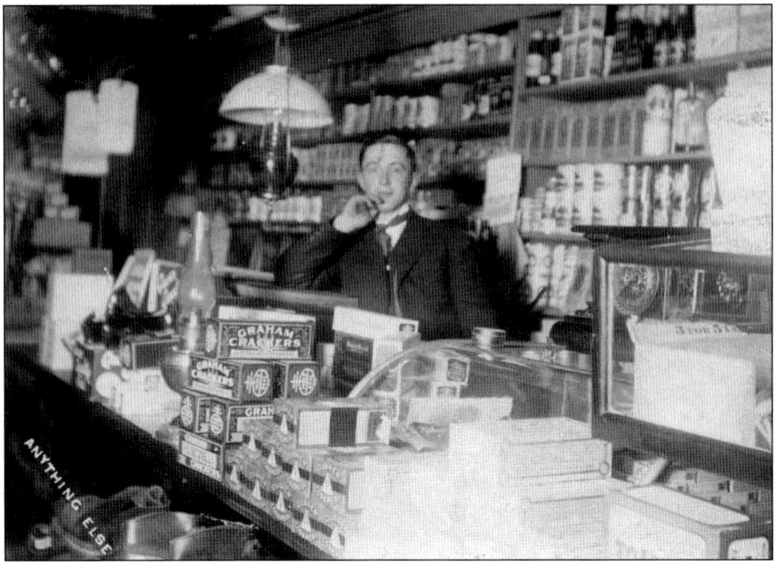

Millard Braman's General Store, around 1890. Millard F. Braman, aged 35 in this 1890s photograph, is shown behind the counter of his Central Bridge general merchandise store, which seems well-stocked with graham crackers, Quaker cornmeal, and other sundries. (Courtesy of Robert Holt.)

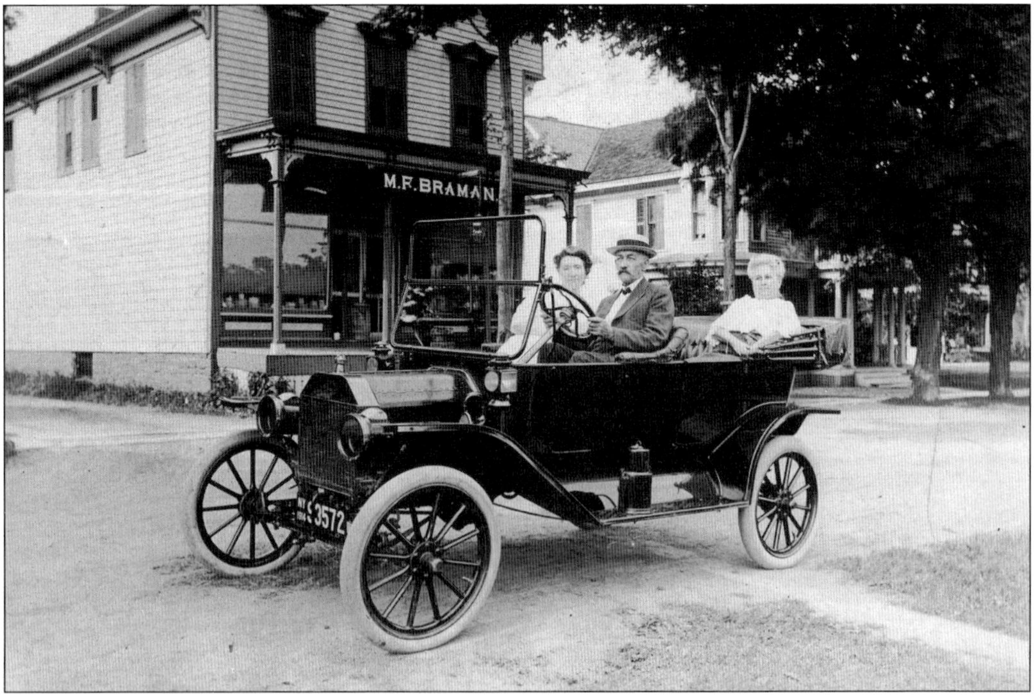

Millard Braman Takes a Drive, 1914. With passenger Emma Hills, Millard F. Braman and his wife, Libby, show off their new Ford Model T touring car in front of Millard's general store located at 25 North Main Street in Central Bridge. Already, the license plates bore high numbers—NY 95372. (Courtesy of Robert Holt.)

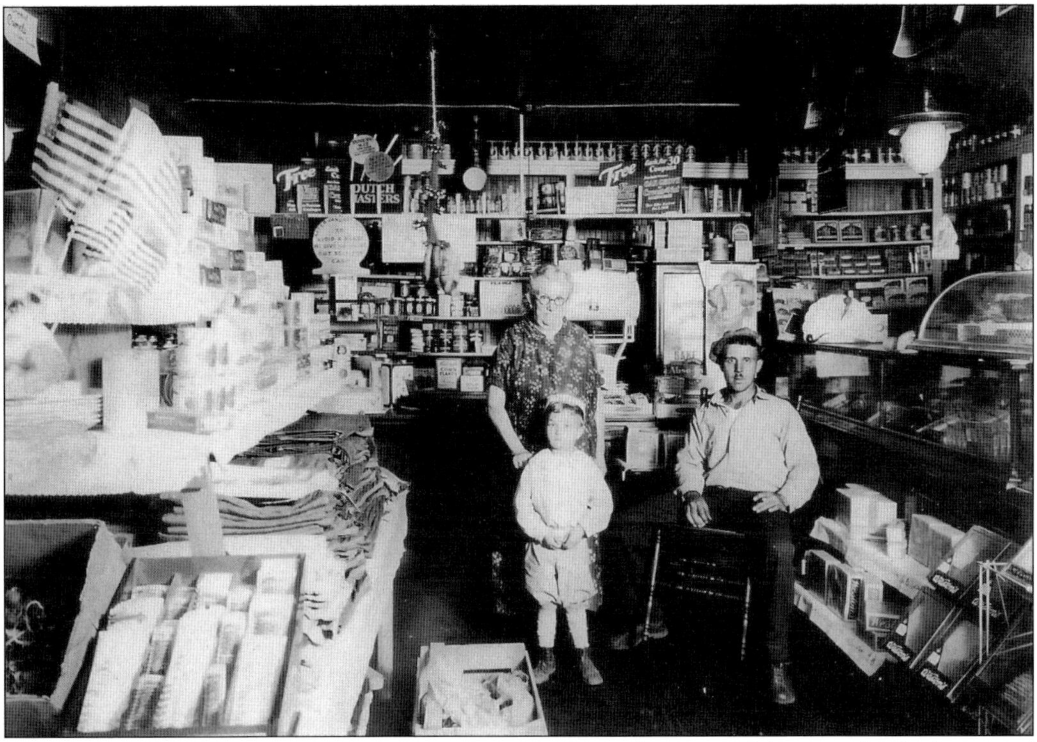

INTERIOR OF THE DIETZ STORE, AROUND 1920. By the mid-1920s, Adelia Mansheffer Dietz and her husband, Byron, owned a grocery store, perhaps made possible by a recent inheritance. Adelia and Alvaro Mansheffer pose with an unidentified child, possibly Adelia's grandson. The store carried a wide variety of goods, including American flags. (Courtesy of Robert Holt.)

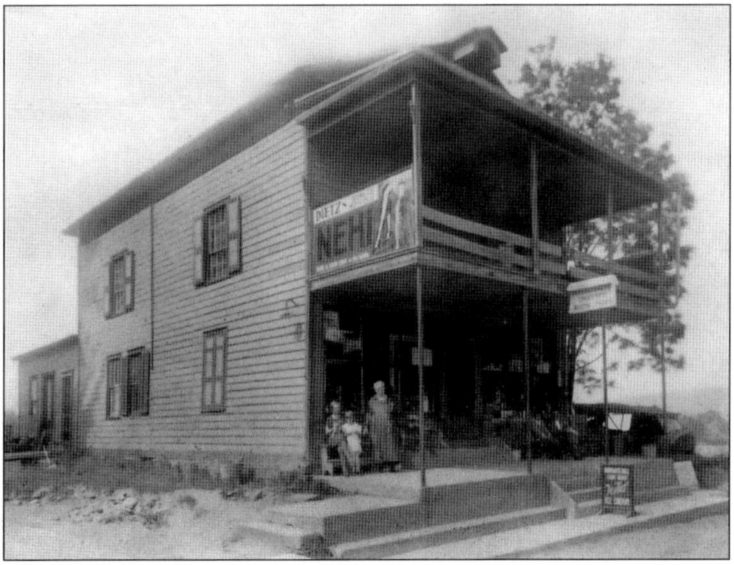

THE DIETZ STORE, AROUND 1920. Adelia Dietz poses with several unidentified people on the porch. Her store carried Nehi, a flavored soda. The sign showing a seated woman's legs, suggesting the phrase "knee high," is on the upper porch. The store carried boots, shoes, a general line of groceries, and Velvet ice cream. The building stood on State Route 7 in "old" Central Bridge but is now gone. (Courtesy of Robert Holt.)

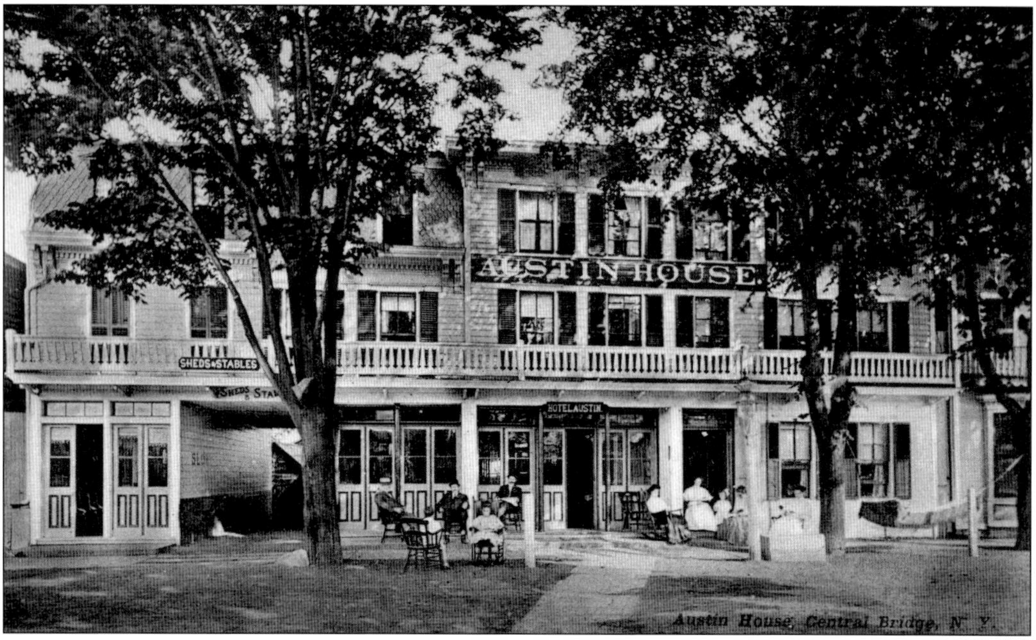

Austin House, Central Bridge. An 1894 advertisement states: "This fine hotel and eating establishment includes a barber shop, livery, stabling and sheds connected. Moderate charges to all. Convenient to trains. Henry Austin, Proprietor." The photograph shows where horses and wagons could drive through the front of the building to the rear where sheds and barns were located. (Courtesy of Robert Holt.)

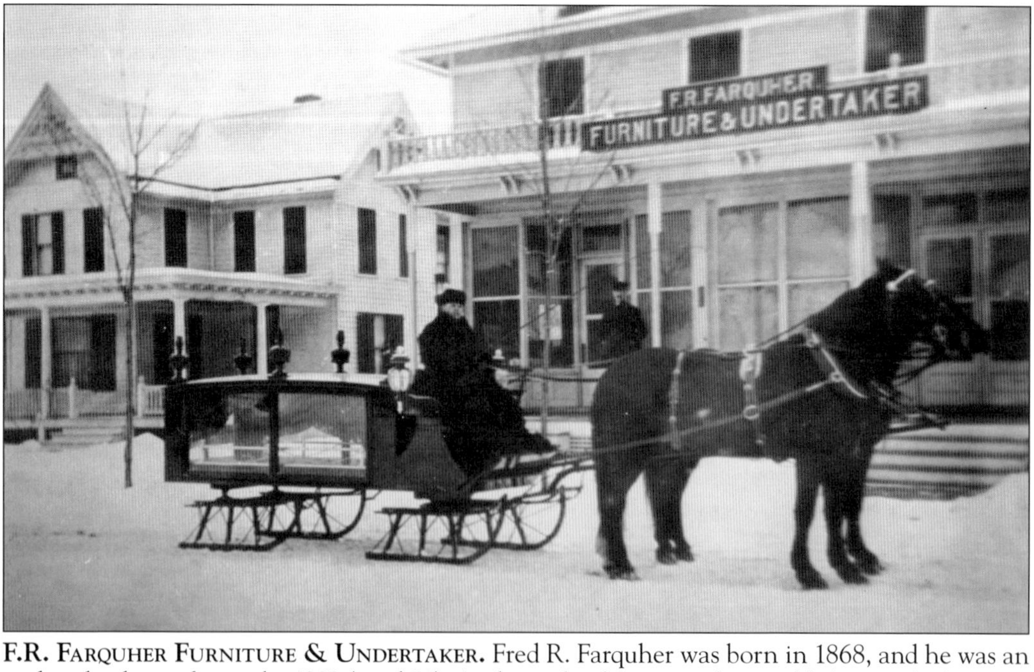

F.R. Farquher Furniture & Undertaker. Fred R. Farquher was born in 1868, and he was an undertaker by profession by 1892 (aged 23). As shown by the sign on his establishment, he handled furniture also. In this 1900s winter scene, he is shown with his horse-drawn hearse, mounted on sleds for use on snow and ice. (Courtesy of Robert Holt.)

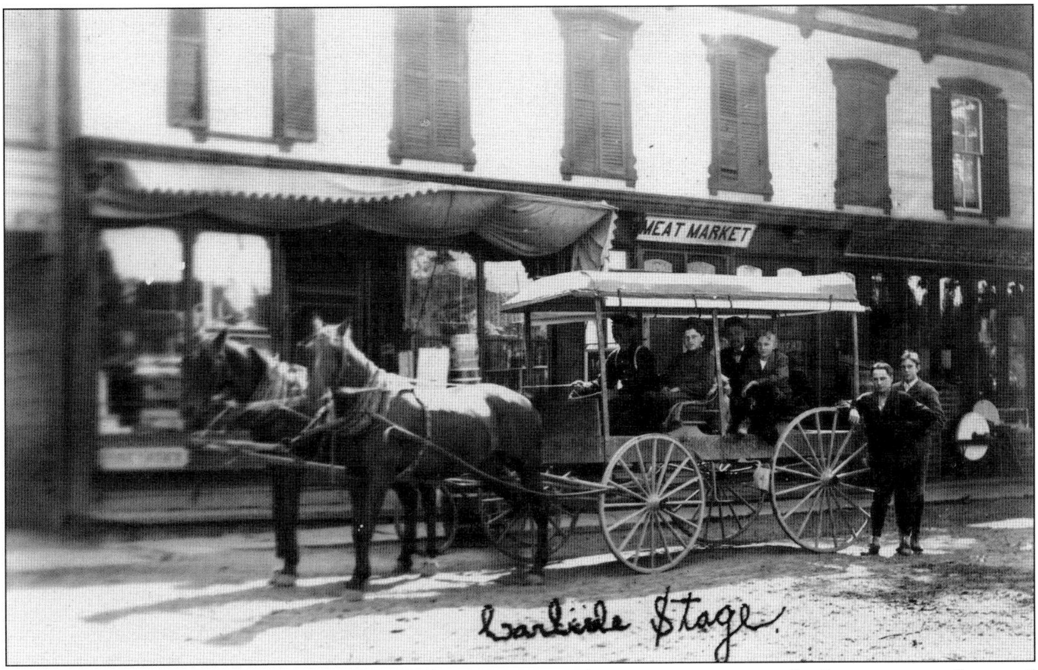

THE CARLISLE STAGE, AROUND 1900. The stage waits for passengers outside the meat market and the Wessell & Becker hardware store in Central Bridge. The uniformed driver and his helper sit in the front seat while a gentleman and a boy are seated behind. Carlisle is some 10 miles from Central Bridge. The stage might have gone north to the Great Western Turnpike (now US Route 20) and then west to Carlisle. (Courtesy of Robert Holt.)

CENTRAL BRIDGE SCHOOL, 1910. The school building still stands on a rise in Central Bridge, though without the bell tower. For the times, this was a rather large school building. There was a gymnasium on the second floor. Here, some 30 schoolchildren pose with their teacher. (Courtesy of Robert Holt.)

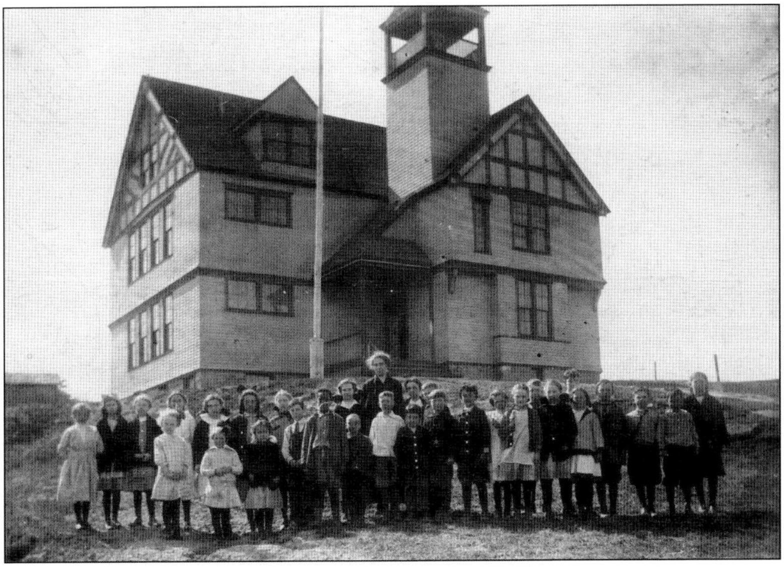

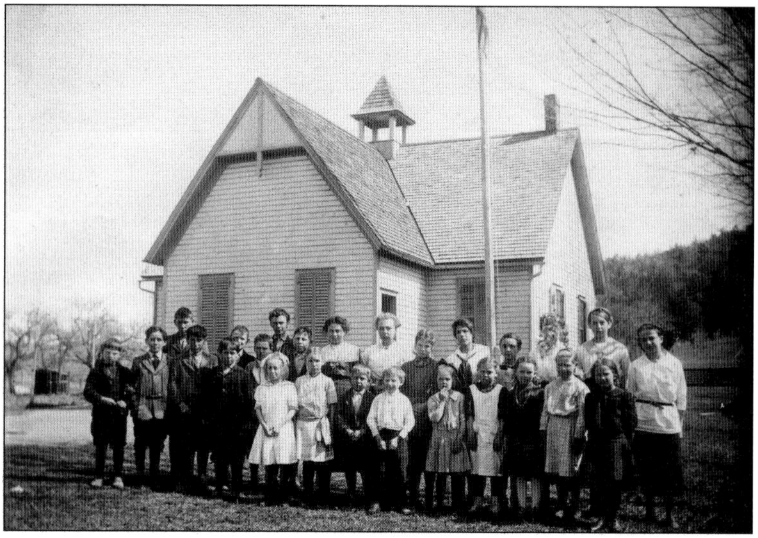

"Old" Central Bridge School, 1910. In "old" Central Bridge, the school building was more modest than that in the "new" village. Here, around 1910, the children line up for their photograph. There are several older pupils as well as younger students. This range of ages was typical in the era of the one-room school. (Courtesy of Robert Holt.)

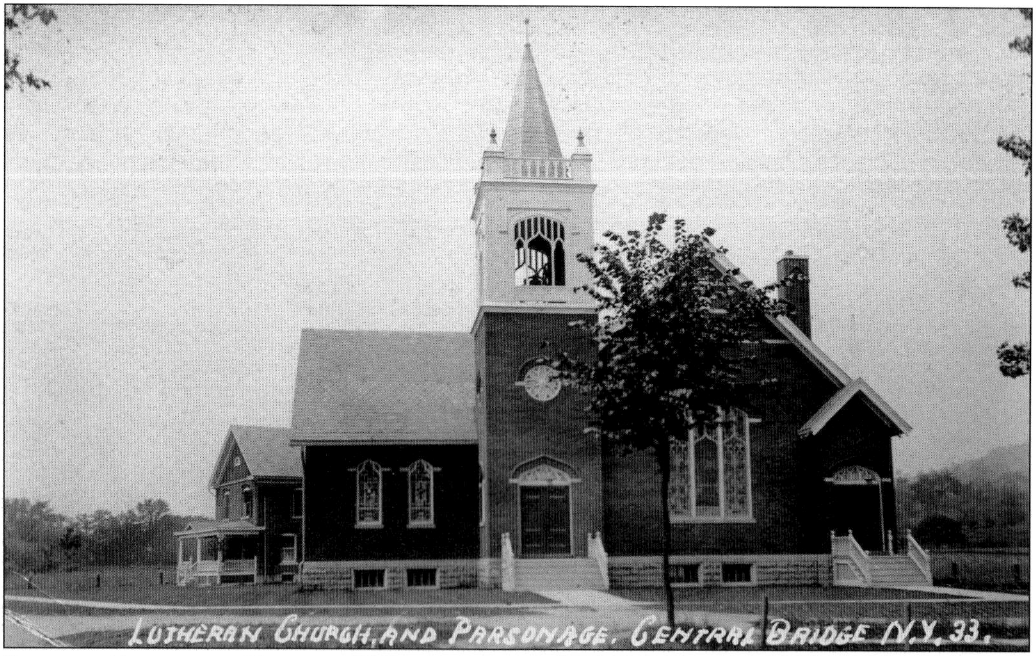

Bethany Lutheran Church. The cornerstone of the church was laid on July 29, 1906, and held a time capsule. The capsule contained various items, such as local newspapers (including the *Schoharie Republican* and the *Cobleskill Times*), a list of church members, and a booklet by Pastor Balfour on the history of the Lutheran church in Schoharie. In 2006, a hundred years later, the cornerstone was reset and more items were added. (Courtesy of Robert Holt.)

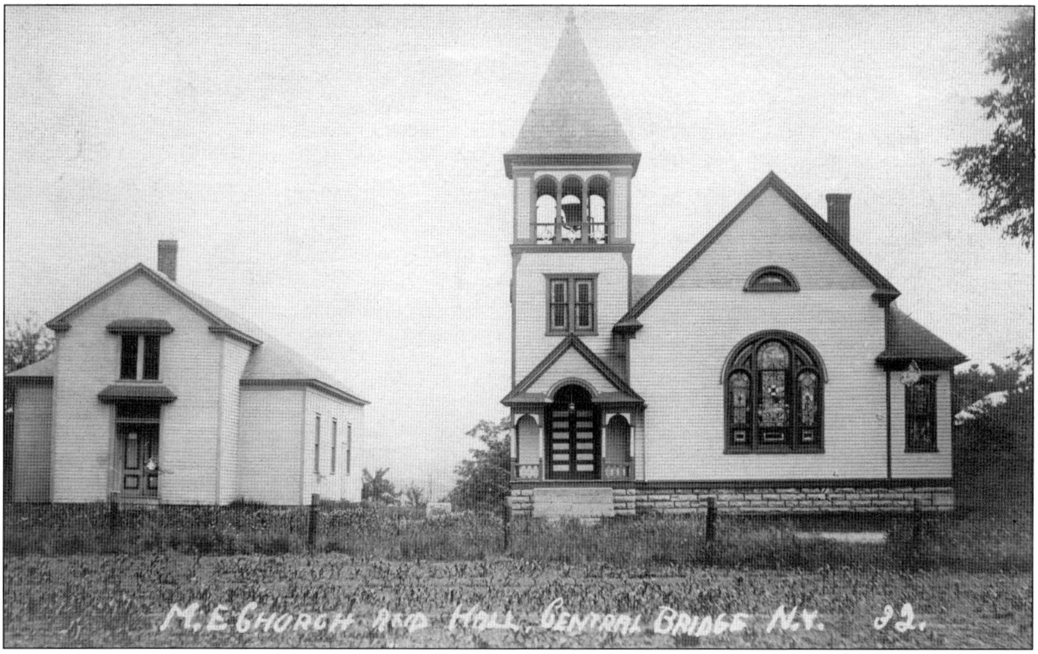

THE CENTRAL BRIDGE METHODIST CHURCH. The first Methodist Episcopal Church was built in "old" Central Bridge in 1869. As the congregation moved toward the depot area and "new" Central Bridge was established, the present church building was erected in 1899. The old church building (left) was moved next door for use as a church hall. (Courtesy of Robert Holt.)

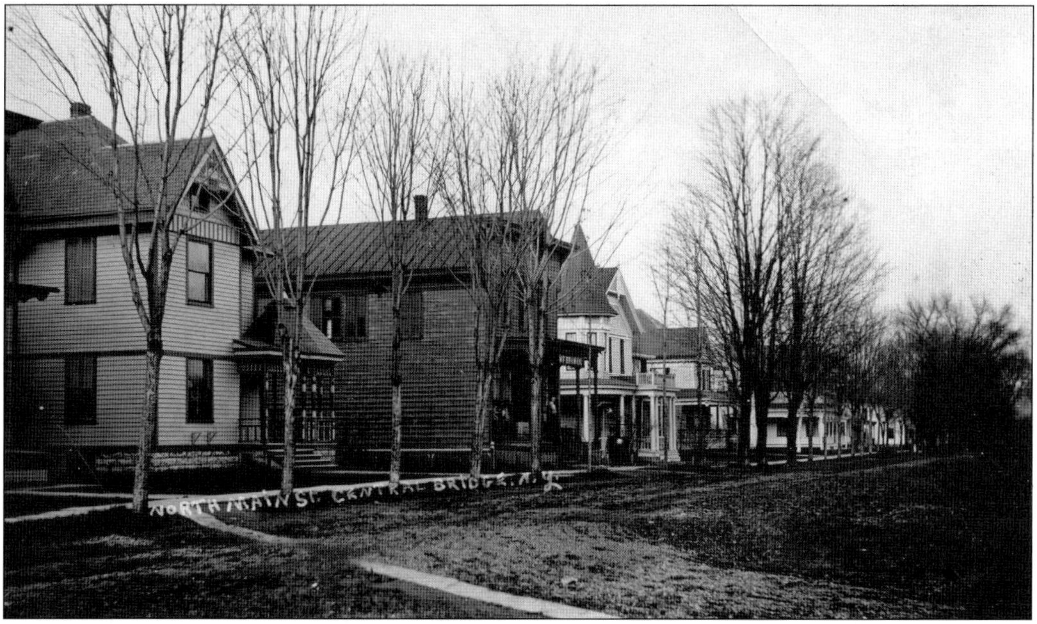

NORTH MAIN STREET, CENTRAL BRIDGE. In the 1910s, houses on North Main Street were either occupied as residences or as stores and offices. The first house on the left with the circular porch belonged to Arthur L. Parsons, who had a Ford dealership by 1930. Later, it was occupied by Dr. Wilhelm Moser until 1975. The house next door was Millard F. Braman's general store. (Courtesy of Robert Holt.)

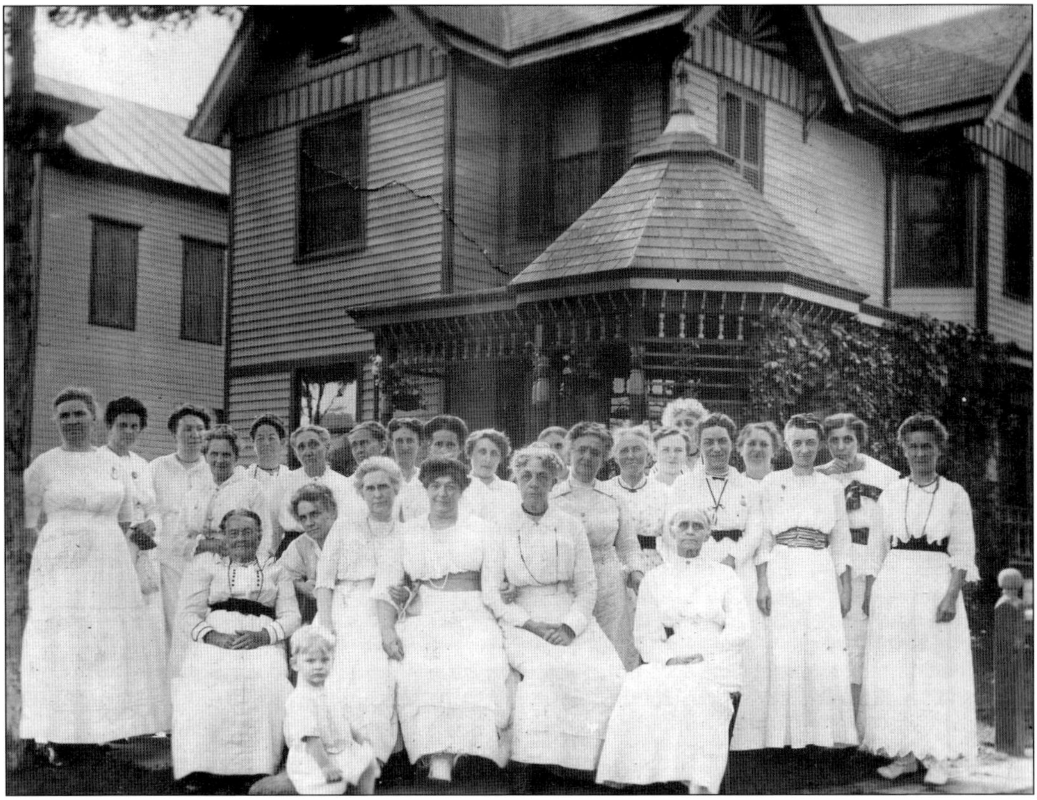

Central Bridge Ladies' Aid Society, 1915. The ladies are gathered in front of the home of Arthur L. and Mary Parsons on North Main Street. The Ladies' Aid Society was a church-oriented organization dedicated to helping with supplies, food, and clean clothes for soldiers in the field during World War I. These ladies wore white outfits with assorted sashes, perhaps a uniform of sorts. (Courtesy of OSFM.)

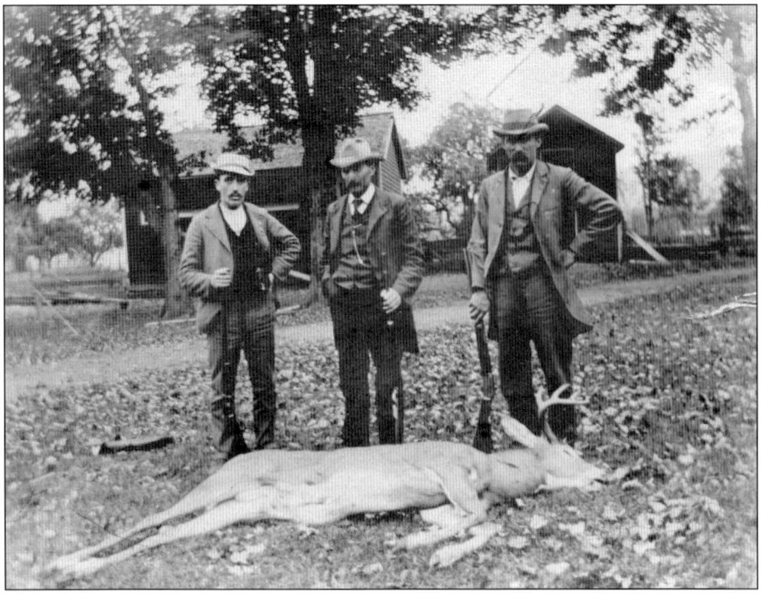

Deer Hunters, about 1905. Standing behind their trophy are, from left to right, Peter Enders, Millard Braman, and the local minister. The men are impeccably dressed with jackets, waistcoats, and even a pocket watch. Deer hunting in the fall provided food for the family and neighbors. (Courtesy of Robert Holt.)

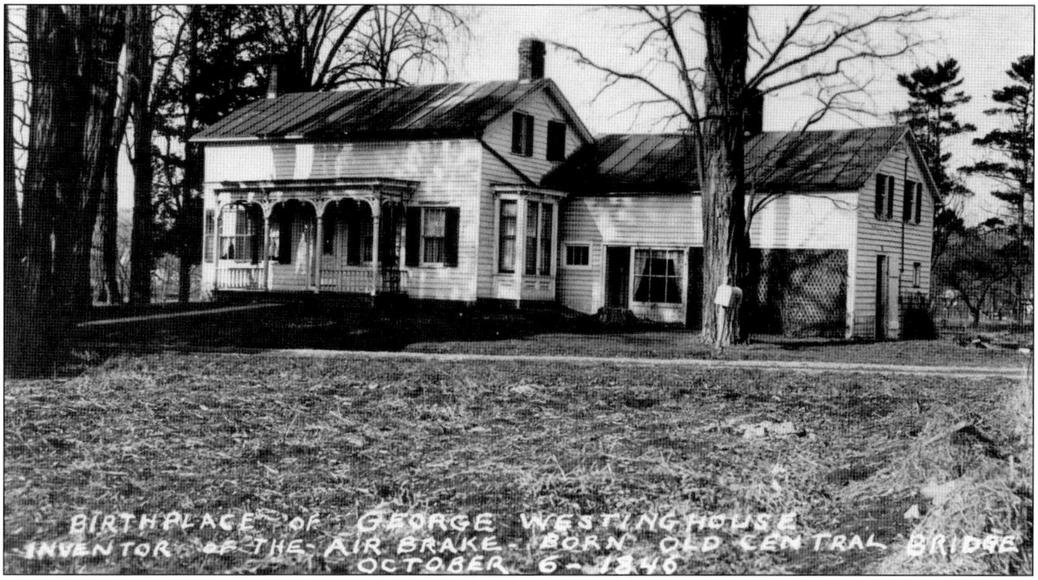

Birthplace of George Westinghouse Jr., Central Bridge. George Westinghouse Jr. was born here on October 6, 1846. Early on, he showed remarkable inventiveness in working with steam engines, farm machinery, and railroad devices. In 1862, at the age of 23, he began the development of the Westinghouse air brake system, a device that would come to be used in most railway cars. Later, his inventions and business savvy led to the creation of the Westinghouse Corporation, headquartered in Pittsburgh, Pennsylvania. (Courtesy of author's collection.)

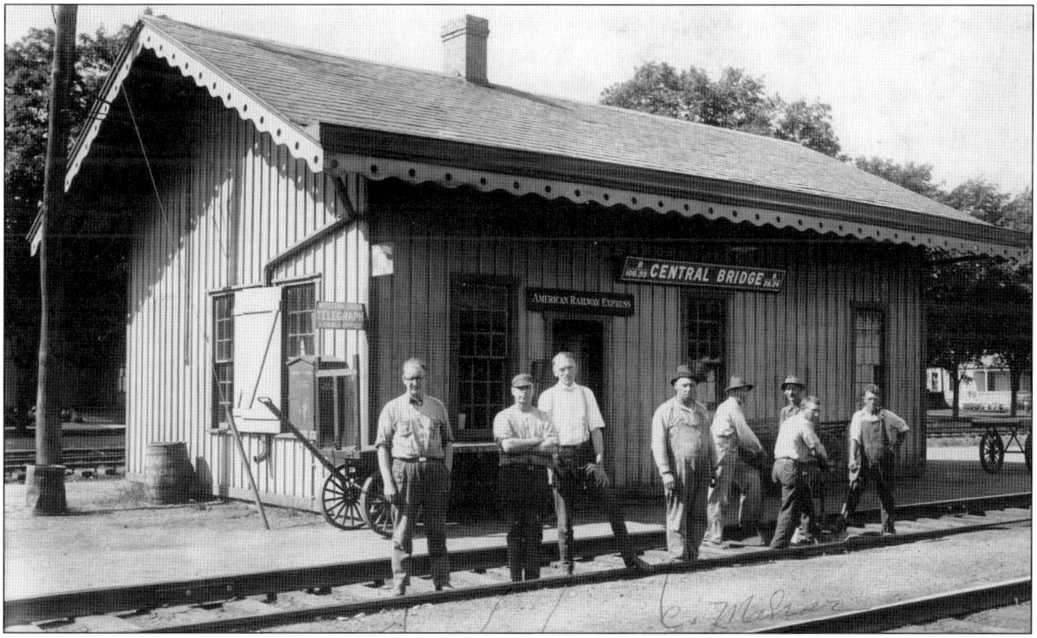

Central Bridge Depot. From left to right, Webster Gardner (station clerk), Clarence Shafer, Burr Newby (station agent), C. Maher, and others stand on the tracks around 1930. The depot sign shows the mileage from Binghamton (106.35) and Albany (36.24). All stations on this stretch of rail had similar mileage signs. Of note are the Western Union telegraph sign and the American Railway Express service sign above the door. (Courtesy of Robert Holt.)

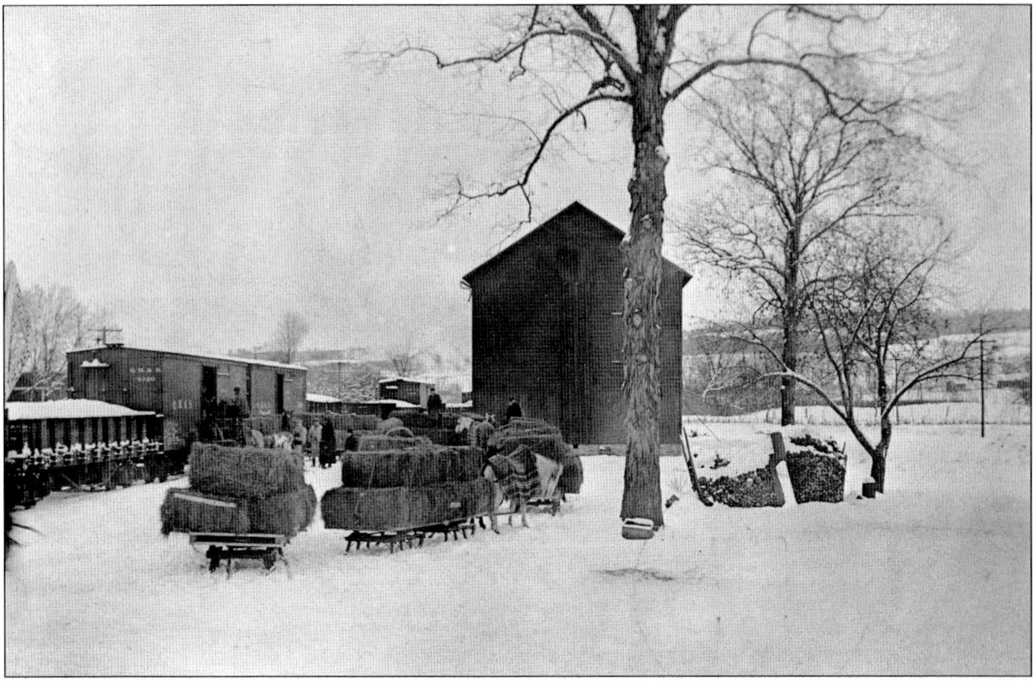

Loading Hay at Central Bridge. Hay is being loaded onto a Delaware & Hudson Railroad boxcar in this c. 1910 winter scene. During the winter, sleds were used to move both goods and people. This must have been a cold day because the horses are well covered with blankets. The barn belonged to W.B. Colyer, a wholesale hay dealer. (Courtesy of Robert Holt.)

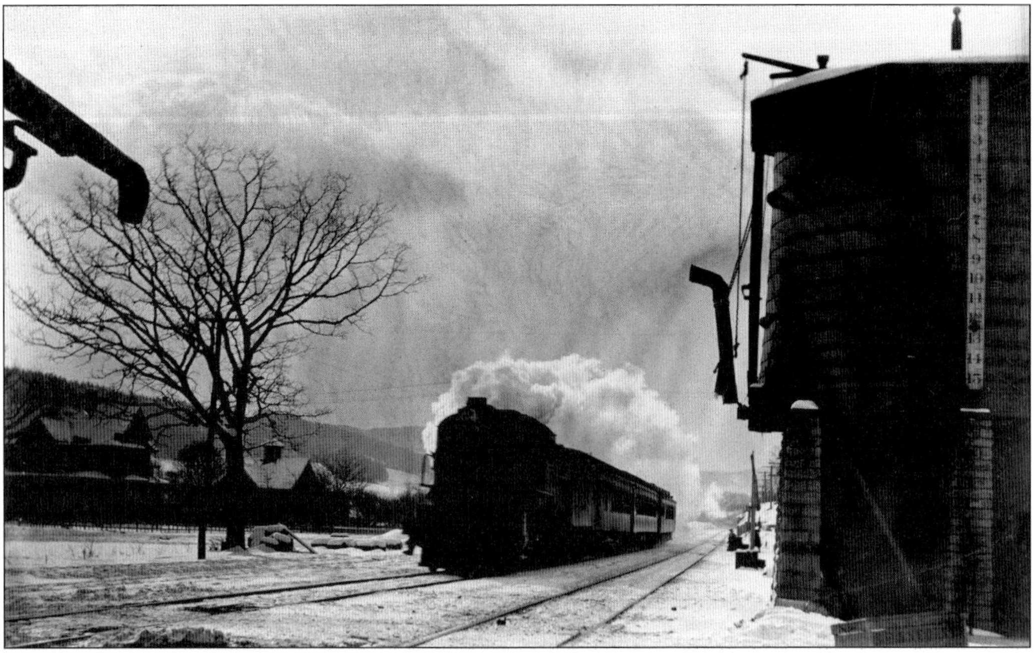

Water Tanks at the Central Bridge Depot. A Delaware & Hudson passenger train steams past the Central Bridge depot on a winter day. The tanks were used to replenish the steam engine's water supply. (Courtesy of Robert Holt.)

Eight

HOWE'S CAVE

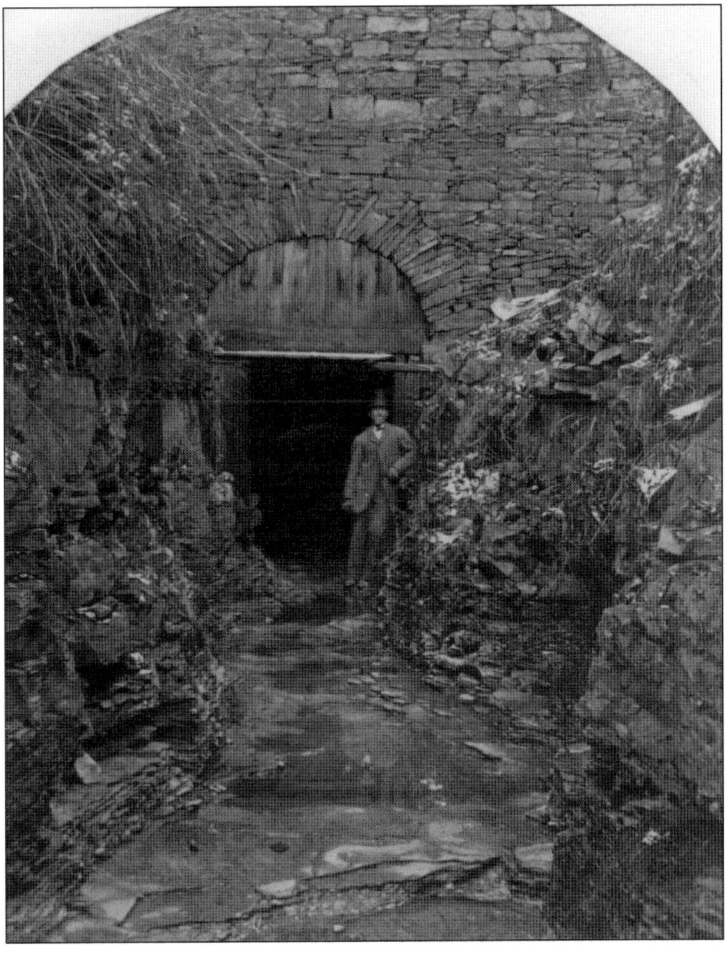

THE OLD ENTRANCE TO HOWE'S CAVE. Lester Howe discovered an entrance to the cave in 1842. Legend has it that he observed that his cows were always near the same spot on his neighbor Henry Wetsel's land. There, he noticed that the air was much cooler and found an entrance to a cave. By 1843, Howe had purchased Wetsel's land. Here, he stands at the cave entrance in his suit and top hat, perhaps ready to receive visitors. (Courtesy of Howe Caverns, Inc.)

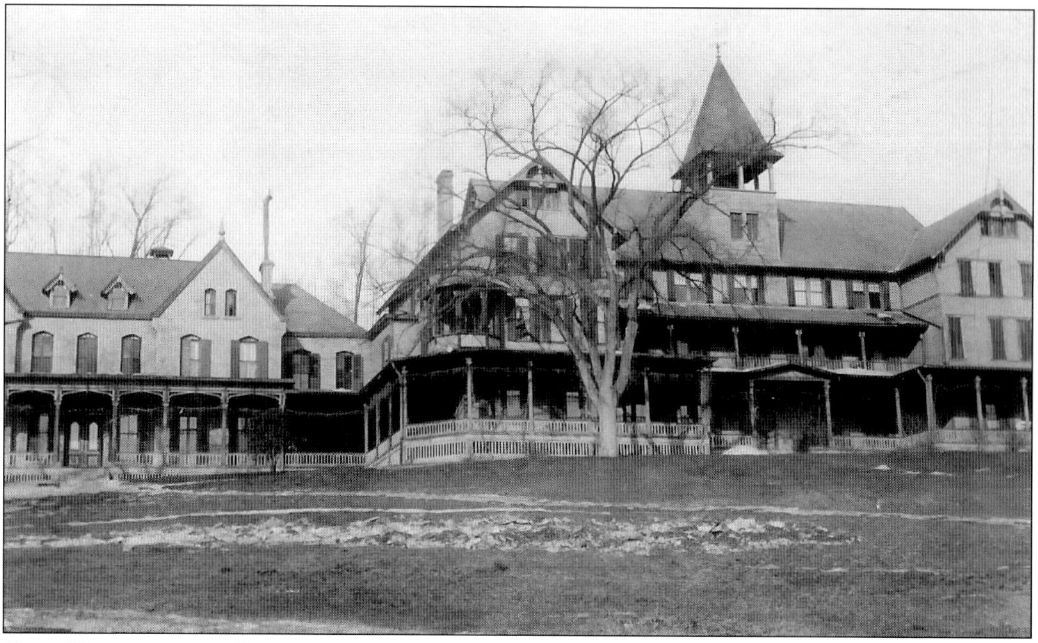

Cave House and the Pavilion Hotel. The coming of the railroad in 1865 with a depot at Howe's Cave allowed more visitors to easily reach the caverns. Rooms were needed to accommodate the guests. Cave House (left) was built in 1872 at the original cave entrance. The Pavilion Hotel (right) was erected some time later. (Courtesy of Howe Caverns, Inc.)

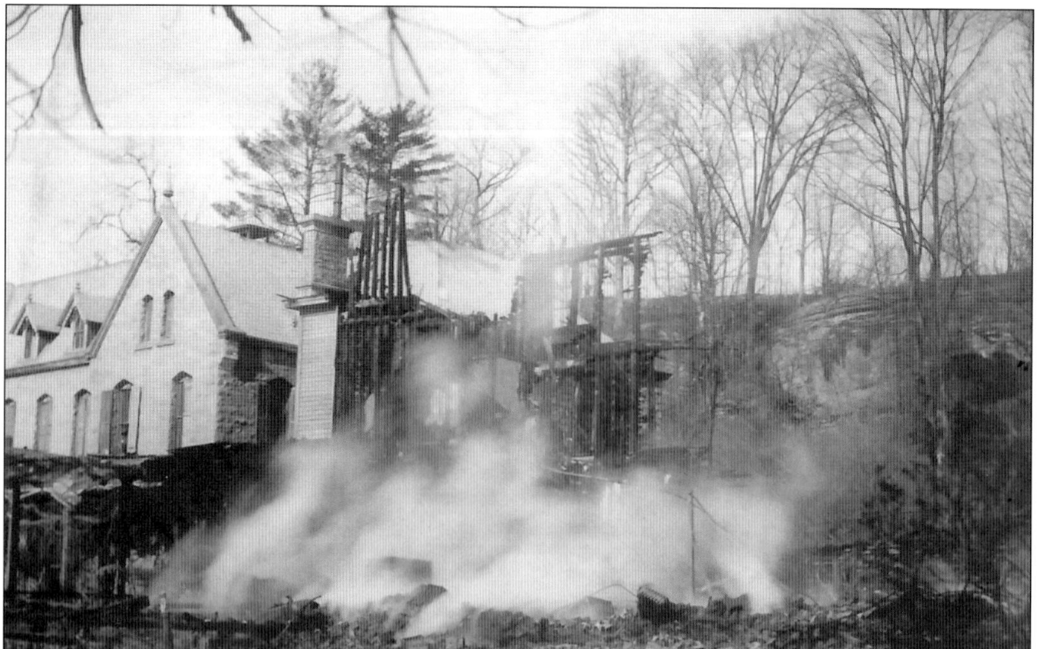

The Pavilion Hotel Burns in 1909. The Cave House remained but fell into disrepair in later years. It is now under restoration as the Cave House Museum of Mining and Geology. (Courtesy of Howe Caverns, Inc.)

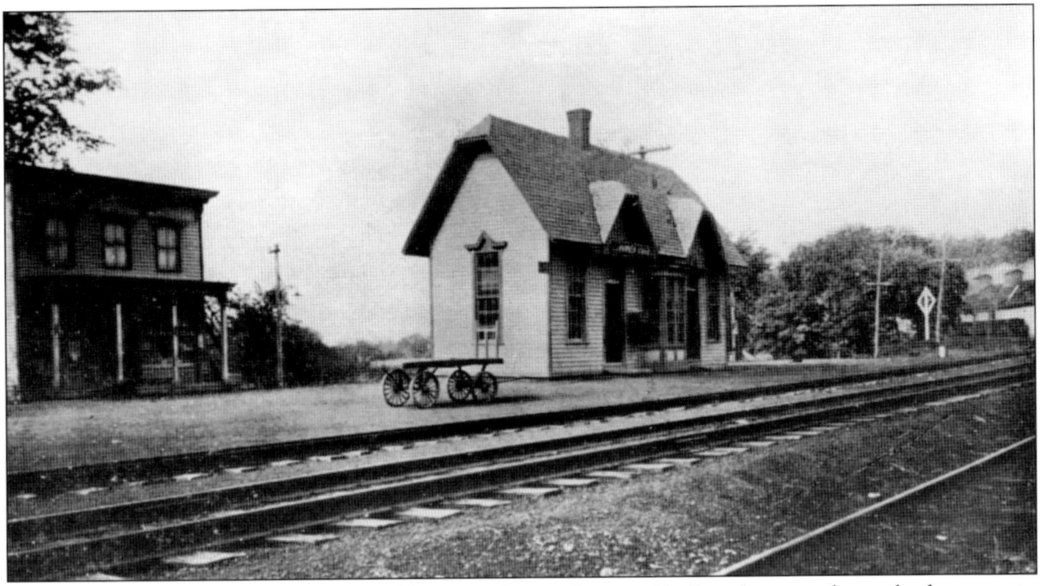

Howe's Cave Depot. When the Albany & Susquehanna Railroad came through the area in 1865, the caverns and the hamlet of Howe's Cave became easily accessible to visitors. Visitors to the caverns could take an easy walk from the depot to Cave House and the Pavilion Hotel. (Courtesy of Robert Holt.)

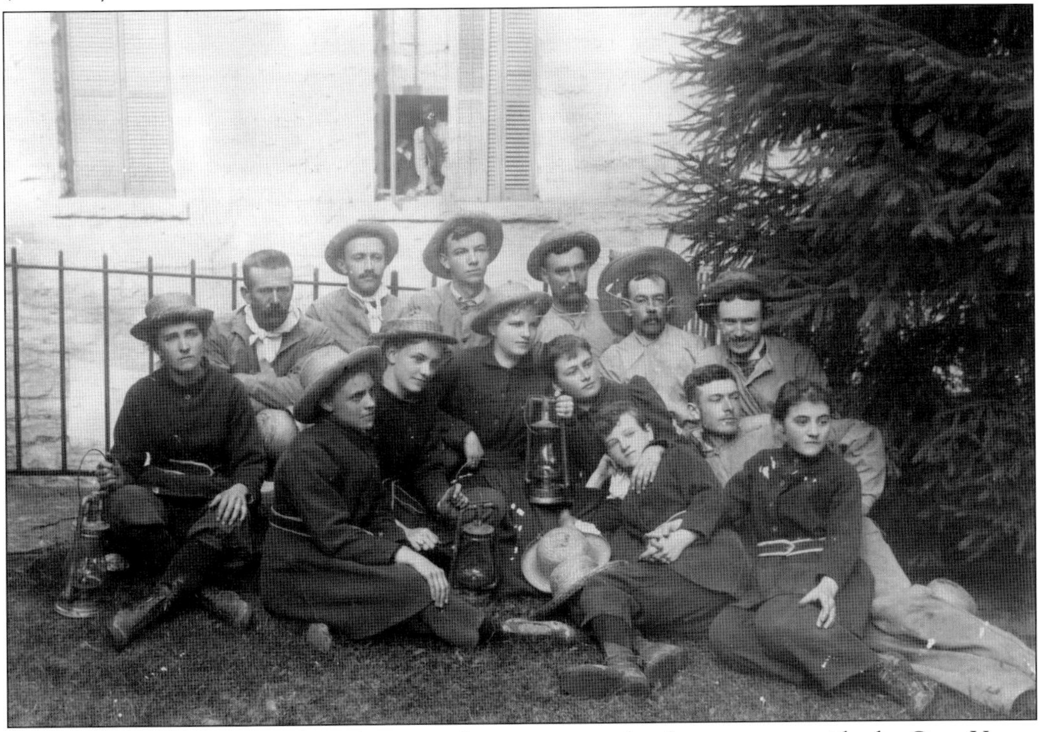

Howe's Cave Tourists, 1880. A group of tourists poses for the camera outside the Cave House around 1880. The women were supplied with heavy woolen trousers and coats while the men were given overalls. All were given straw hats and whale oil lanterns. This group has yet to venture underground, so their clothes and boots are clean. (Courtesy of Howe Caverns, Inc.)

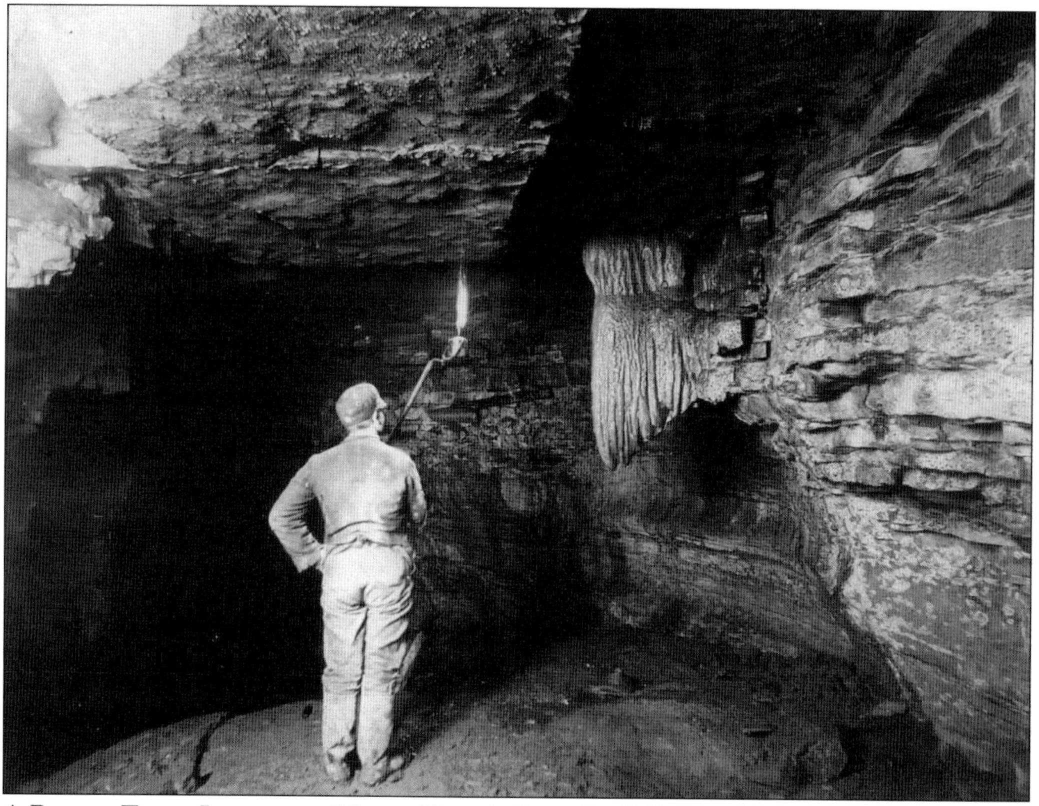

A Parade Torch Lights the Way in Howe's Cave. In 1888, noted Adirondack photographer Seneca Ray Stoddard made a series of photographs in the caverns. Here, a man holds a parade torch to show a cave formation known as the Epaulette. This section of the cave was consumed in mining operations in the 1920s and no longer exists. (Courtesy of Howe Caverns, Inc.)

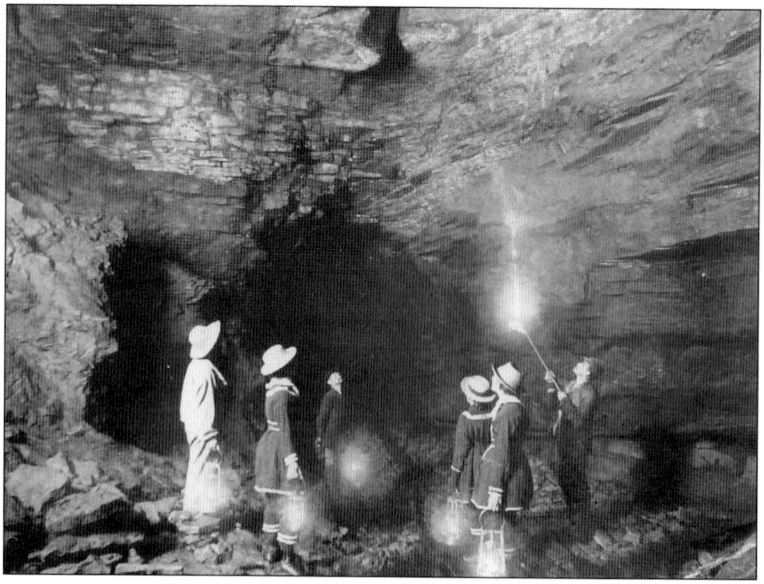

Washington Hall, Howe's Cave, 1888. A man and four women look at the cave formations in Washington Hall as the guide (right) holds a parade torch to light the space. The tourists hold whale oil lanterns. These were the only lights the tour had while underground. Tours often lasted 8–10 hours. (Courtesy of Howe Caverns, Inc.)

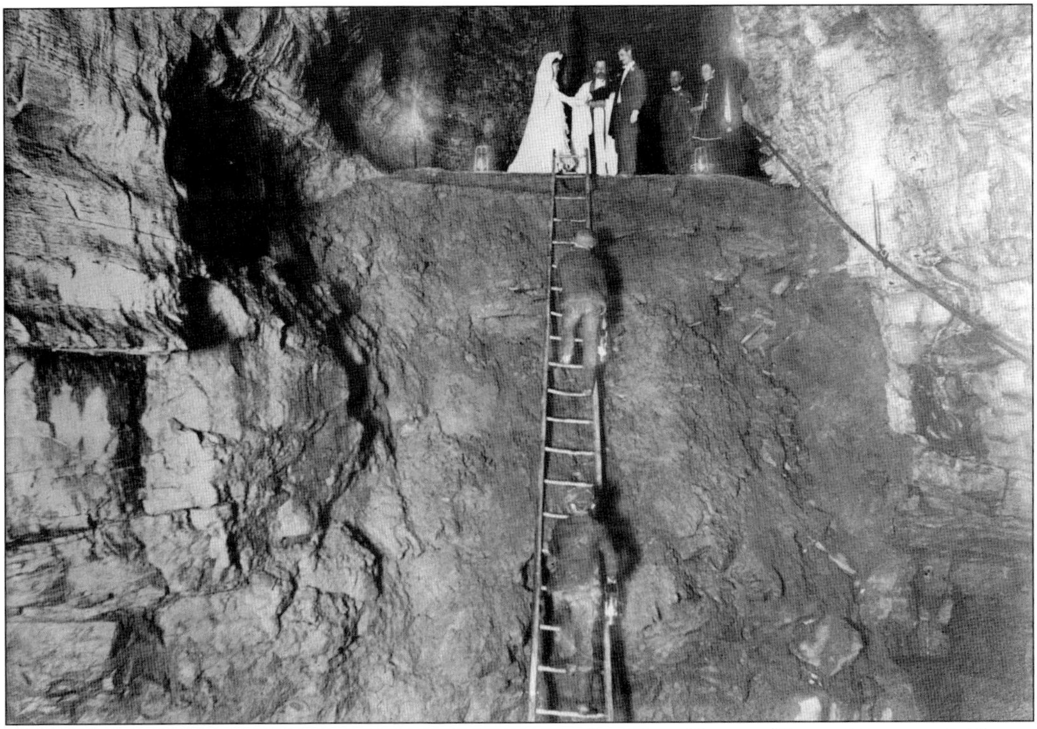

The First Underground Wedding. Lester Howe's daughter Harriet Elgiva Howe and Hiram Shipman Dewey were married in the caverns on September 27, 1854. This was the first wedding in the Bridal Chamber of the cave. This 1880 photograph was a re-creation of the event done as a publicity stunt. Since 1929, well over 600 weddings have taken place at the new Bridal Altar. (Courtesy of Howe Caverns, Inc.)

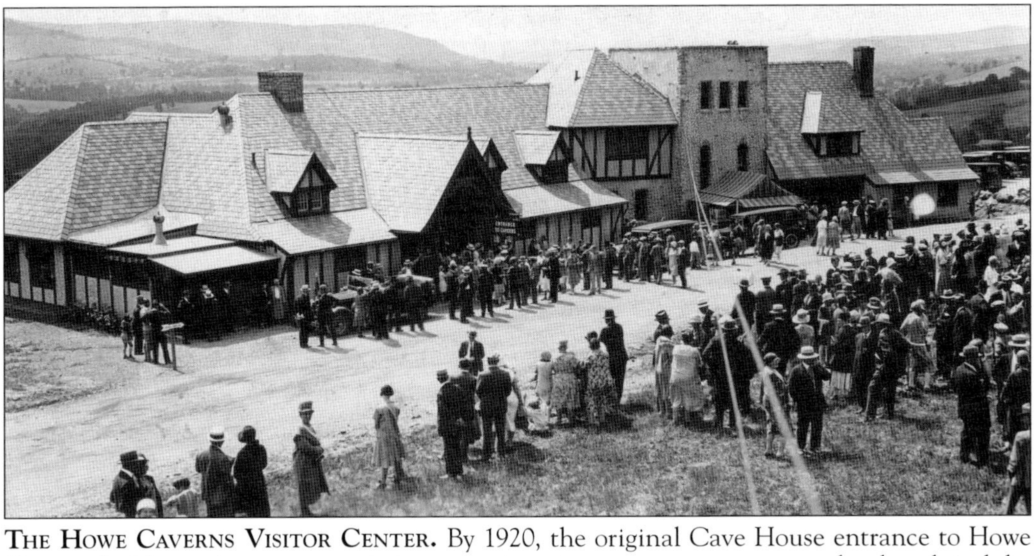

The Howe Caverns Visitor Center. By 1920, the original Cave House entrance to Howe Caverns had been given over to mining operation. A new cave entrance was developed, and the present Tudor-style building was erected. This 1920s photograph may show the opening of the new welcome center. The name of the caverns was officially changed to Howe Caverns in 1929 when the enterprise was incorporated. (Courtesy of OSFM.)

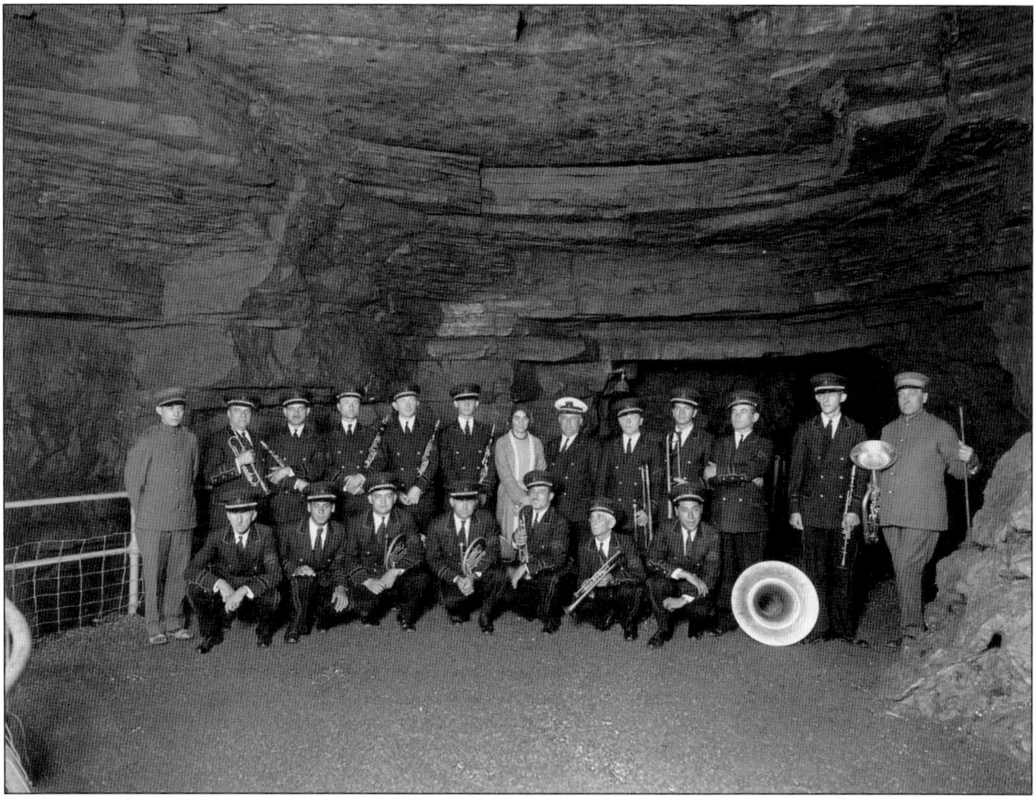

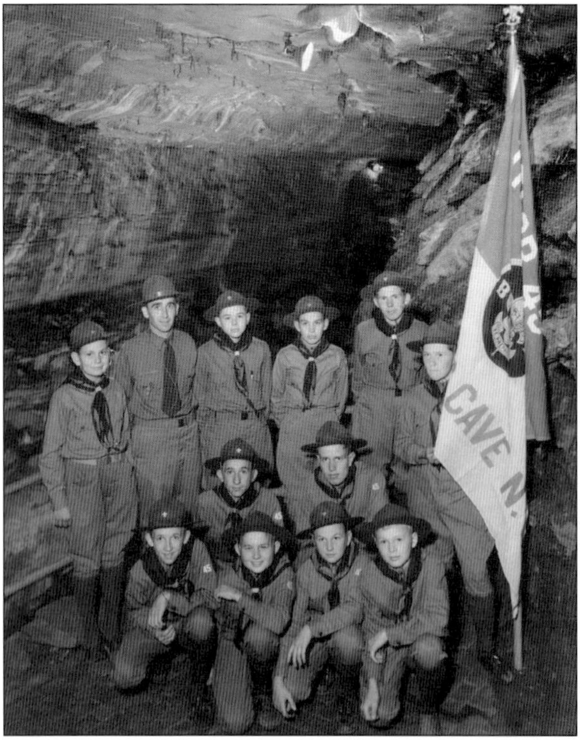

Bands Play Underground. In September 1930, Joe Basile's Madison Square Band performed in the caverns. Chauncy Rickard, the guide on the right, heard the band play at the Cobleskill fair and persuaded them to play here. Special guests marveled at the acoustics. The guides on the left and right of the group are uniformed. (Courtesy of Howe Caverns, Inc.)

Howe's Cave Scout Troop 45. In December 1940, members of the troop pose in the caverns. From left to right are (first row) Carlton Stanton, Francis Holloway, Arthur Emery, and LeRoy Stanton Jr.; (second row) Milton Stanton and Roger King; (third row) Stanley Tilison, scoutmaster Lyman Stanton, Roger Holloway, Donald Tilison, Edward Livingston, and Robert Livingston. (Courtesy of Howe Caverns, Inc.)

The Chinese Pagoda, Howe Caverns. Today, guided tours are given every day of the year except Thanksgiving and Christmas. An elevator provides access underground. Howe Caverns is well lit and has safe pathways for visitors to enjoy guided tours of the magnificent underground scenery. Here, the path moves by a stalagmite known as the Chinese Pagoda. (Courtesy of Howe Caverns, Inc.)

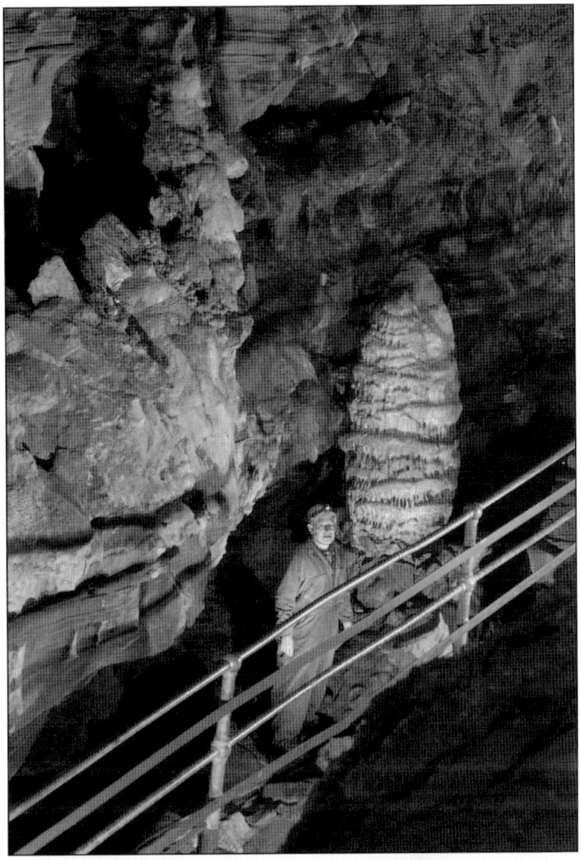

Boat Ride on the Lake of Venus. The tour of Howe Caverns includes a guided boat ride on the Lake of Venus past flowstone formations and a stalactite. The boat is handled by two guides who give a commentary on the cave formations. (Courtesy of Howe Caverns, Inc.)

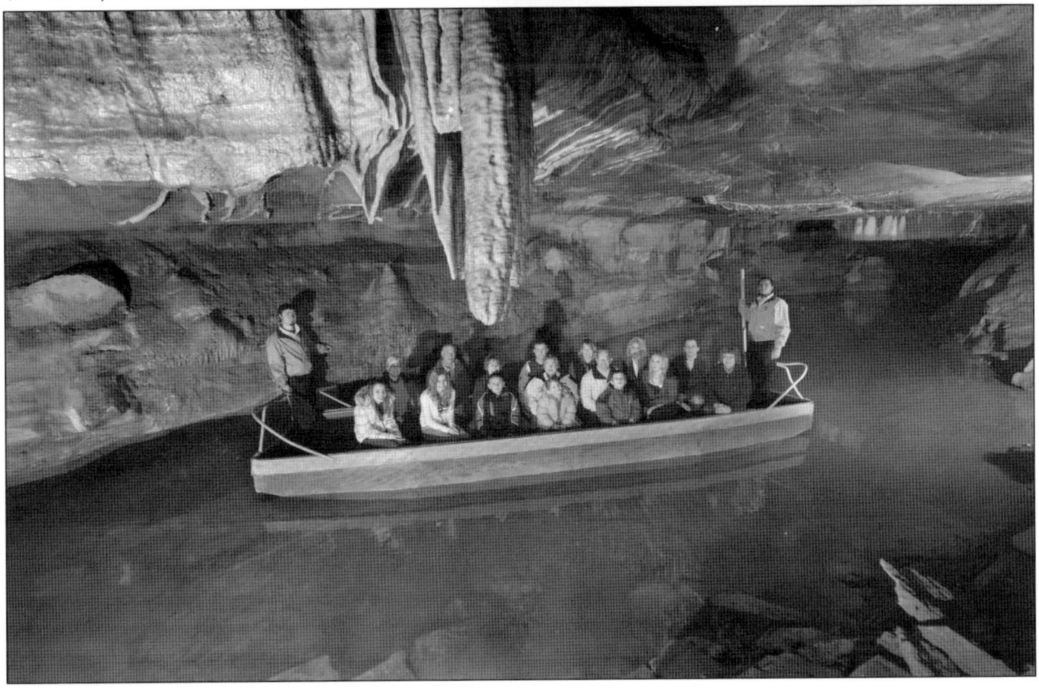

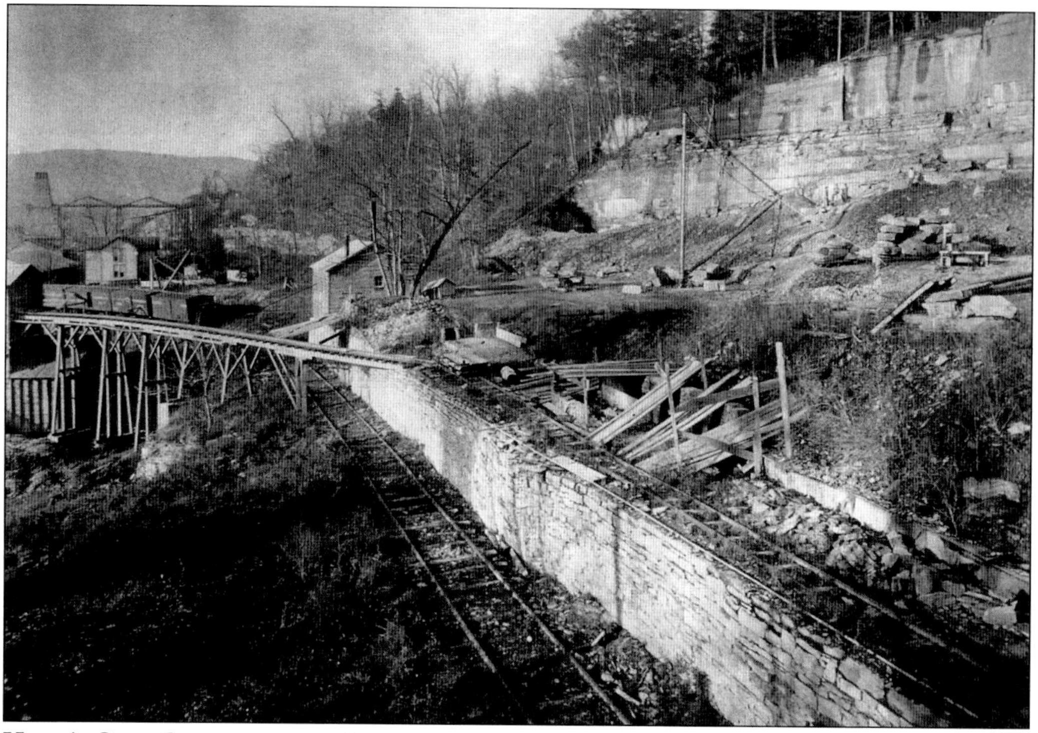

HOWE'S CAVE QUARRY, 1888. A quarry had long been established near the original entrance to Howe's Cave. This 1888 photograph by Seneca Ray Stoddard shows an early view of the operation. Over the years, mining encroached on the caverns, and many of the areas photographed underground by Stoddard no longer exist. (Courtesy of Howe Caverns, Inc.)

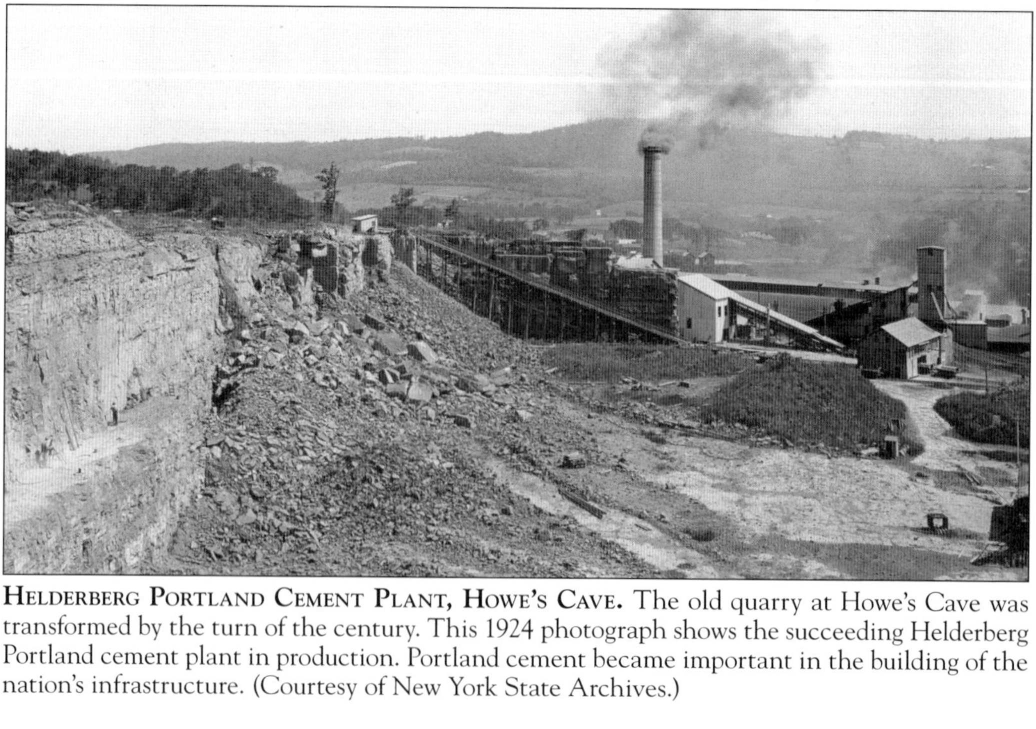

HELDERBERG PORTLAND CEMENT PLANT, HOWE'S CAVE. The old quarry at Howe's Cave was transformed by the turn of the century. This 1924 photograph shows the succeeding Helderberg Portland cement plant in production. Portland cement became important in the building of the nation's infrastructure. (Courtesy of New York State Archives.)

Nine

Esperance and Sloansville

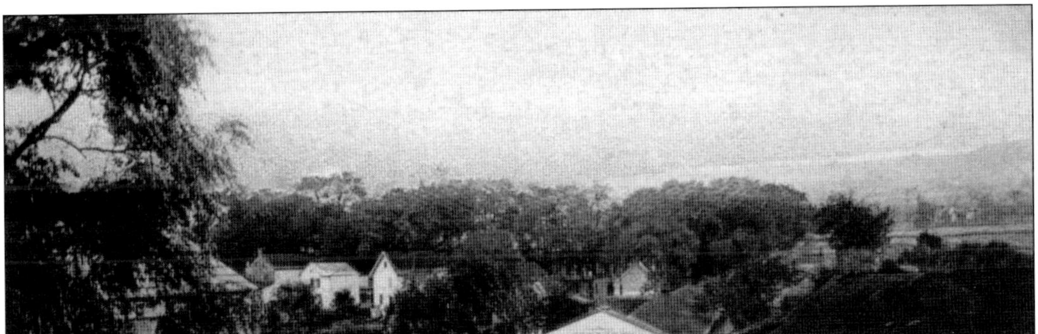

East Entrance of the Covered Bridge, Esperance. Esperance was located on the Great Western Turnpike, which ran from Albany to Cazenovia and beyond. The turnpike was heavily used before the construction of the Erie Canal in 1825. At the entrance of the bridge is the Brooklyn Hotel (right), built around 1800. It was in business until 1928 when the turnpike became US Route 20. (Courtesy of OSFM, Robert Mahar Collection.)

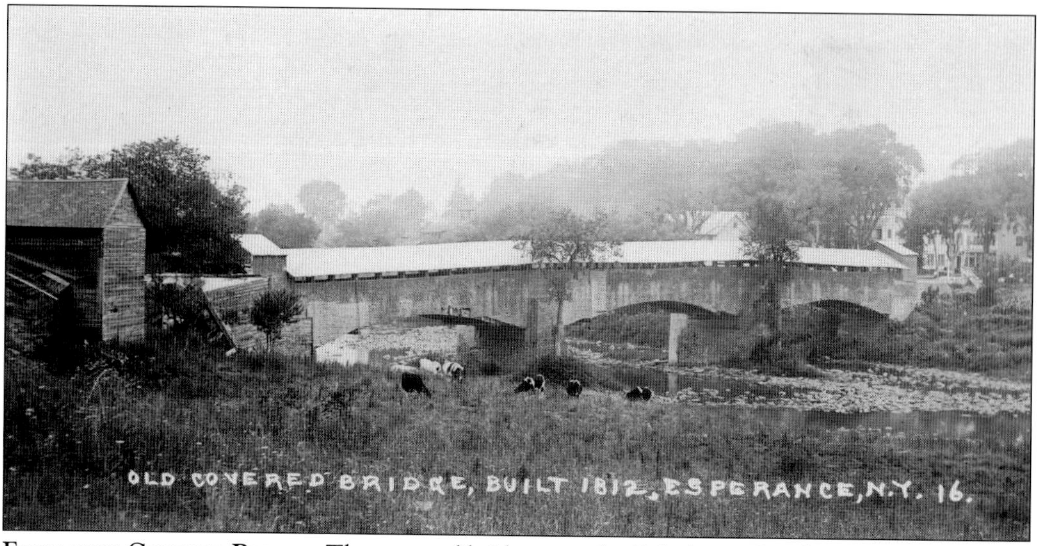

Esperance Covered Bridge. The covered bridge over the Schoharie Creek was built in 1812 by Theodor Burr, a prominent builder of covered bridges in New York and Pennsylvania. At first, the bridge was a toll bridge. At one time, it generated over $700 a month, a considerable sum considering the tolls were measured in pennies. The bridge was torn down in 1930. (Courtesy of the Esperance Historical Museum.)

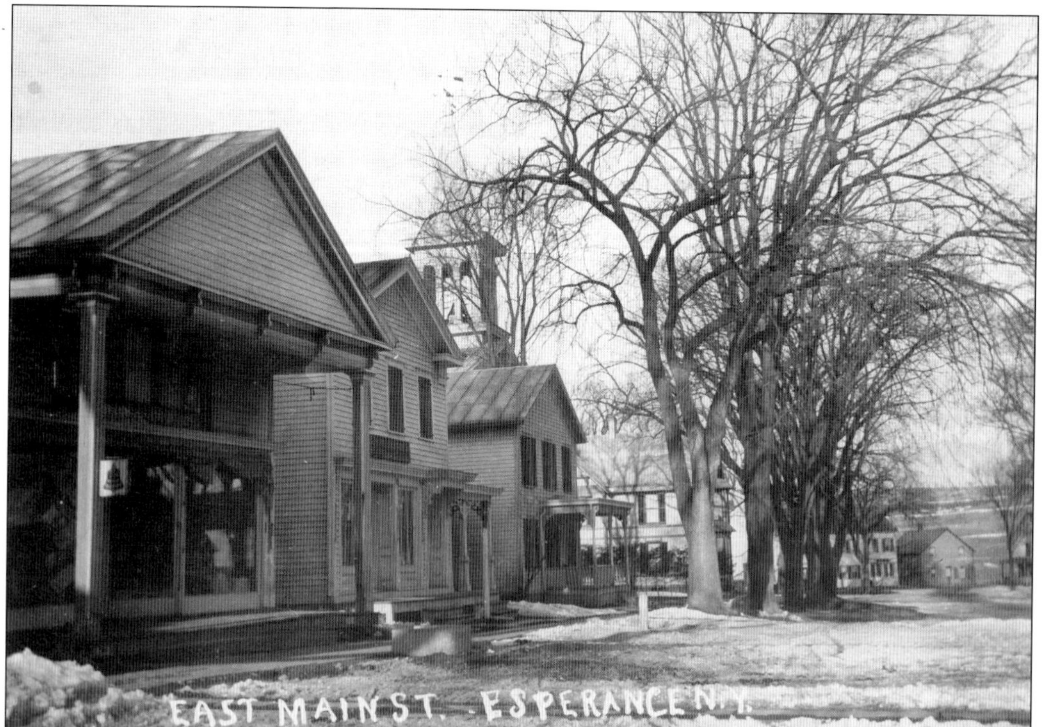

East Main Street, Esperance. The store on the left is the Van Vechten and McIntosh general store (now the Quilt Bug). Even in this 1906 view, there was telephone service at the store. Next door is the Briggs drugstore and farther on, the Methodist church and parsonage. At the right is the tollhouse for the covered bridge. (Courtesy of author's Collection.)

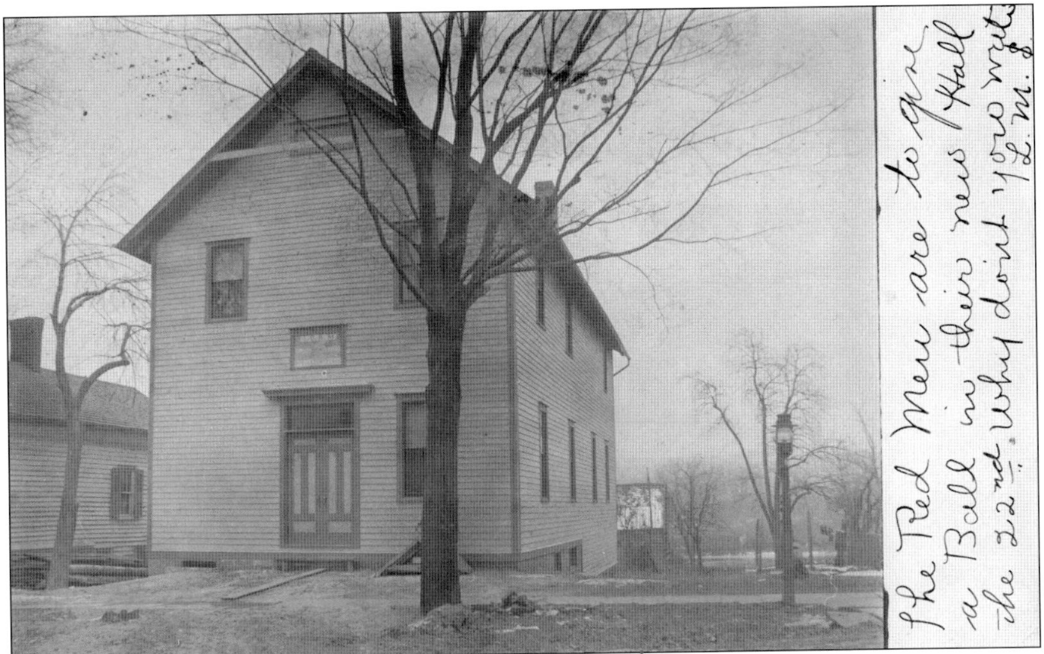

IORM Hall, Esperance, 1905. The Improved Order of Red Men (IORM) is one of America's oldest fraternal organizations, dating back to 1765. The Esperance IORM Hall was relatively new in 1905 when this postcard was mailed. The card says, "The Red Men are to give a Ball in their new Hall the 22nd. Why don't you write. L.M.S." (Courtesy of OSFM, Robert Mahar collection.)

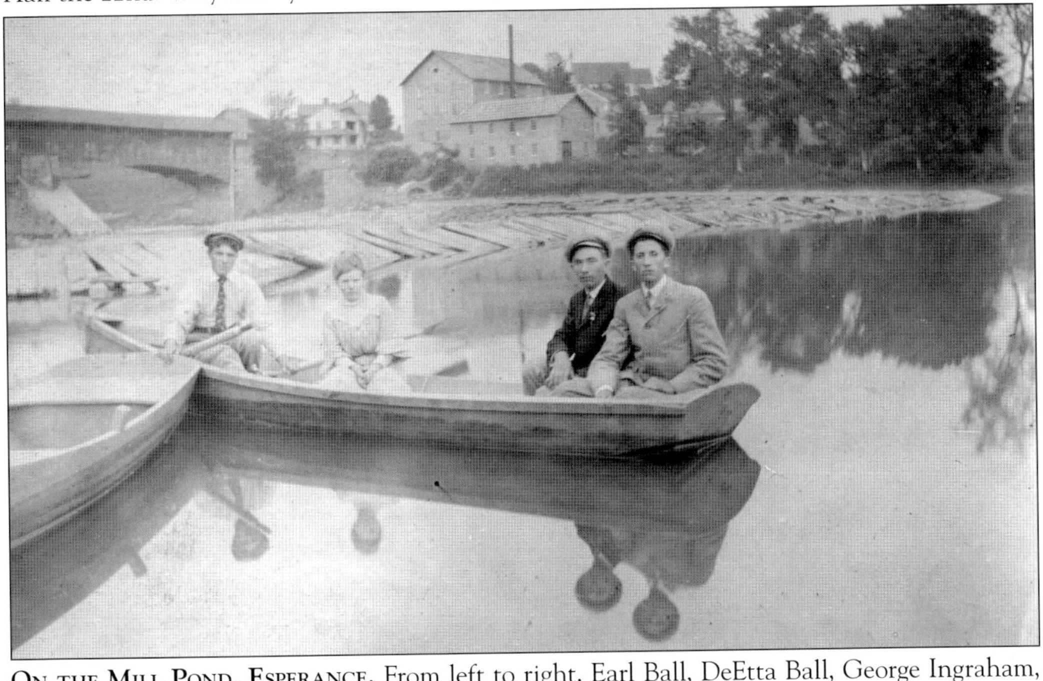

On the Mill Pond, Esperance. From left to right, Earl Ball, DeEtta Ball, George Ingraham, and Oscar Jackson enjoy a boat ride on the Schoharie Creek above the mill dam. Many people in Esperance owned small boats and fished in the creek. In this 1900s view, the covered bridge is to the left and Grantier's mill is at the upper center. (Courtesy of OSFM.)

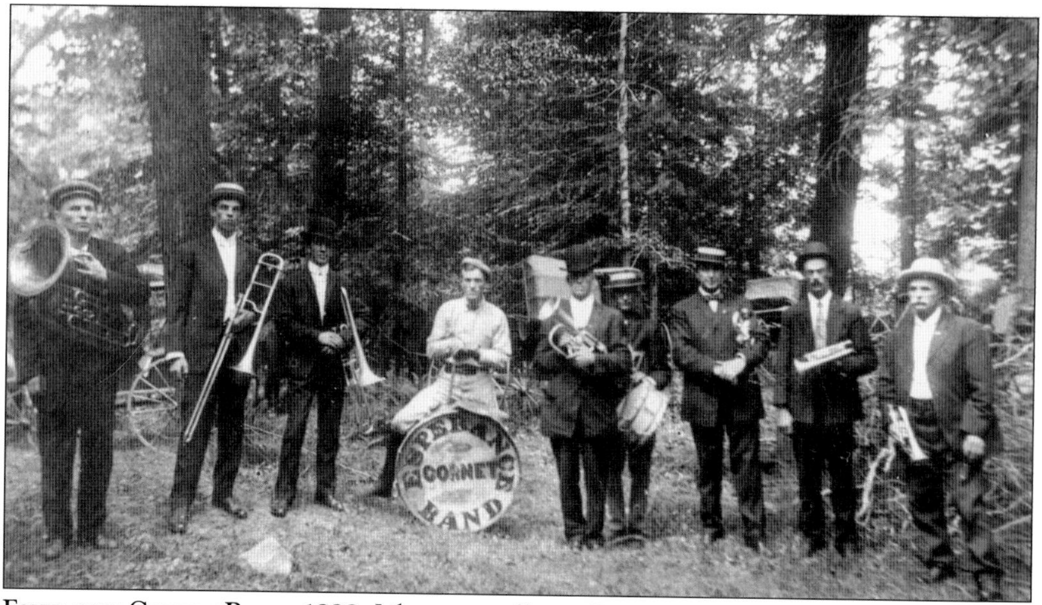

Esperance Cornet Band, 1898. Like many villages, Esperance had a cornet band, which was formed in 1877. The present Esperance Band traces its heritage to the cornet band. From left to right are Russell Young, Roe B. Rockwell, Bliss Adell, Dewitt Rockwell, Rex Rockwell, Samuel Armstrong, Avery L. Vunck, Fay Winslow, and Charles E. Barrup. (Courtesy of the Esperance Historical Museum.)

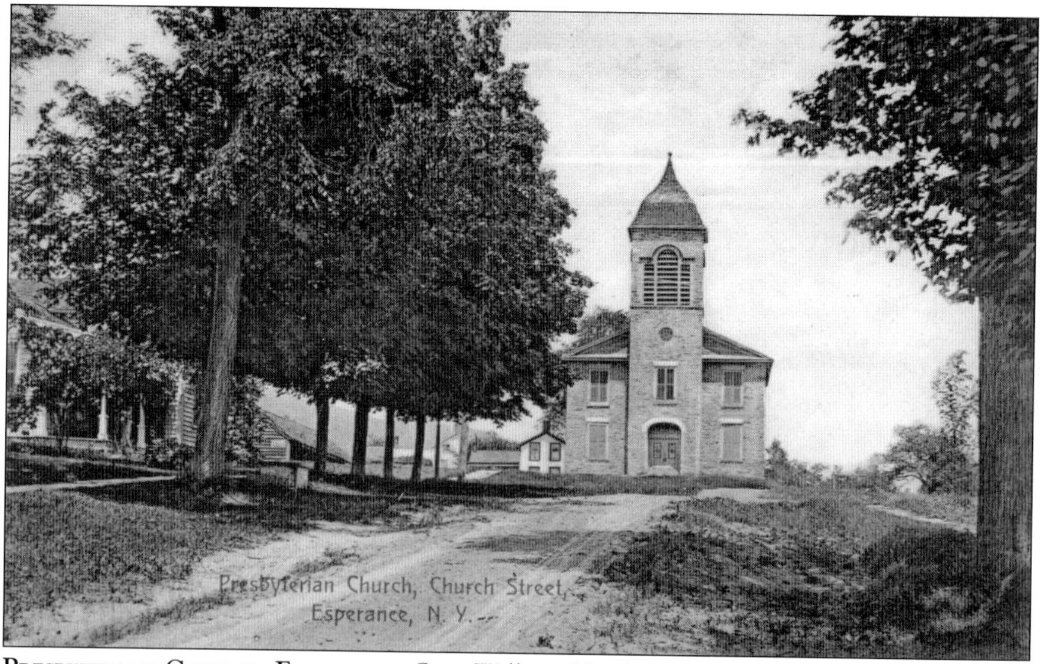

Presbyterian Church, Esperance. Gen. William North gave two acres of land for religious and educational purposes, which are now known as the Esperance Commons. The Presbyterian church was built here in 1824. It is made of local red sandstone and was enlarged with the tower and redecorated in 1896. (Courtesy of author's collection.)

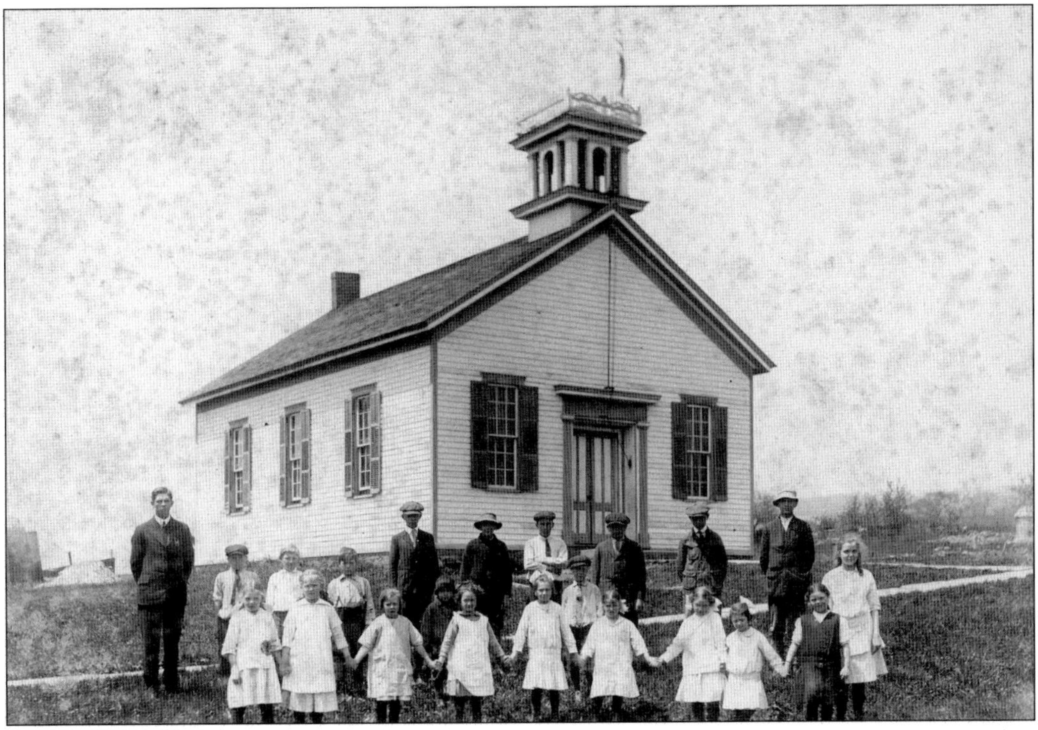

ESPERANCE ONE-ROOM SCHOOLHOUSE, 1916. The schoolhouse was built in 1878. Here, teacher Rea Rockwell (left) stands with his students in front of the school. Though most of the children are unidentified, two of the boys are Jim and Roland Gage while the fourth girl from the left is Nellie Warner Shafer. The building now houses the Esperance Historical Museum. (Courtesy of the Esperance Historical Museum.)

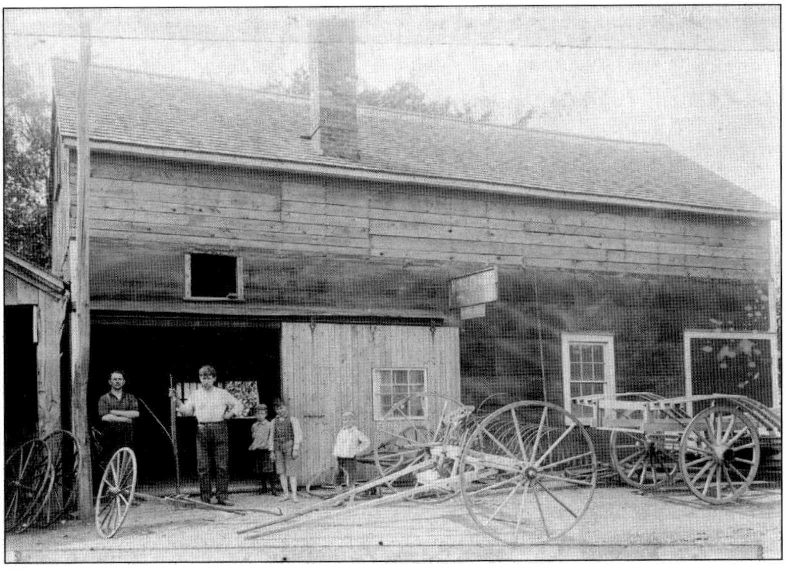

GEORGE WARNER'S BLACKSMITH SHOP, ESPERANCE. George Warner's sign proclaims that he does horseshoeing and jobbing. Here, from left to right, are Russell Young and George Warner with several youngsters, some of whom are shoeless. (Courtesy of the Esperance Historical Museum.)

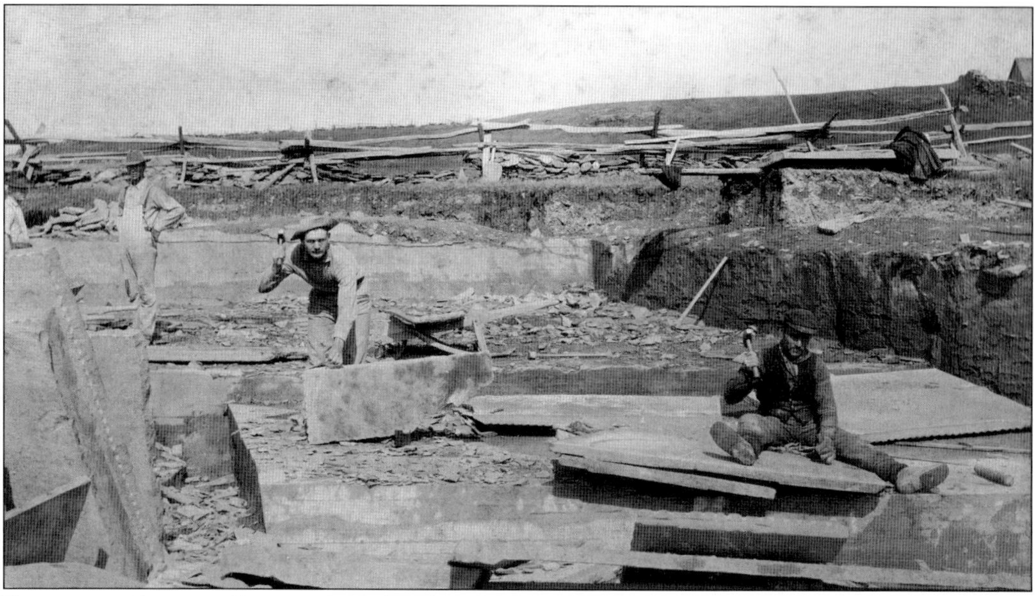

Bluestone Quarry, Esperance. The bluestone quarry was discovered in 1863 on a six-acre plot on the Connover and Collette farms above the village of Esperance. Bluestone was used in city sidewalks. At its peak, the quarry required 26 teams of wagons to transport the bluestone to the Esperance depot, a distance of five miles, where it was loaded on Albany & Susquehanna railway cars. (Courtesy of the Esperance Historical Museum.)

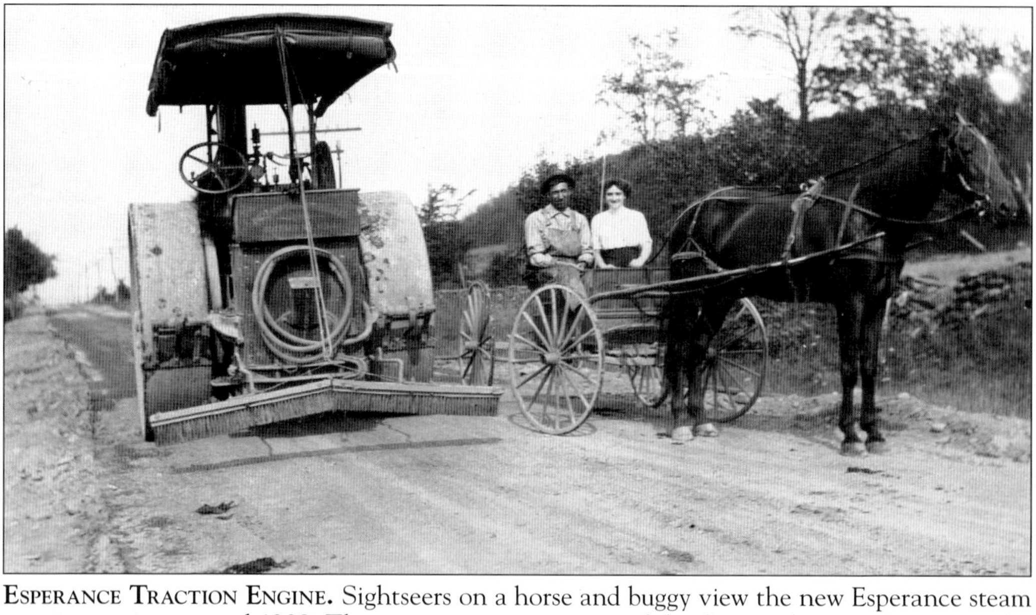

Esperance Traction Engine. Sightseers on a horse and buggy view the new Esperance steam traction engine around 1908. The steam engine was one of the first in the area for use on the roads. The town borrowed $796.58, which paid for the engine, its transportation, a scraper, and a teaching engineer. (Courtesy of the Esperance Historical Museum.)

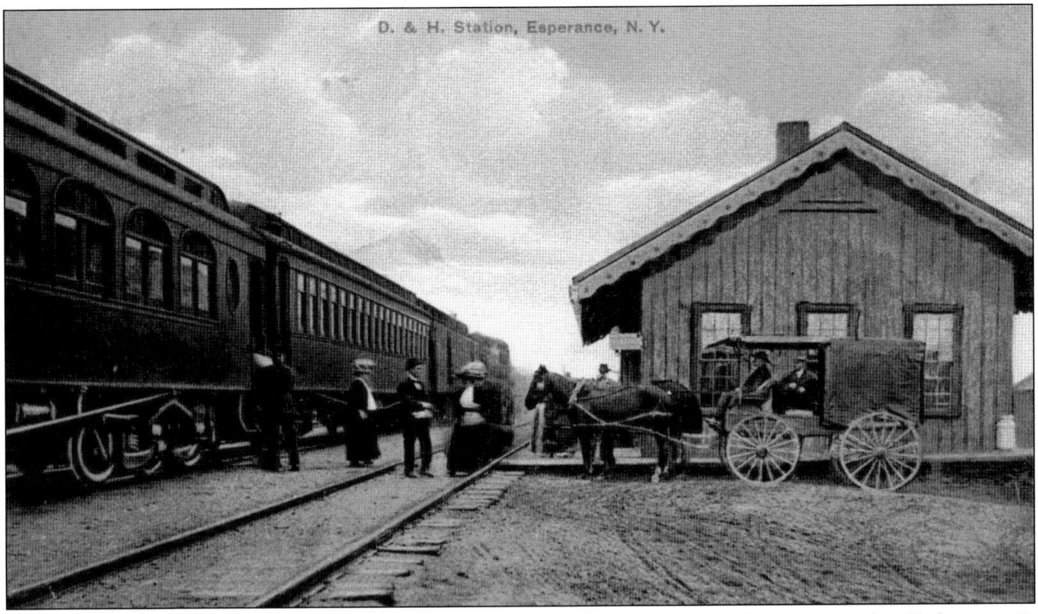

Railway Station, Esperance. Passengers arrive at the Esperance Station on the Delaware & Hudson train around 1905. John Hunter was the station agent. Richard Hunter ran the express wagons, which brought mail, goods, and visitors to the village some three miles away. (Courtesy of OSFM, Robert Mahar collection.)

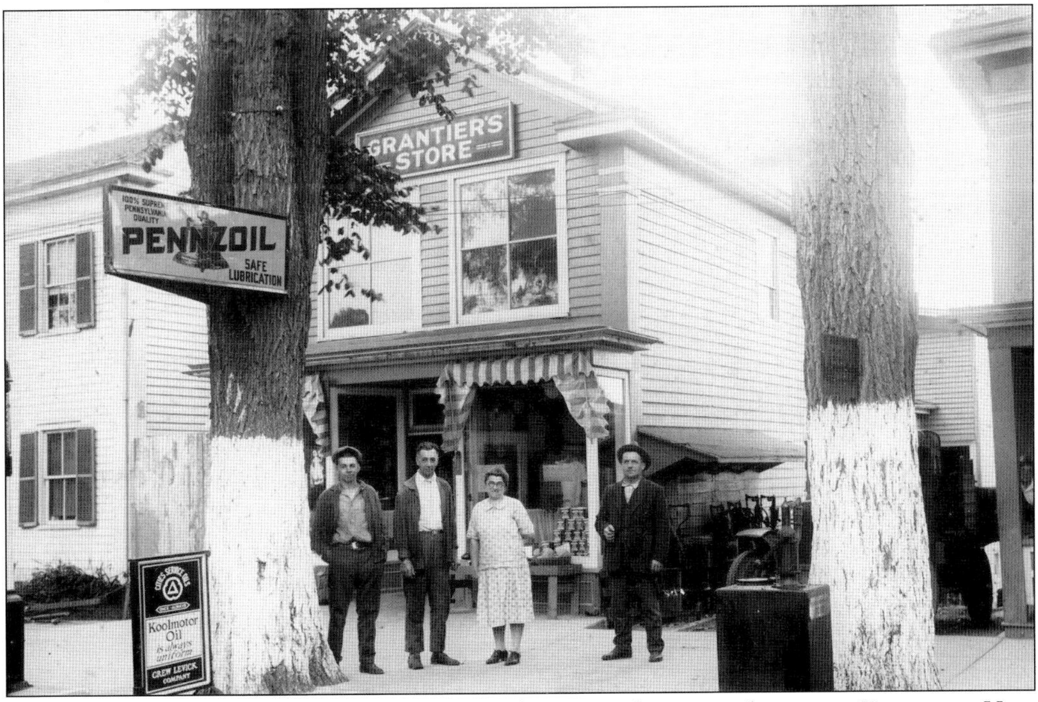

Grantier's Store, Esperance. In the 1920s, there were five general stores in Esperance. Here at the Grantier store are, from left to right, Reginald, Charles, and Laura Grantier and Fred A. Montanye. The store partially burned in the 1940s and is now a residence. Of note are the Pennzoil and Koolmotor Oil signs. (Courtesy of the Esperance Historical Museum.)

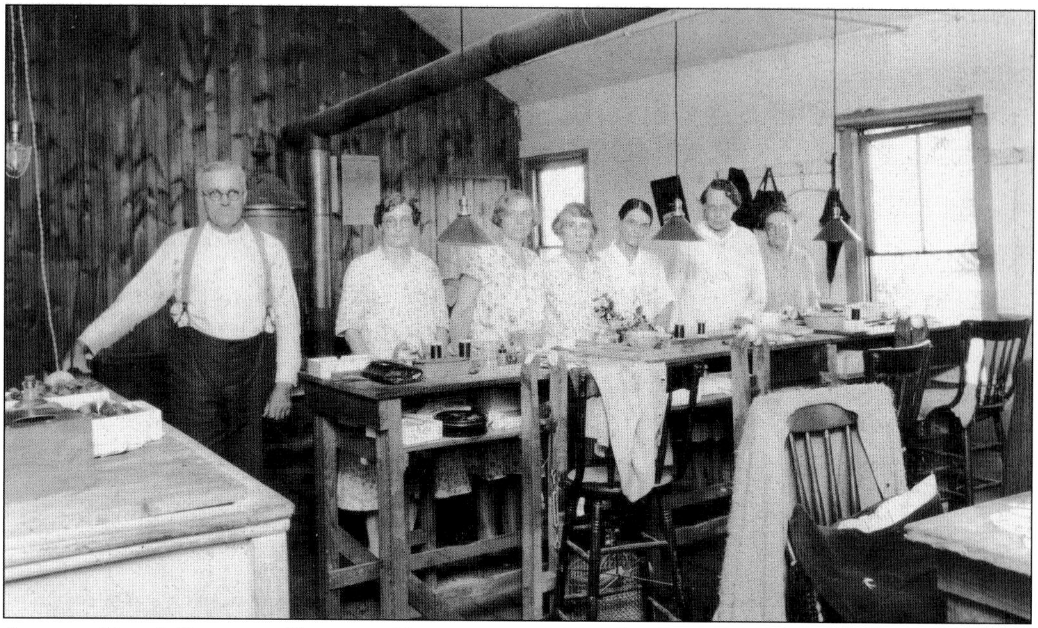

ARTHUR FERO'S BASEBALL FACTORY, ESPERANCE, 1928. The factory was located near the corner of Esperance Road and US Route 20, above the old post office where Fero was postmaster. From left to right are Fero, Flora Van Natta, Winnie Lettis, Jennie Moore, Emma Lape, Anne Rockwell, and Ella Montanye. (Courtesy of the Esperance Historical Museum.)

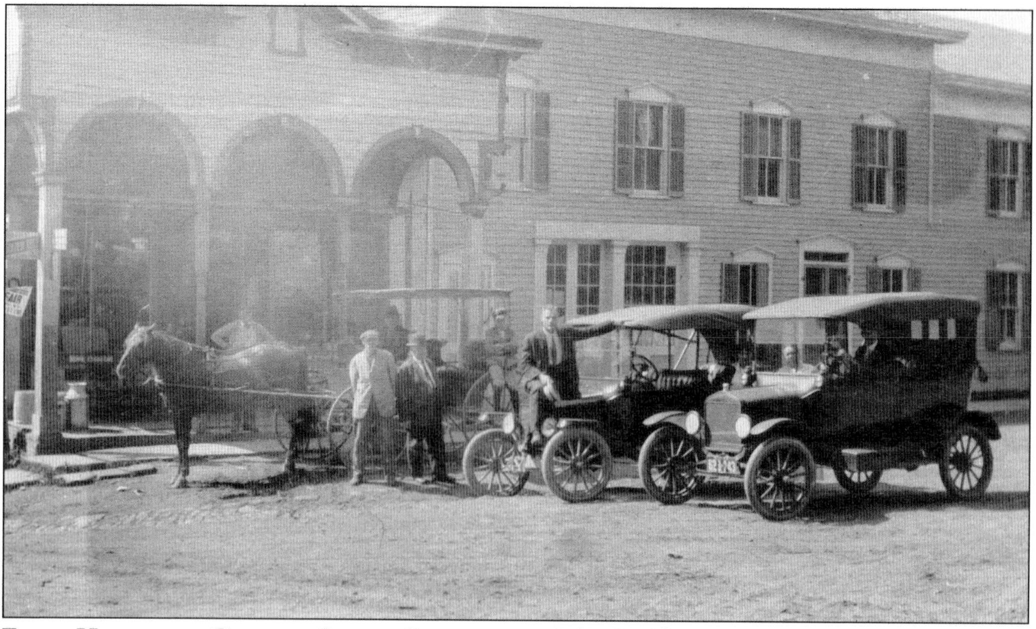

EAGLE HOTEL AND GENERAL STORE, SLOANSVILLE. John R. Sloan was the first postmaster here and had the privilege of naming the hamlet. In this 1920s view, the store on the left is the Pettys and Boyd store, later the Delwin H. Gordon store. The Eagle Hotel is at center, one of several hotels built in the 1820s and 1830s. It burned in 1941. (Courtesy of author's collection.)

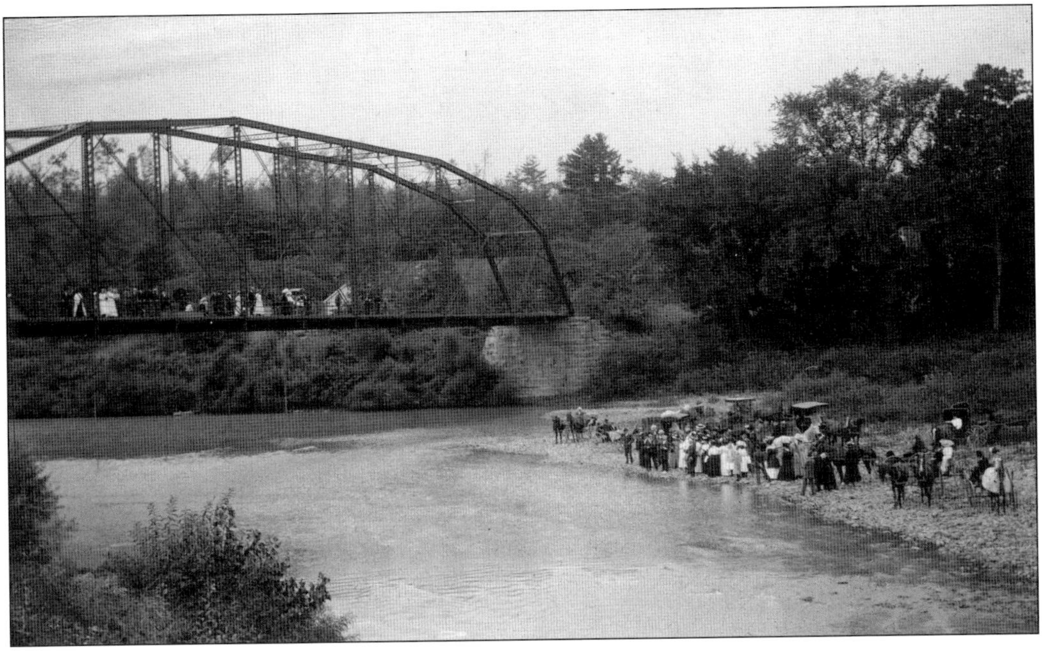

Baptism in the Schoharie Creek, Sloansville. Members of the Christian Church of Charleston are gathered at the Schoharie Creek near Sloansville to witness the baptisms of new members. Horse-drawn carriages have been brought creek side. Spectators also view the proceedings from the bridge. Below, the minister brings a woman dressed in white to be baptized in the waters of the creek. These photographs date from the late 1890s. (Above, courtesy of the Esperance Historical Museum; below, courtesy of Ken Jones.)

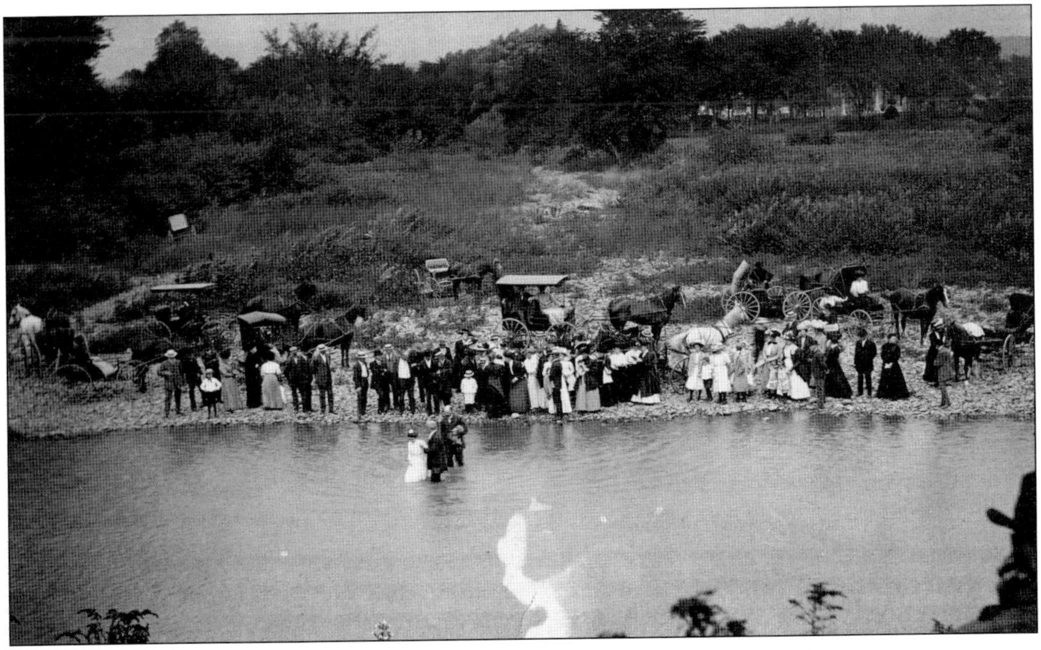

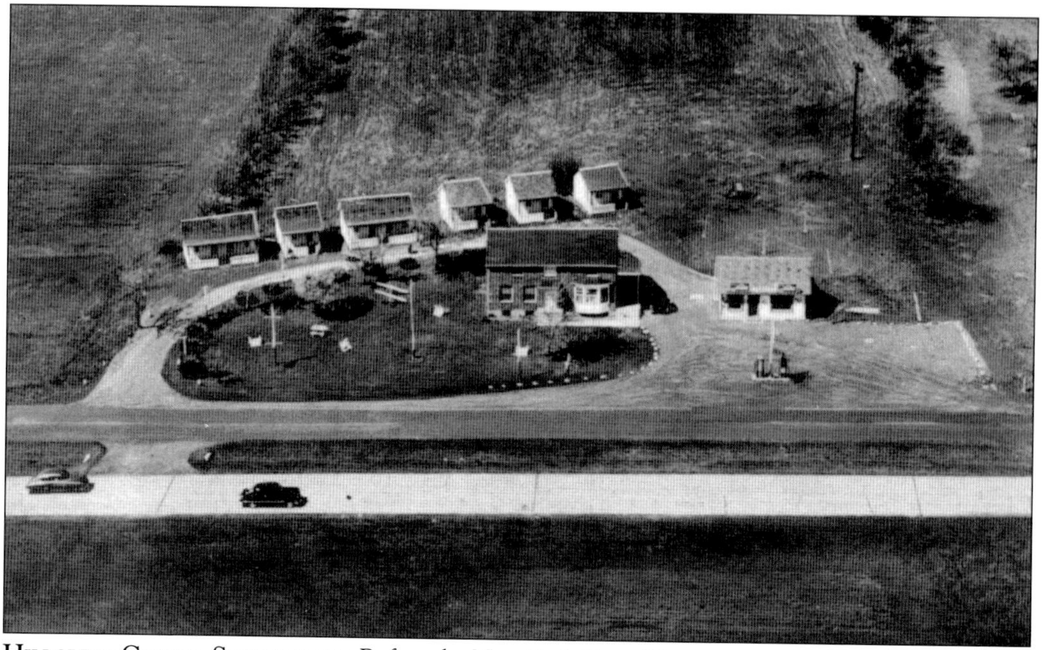

Hillcrest Cabins, Sloansville. Before the New York State Thruway was built, US Route 20, the successor to the Great Western Turnpike, was the main road from Albany to western New York. Many small tourist cabins were built along the route to accommodate travelers. This 1950s aerial view shows a typical row of cabins behind the owner's home. (Courtesy of author's collection.)

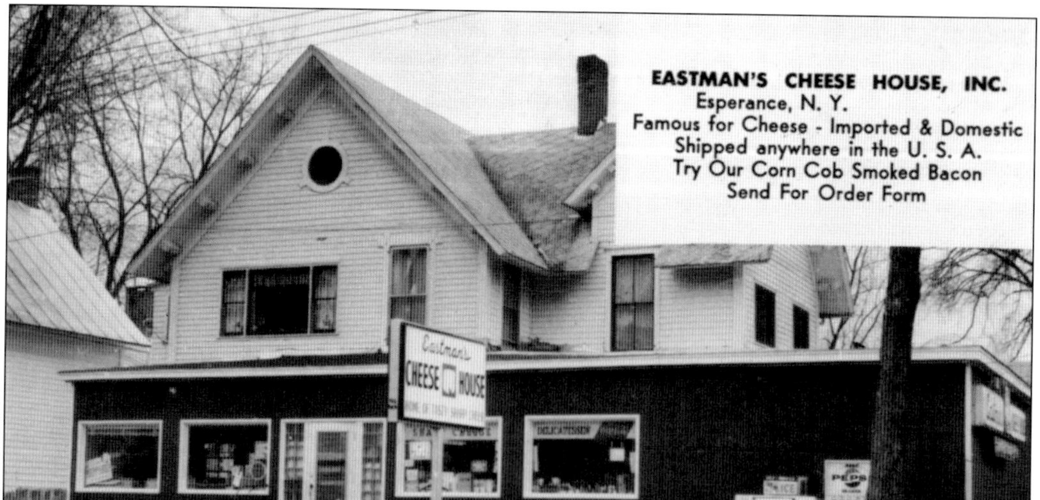

Eastman Cheese House, Esperance. Floyd and Ella Eastman began aging cheese and selling it from their home in the mid-1940s. Their store became popular and grew to be the Eastman Cheese House, where they sold aged cheeses, cheese bread, and many other food items. It remained in business until the 1980s. (Courtesy of author's collection.)

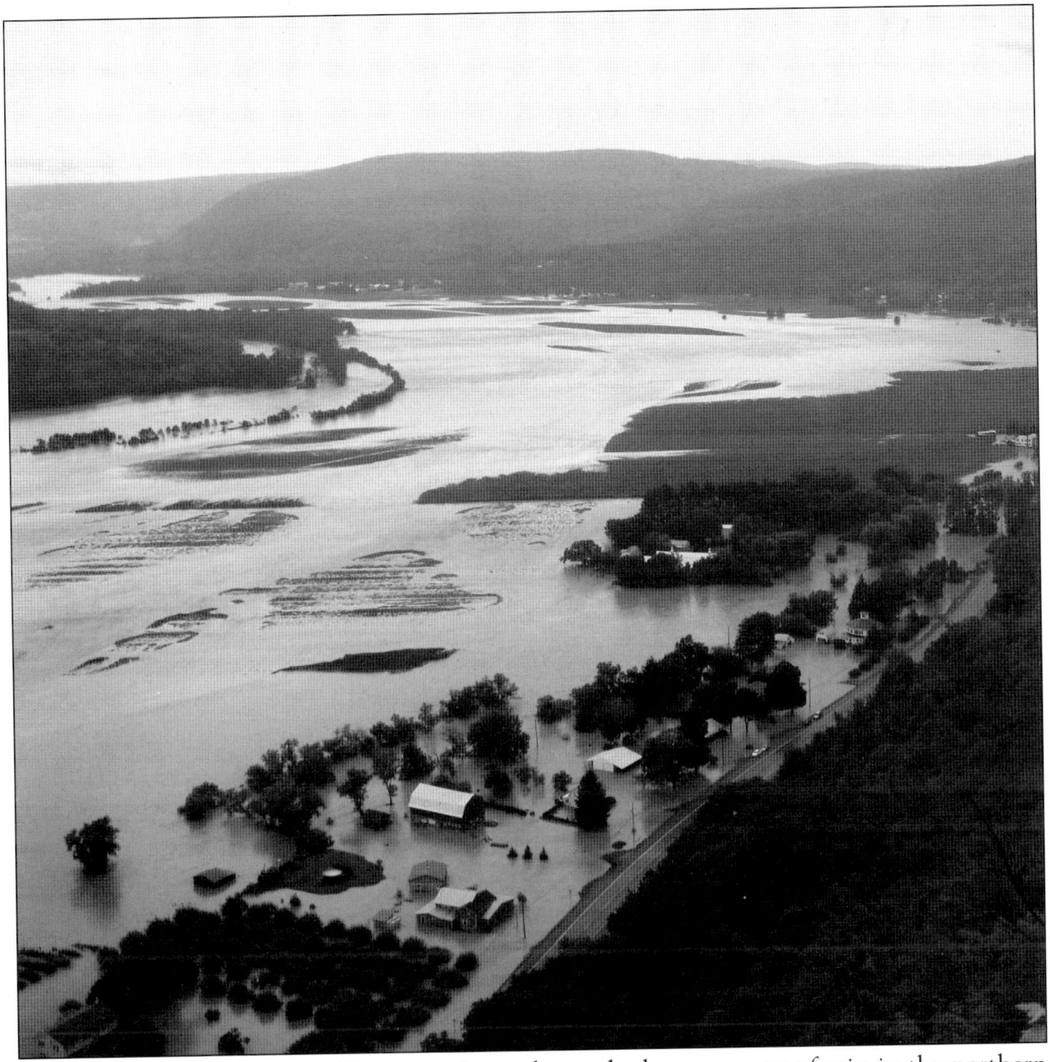

The Great Flood of 2011. Hurricane Irene dropped a huge amount of rain in the northern Catskill Mountains, much of it in the Schoharie Creek's watershed. The resulting great flood of August 28, 2011, caused damage to homes, businesses, farms, and crops in the Schoharie Valley and beyond. Houses were moved off their foundations or had their entire first floors under water. The historic Blenheim covered bridge was destroyed. Though the valley floods occasionally, this flood was the worst in recorded history. This view of the valley taken from near the top of Vroman's Nose, which is from nearly the same vantage as that on page 18, shows the initial progress of the floodwaters in the town of Fulton. State Route 30 runs diagonally at the lower right. Though the destruction was enormous, the residents of the valley will find the strength to recover. (Courtesy of Amy Colyer Frogley.)

Discover Thousands of Local History Books Featuring Millions of Vintage Images

Arcadia Publishing, the leading local history publisher in the United States, is committed to making history accessible and meaningful through publishing books that celebrate and preserve the heritage of America's people and places.

Find more books like this at
www.arcadiapublishing.com

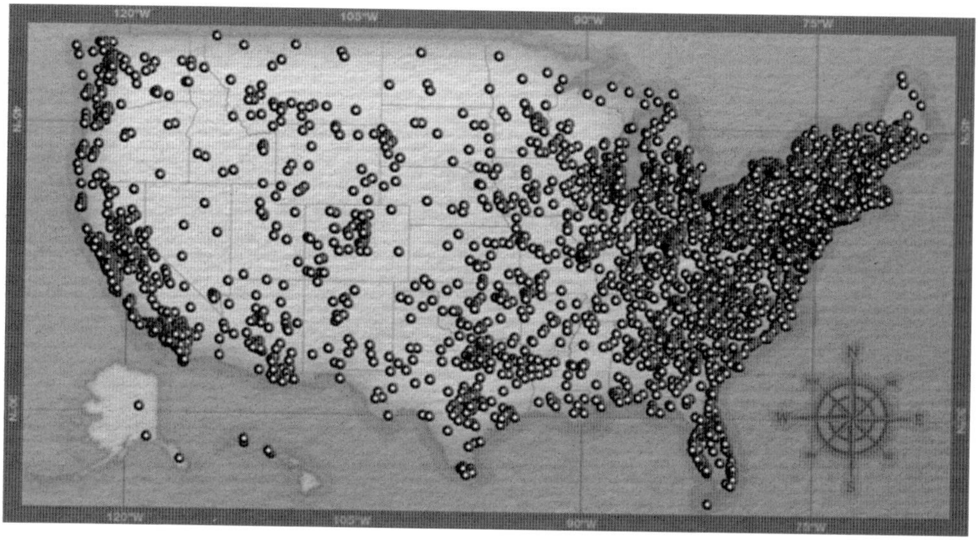

Search for your hometown history, your old stomping grounds, and even your favorite sports team.

Consistent with our mission to preserve history on a local level, this book was printed in South Carolina on American-made paper and manufactured entirely in the United States. Products carrying the accredited Forest Stewardship Council (FSC) label are printed on 100 percent FSC-certified paper.

MADE IN THE USA